A MOTHER'S
TOUCH

A MOTHER'S TOUCH

The Tiffany Callo Story

JAY MATHEWS

HENRY HOLT AND COMPANY
NEW YORK

Owing to limitations of space,
acknowledgments for permission
to reprint may be found
following the index, on pg. 267.

Library of Congress Cataloging-in-Publication Data
Mathews, Jay.
A mother's touch / Jay Mathews.—1st ed.
p.   cm.
1. Handicapped parents—United States.   2. Handicapped parents—
Legal status, laws, etc.—United States.   3. Parent and child
(Law)—United States.   I. Title.
HQ759.912.M38   1992
306.874'3'092—dc20   92-6472
                                                                          CIP

ISBN 0-8050-1714-3

Henry Holt books are available at special discounts
for bulk purchases for sales promotions, premiums,
fund-raising, or educational use. Special editions
or book excerpts can also be created to specification.

For details contact: Special Sales Director,
Henry Holt and Company, Inc., 115 West 18th Street,
New York, New York 10011.

First Edition—1992

Printed in the United States of America
Recognizing the importance of preserving
the written word, Henry Holt and Company, Inc.,
by policy, prints all of its first editions
on acid-free paper.∞
1 3 5 7 9 10 8 6 4 2

To Joe, Peter, Kate,
and their mother,
the best one I know

A five-year-old told her paraplegic mother:
"When I grow up I want to be a mommy,
and have a van and a blue wheelchair."
"Oh, you won't need *that*," the mother said.
"But I *like* blue," the child insisted.

—Megan Kirshbaum

PREFACE

This book began five years ago with what I thought would be a simple inquiry into one woman's fight to recover her two children. As I found myself drawn into Tiffany Callo's life, however, I discovered I could not explain to my satisfaction what had happened to her without learning a great deal more about the disability rights movement and the disintegration of the American family. What had been dozens of interviews grew into hundreds.

I met many productive and creative people. They had goals and projects unrelated to their handicaps, but stubborn stereotypes about the disabled, and sluggish official response to their requests for fair treatment, had forced them to spend much of their time seeking public sympathy.

Many minority group members know that feeling. They are put into boxes which are hard to escape. Tiffany's story, I think, shows that the trap for people with disabilities is the most treacherous of all, for it is often woven out of love.

I wager that almost everyone reading this is either disabled or has a close friend or relative with a significant handicap. Disabled people are far more numerous than most people imagine. They represent nearly one out of every five Americans, but are so scattered and often isolated that their place as the nation's largest minority group is usually overlooked.

People with disabilities often begin life cut off from other people who share their characteristics. Their ability to organize to remove barriers to creativity bumps hard against the understandable failure of the nondisabled people around them to appreciate how they feel.

In their individual, isolated lives, their access to life, liberty, and the pursuit of happiness is unnecessarily limited without there ever being much debate about it. This is wrong, and terribly shortsighted, for the most overlooked fact about disabled people is that millions of us nondisabled will eventually join their ranks.

Modern medicine is helping us live longer even as our bodies break down at the same ancient rate. The National Center of Health Statistics calculates that Americans who live to age seventy-five will, on the average, find their activities in almost thirteen of those years limited by some disability.

We are the disabled, if not now, then some day.

In writing this book, I tested the patience of several experts on disabilities and made frequent demands on Tiffany's remarkable memory, which nearly always proved accurate when checked against documents and the recollections of others. I interviewed her friends and relatives, and some of her adversaries. I examined thousands of pages of court documents and transcripts, many of them still not part of the public record. For the testimony at the June 1988 Juvenile Court dependency hearing for Tiffany's two children, closed to the press and to me, I relied on a 298-page transcript, augmented by the memories of people who were allowed to attend.

Nearly every person interviewed for this book has been given relevant portions of the manuscript to check for errors. I want to thank all of them for their help, but any mistakes remain my responsibility. Conversations and events that I did not hear or see have been reported as the participants remembered them, with emphasis on those elements found in more than one account. In a few minor instances I corrected errors in the transcript brought to my attention by witnesses who testified at the hearing.

The Santa Clara County officials who handled Tiffany's case

were prohibited by state law from discussing it with me. Their view of the case is laid out in some detail in activity logs, court records, the hearing transcript, and my interviews with individuals who spoke to them, but I was not permitted to question them directly and they were not permitted to rebut my conclusions. I gave them a draft manuscript of this book and asked them to correct any errors, but they again declined because of the confidentiality laws. As they explained several times, Tiffany had waived her confidentiality rights but her children had not, and there was no feasible way for them to do so.

I want to thank my editor, Channa Taub, and my agent, Diane Cleaver. Lee Bennett, Megan Kirshbaum, Tari Susan Hartman, Carol Gill, Margaret Jakobson, and Lonnie Nolta read the manuscript and made helpful suggestions. I received valuable assistance from James Fare, Paul Longmore, Bart Everett, Anne Finger, Gertrude and Jim Corcoran, Tom and Frances Mathews, Lou Cannon, Matt Lait, Jill Walker, and Leef Smith. My editors at the *Washington Post,* Bill Elsen, Fred Barbash, Karen DeYoung, Robert G. Kaiser, Leonard Downie, Jr., and Benjamin C. Bradlee, were as usual very supportive.

All the people in this book are real, but two of the names are pseudonyms. To avoid both confusion and what might seem inappropriate familiarity, I refer to Tiffany and her relatives and close friends mostly by their first names and to others in the story by their last names. In some cases I have identified people by only their first names.

With some exceptions when quoting people or making a particular point, I have honored the preference of the disabled people in this book by referring to them as either disabled or handicapped, although the latter term is now frowned upon by many disability rights advocates. The terminology, like everything else associated with disabilities, is in a state of flux. The day may come when euphemisms like "disAbled," "differently abled," or "physically challenged" become standard, and when terms used by the disabled in referring to the nondisabled, such as "ABs" (able-bodies), "normies," "regulars," or "walkers," are also in common use.

I am not disabled myself, at least not yet, and I am indebted to dozens of people with disabilities, particularly Tiffany Callo, for their candor and trust that allowed me to try to present the world from their perspective.

I rode a wheelchair for a week, not expecting to come close to re-creating the experience of a truly disabled person but hoping for an additional insight or two. I was impressed by how kind, and blessedly offhand, most strangers were toward me, and how distressingly high and cluttered the world had suddenly become. Even with modern equipment, it was difficult for me to plan the simplest excursion.

I felt, for a fleeting moment, the psychological and physical demands on people like Tiffany who want to live in the real world. The forces that keep so many disabled people at home, socially invisible and unaware of their strengths, became clearer to me, as did the annoyance of being thought of as nothing more than a disabled person.

Like members of other minority groups, people with disabilities prefer to be judged on their own merits, not on their differences from the nondisabled majority. Some succeed in that effort. My brother, Jim Mathews, was born with a birth defect that made it difficult for him to walk as a child and limited his access to sports. But his social, intellectual, and musical talents more than made up for his handicap. People who know him today associate him with the college audiovisual work he supervises, his amateur musical comedy performances, and his church leadership. They hardly ever think about his handicap, which is as it should be.

As I was finishing this book, I happened to cover the national finals of the U.S. Academic Decathlon, a rapidly growing competition for high school scholars. I noticed one of the members of the Jefferson High School team from Fairfax County, Virginia, was a blond sixteen-year-old in a wheelchair named Bliss Temple.

In the first draft of my story about the event, I said she was the only disabled person in the competition. I showed the story to her to make sure it was accurate. She objected to my identifying her as a right hemiplegic. It had nothing to do with her expertise in literature and the arts, the reason she had been picked for the Academic Decathlon team. She preferred her disability not be mentioned.

I resisted at first, and then, after some thought, saw her point. If I had the good fortune to receive such an honor, would I want it accompanied by a reference to my being the shortest member of my team, or the one with the biggest ears, or the one with freckles? Would the readers of the story benefit from such information?

I took the reference out. I had been distracted, I realized, by the writer's temptation to take any achievement by a disabled person and turn it into another Helen Keller story, a heroic battle against great odds waged by an imperfect body with a pure heart.

That is not what this book is about. Tiffany Callo is as human as she can be, with weaknesses and excesses we all share. She had a dream that she be allowed to live her life like any mother—to seek help when she needed it, reject it when she didn't, and not be held out as a model for anyone.

Nonetheless, she inspired other people to test their own dreams in the nondisabled world. The more people we have reaching out like Tiffany, risking mistakes, the richer life will be for all of us—standing, sitting, or just lying down and thinking.

PART
ONE

Two Babies

1

Some nights she dreamed she was an ice skater in the Winter Olympics. She glided across the frosty gray-white rink and kicked up shavings in tiny white clouds that marked her icy wake. Other nights she was an actress and model, putting one long leg after another at the marks she imagined she herself had choreographed.

Her conscious mind had grown used to the atrophied muscles and the mixed messages they received from the damaged tissue of her brain. They were part of her, neither bad nor good. But her subconscious, perhaps infected by society's bias in favor of movement on two legs, invented fantasies in which she walked and ran and danced with a fluidity her real limbs could never achieve.

She had always had a wide, somewhat mischievous smile and a kindness and charm that had won her a wide circle of friends. People were first struck by the way she ignored her disability, and then intrigued by her evident intelligence and almost immediate grasp of the word or gesture that would put them at ease.

"Come over *here* and tell me *what's going on!*" she insisted, the high pitch of her voice indicating delight and curiosity. She listened and asked questions and exchanged jokes about mutual failings and triumphs. Time went fast with her around.

She carried herself proudly, and had a habit of lifting her chin before gently skewering a silly remark. She had soft brown hair and perfect milky skin. Her eyes were a light, luminous blue. Her nose turned up slightly. She had a model's cheekbones and a dimple below her right cheek that gave her smile an extra morsel of allure.

A few people, upon first encountering her, thought she was stupid. To the uninitiated her speech sounded odd and her eyes did not seem to focus. But anyone who spent more than a few minutes with her discovered her quick sense of humor, keen grasp of business and finance, and extraordinary memory.

On that early morning in January 1988, with her bedroom fan stirring the rancid warmth of a midwinter California hot spell, Tiffany Ann Callo was happy for any diversion her dreams and memories could provide.

Her small ground-floor apartment on a shabby stretch of San Jose's Tenth Street was full of people. She liked having friends around. She was a sun that needed planets, and this group she had handpicked to help her handle the approaching birth.

But the crowd had also drained her. She was spending more time in bed. It was difficult to muster her usual delight in daily living—radio contests, hot showers, long wheelchair rides from Lucky's with bulging grocery bags looped around the armrests and piled high in her lap.

It was 6 A.M. She was not quite awake. What was that tugging sensation? Why was she drenched in sweat? She knew the baby was almost due, but the thought nestled in a far corner of her mind. The bed was soft. The coming day offered little comfort. Why should she rouse herself when there was as much to dread as to celebrate?

They had said several times they would take the baby away, just as they had David. Why should she rush to surrender him?

A warm, moist, almost gushing sensation roused her. Her diaper—the beige, pink, and blue box called them "Adult Pads"—soaked up some of the amniotic fluid, but a misty spray flew into the air and tiny drops landed on her face. Her slumbering brain told her this, finally, was it.

She opened her eyes and issued the first order of the day: "Patty! Patty! Come in quick!"

Patty Smith, her attendant, appeared in the doorway, blinking her eyes. She wore the gray sweat suit she used for sleeping. Patty had talked often with Tiffany about what they would do. Both had memorized the number of the ambulance service—the only practical emergency transportation for a disabled person on Medicaid.

Tiffany lay flat on her back. Patty saw her face tighten as a contraction passed through her. The attendant did not like the sight of the water-soaked bed.

"Oh my God," she said. "Oh my God. Hold on, Mommy. Hold on. We got to get you to the hospital."

They often called Tiffany Mommy. It was partly a joke to ease the tension of her legal fight and partly an acknowledgment of her love of maternal titles. She wanted to have this baby and rescue her older child, David, from the bureaucratic fortress. They would be a family and her unusual energies and talents would finally have a purpose. She knew unhappy children—she had been one once—and she thought she knew how to make them happy.

She had not been ashamed to discover that she did not want a disabled child. It was a common feeling among disabled parents. Anne Finger, a writer who had had polio as a child, explained it in her book *Past Due*: "I wanted something perfect to come out of my body. All my life I'd had to fight for everything. Walking across a room is work. I wanted something just to happen. I wanted something not to be hard."

When Tiffany had been pregnant with David, she had asked her doctor to check the records of her own birth for any evidence of genetic deformity. Cerebral palsy did not work that way, the doctor reminded her. It had no genetic component anyone had been able to isolate. Still, she insisted he check, so he wearily pulled the file and scanned the record.

"Nope, nothing here," he said, too quickly for her taste.

She drove her chair right to the corner of his desk, as close to him as she could without scratching the metal. She had spent six hours at the hospital that day, taking some tests, waiting for others. "Listen," she said, the pitch of her voice rising. "I don't want you to lie to me. I don't want you to not tell me. I want you to show me what it says." She reached over, her left arm quivering, and managed to snatch the file.

She took her time inspecting it. Not everything she read made sense. But there seemed to be nothing in it to fear. How about the father's juvenile rheumatoid arthritis? Not genetic, as far as we know, he said, waiting stoically for his patient's next outburst.

All right, fine, she thought. She knew where she stood. She had been very careful throughout the pregnancy, rejecting invitations to parties and watching what she ate and drank. She was going to make sure that the doctor was equally careful at the birth. Her own condition might have been triggered by the failure to provide enough oxygen in the crucial minutes after her premature birth nearly twenty years before. That was not going to happen to her baby. She had asked that an incubator be placed outside the delivery room, just in case.

Childbirth was unpredictable. She wanted to be prepared, to know if the child would need special help and where to get it.

Wouldn't any mother want that? And what mother would be better at raising a child with disabilities? She could say the words her grandmother had often said to her. She imagined folding her child in her arms and softly whispering: "There isn't a whole lot that you can't do. You're only limited if you limit yourself."

Yeah, yeah," Patty said on the telephone. "Yeah, her water's broke and she's got CP, so we'll need some help. Yeah, it's 560 Tenth Street. Yeah. Hurry."

Tiffany was too excited to pay much attention to the pain, but her disability had not dulled her senses. At their first meeting, it had taken her a while to convince her doctor of that. She enjoyed lovemaking and she could feel like any woman those awful birthing spasms, that sensation of being lovingly ripped apart.

She seemed deceptively quiet and strong to those hovering around her, a peaceful demeanor that Patty, in a growing panic, did not appreciate.

"So where are they?" Patty said to her friend Pat, who had come over to help. "Bleeping paramedics, never get it right." She moved nervously from one room to the other, looking at her watch. It was 6:45 A.M. "Where the hell are they? Did I give them the apartment number?" She had not, she decided. She hurried out to the street, while Tiffany gazed at the cracked and stained ceiling, wondering if she could time the contractions.

One was coming. OOOoowhhhhoaaa.

An intense muscular reaction, an irresistible need to expel every organ in her body, raced through her. The sheet was off. The diaper was spread open below her knees. She flopped on the bed helplessly, wearing only a T-shirt. She strained every recalcitrant muscle to push the baby out.

She heard a sound, a swishing gurgle like ketchup oozing from a bottle. She peered down over her chin and saw something move. A snake? A rope? Oh, God, she thought. It's the *umbilical* cord. This is the world's fastest labor! *Where is the baby?* Is he on the floor? Is he on the bed? Is the damn cord around his neck?

"Help! Somebody help me! I need some *help* in here."

Patty's friend Pat saw what had happened and gasped. Her sharp intake of breath seemed to paralyze her, as if she were afraid ever to let it out again. When she finally relaxed her lungs, she emitted a small, high-pitched scream, the extended yelp of a small dog. She stood there, breathing fast and shallow, not moving.

Tiffany felt both amusement and disgust. "Pat! Pat! Get it together." She intentionally raised the volume of her words to the highest setting, her voice being one of the few ways she could control her environment. "*Quit screaming and tell me!* Is he *okay* or is the damn cord *around his neck!?*"

Patty rushed in and saw that there was not much left to do. Tiffany heard a vibrant wail, the cry of a healthy baby insisting on food, comfort, love, and attention.

Thank God, she thought, closing her eyes and letting her head flop back on the pillow. I've done it.

The Santa Clara Valley Medical Center sprawled along Bascom Road just south of Interstate 280, one of the more crowded of San

Jose's perpetually clogged freeways. It was a neighborhood of gas stations, two-story medical offices, well-tended maples and firs, and an odd assortment of commercial establishments. This mix was typical of the booming, multilayered economy of the southern San Francisco Bay Area. People looking for jobs were moving into what the world called Silicon Valley and adding to the growing pains of its capital city, San Jose.

The ambulance whined past the Burbank Theater (ADULT XXX SHOWS EVERY NITE), Stan's Skin Diving School, the Mini Gourmet, CTV Videos, and into the dark shade of the emergency room entrance. Valley Medical had been born a century before as a county clinic to serve the farmers and day laborers picking plums and peaches on the plain and in semi-arid valleys to the west. Eventually the huge hospital grew into a city in itself. Its glassy towers with blue siding and white stucco walls jutted six and seven stories above the low-slung neighborhood full of young job-seekers from rural America and Latin America.

Failure to anticipate the painful consequences of growth was traditional in San Jose, even though the city was about to pass San Francisco in total population. Tiffany's hurried arrival at Valley Med, with her baby wrapped snugly on her chest, fit the municipal habit of playing life by ear.

Tiffany had teased the paramedics. The two large men acted as if they were rescuers even though, as she loudly pointed out, the crisis had passed. Tiffany's hand-picked team of attendants had cleaned the baby and wrapped him in a blanket, the cord still linking him and his smiling mother. The paramedics had nothing to do but cut the cord and suffer abuse from Tiffany when she caught them writing on their form that they had delivered the baby.

The infant was quiet in the warm embrace of the blanket. She planned to name him Jesse after his great-grandfather, and Robert after his grandfather.

Anyone who peered down on him could tell that he was Tiffany Callo's son. The slightly lifted nose, blue eyes, and creamy skin affirmed the unmistakable connection. Jesse Robert Callo was eight pounds, nine ounces, and twenty and three-quarters inches long.

Tiffany thought she could sense the infant's mood—bewildered, frightened, alarmed by the bright life outside the womb but comforted by her presence and her running stream of coos and high-pitched conversation. She had given birth with dazzling speed, but usually time moved more slowly for her than for other people. Buttering toast, changing channels, pouring water, diapering a baby—all could take many minutes rather than seconds, a pace she could make very soothing to a baby.

Tiffany thought people could live full, interesting lives at far less than the speed of a television pizza commercial. Glorious civilizations had arisen in China and Egypt, Rome and Athens, before anyone knew how to divide time into seconds and minutes. Why did she and her babies need to watch the clock?

Tiffany had visited Valley Medical many times as a child to see doctors about her frequent urinary problems, or to prepare for operations on her legs and feet. She did not like the hospital very much, but at least it provided a platform for one more assault on the people who had David and were coming to get Jesse.

She was taken to the delivery room to remove the placenta while Jesse was hustled off elsewhere. This troubled her. When would she see him again? She was caught in one of those currents of hospital gurneys and trays and regulations and forms in triplicate that had washed through her life so many times she knew it was futile to resist. She had to regain her strength and summon her allies.

A nurse and two orderlies wheeled her out of the delivery room, past the wood-paneled reception area, to the right past the nursery, and into Room 348. The maternity ward had been built in 1960 when hospital architects still had sufficient budgets to make ceilings high and rooms large enough to turn around in. Since then the population boom and tax revolts of the 1970s and 1980s had forced hospital administrators to settle for less, evidenced by the five beds crammed inside Room 348. Plastic and cloth curtains suspended from ceiling tracks offered minimal privacy. Three Magnavox television sets peered down from ceiling brackets like vultures.

Tiffany, true to form, ignored everything but the telephone.

Her first call went to Clay Bedford, the attorney who was spending much of his time trying to pry her son David away from the Santa Clara County Department of Social Services, "DSS," as most people called it.

"God, you're late. *God*, you're slow," she said, the pitch of her voice soaring again in agitation. "This baby's already *born*. Two *hours* ago. What are you waiting on?"

"I'm coming," he said. He put the telephone down and sighed. This was not going to make his life any easier, but it would bring out the media.

Two new mothers already occupying beds in Room 348 watched with growing curiosity as small packs of television people—camera operators in Saturday-morning jeans, correspondents in hastily applied makeup—dragged their equipment into the room and surrounded the bed of the new arrival.

Tiffany welcomed the reporters while, still on the telephone, she spoke to her social worker, a woman named Shirley Silvani, who was near the top of Tiffany's list of demons.

"Tiffany, I wonder if we could talk about—" Silvani had begun.

Tiffany cut her off. "The baby's fine. I'm fine," she said. She struggled to control her temper while lifting her right arm in aimless fury, the flapping wing of a new mother bird. "I prefer not to talk to you now. I'll talk to you later."

With the waves of television people came a few members of the Tiffany entourage. Her attendant, Patty, arrived. Tiffany's father, Bob Callo, and his girlfriend, Beth Stuart, were there.

Tiffany was polite to the nurses. She had been treated well by most of them in the past. It was the doctors who often belittled her fears and shrugged off her questions. She asked the first nurse if she had a report on the baby. The young woman left and returned in fifteen minutes. "It looks good," she said. "They've got him resting."

"Will I be able to see him in a little while?"

"I'm sure you will."

For two months she had been a minor celebrity in San Jose.

The television news had captured her motorized chair rattling down the sidewalk on the way to a Saturday visit with David at the DSS offices. It was an irresistible story. In an era when childbirth was coming back into vogue, when millions of women were overlooking the difficulties of career and tight budgets in order to have children, the county government had taken a baby away from a bright and beautiful young woman because she could not pick him up unassisted. The reporters and photographers always found Tiffany full of jokes and effusive gratitude. She became very adept at producing vivid quotes and sound bites.

"So, Tiffany, are they going to take this baby too?" the reporter from Channel 7 asked.

"If I wasn't handicapped, they would not *dare* to take any of my babies away," she said. "And yet they give drug addicts second chances and third chances to have their kids." Her cerebral palsy forced her to pronounce one word at a time, giving her speech a clarity on television that caught people's attention.

The bright television lights and the need to repeat herself began to aggravate her headache. She had not seen Jesse in three hours. She began to wonder if she would be allowed to. When Bedford arrived and she sent him to see about it, he returned with a nurse and a small, blue-eyed infant whose lips moved rhythmically with hunger.

As far as Tiffany could see, he was absolutely perfect.

Jesse shut his eyes tight as the television lights snapped on again. Tiffany felt her headache surge, but she needed the publicity. As long as Jesse seemed content to squirm and cuddle in the warm electronic glow, she could stand the pain. The camera operators experimented with a few close-ups in natural light. The baby cautiously opened his eyelids a small crack and gurgled slightly. Tiffany managed to pull out one of his tiny hands, and he held her thumb tightly.

Visiting hours on the maternity ward were loose—10 A.M. to 6 P.M. every day. But the parade of cameras began to unnerve the nursing supervisor. "Listen," she said, as the media force filled 348 to overflowing, "we can't have this many people in the room at one time. Somebody's gonna have to leave." No one moved.

Jesse, hungry again, began to whimper. Tiffany lowered him so he could move toward her breast. She watched with pride as he lustily took hold.

The news crews wandered away. The pace of the day slowed as Tiffany's friends sought food in the second-floor cafeteria—a favorite teenage Tiffany haunt. During the lull, Bob Callo approached his daughter about the possibility of Jesse moving in with him, something he had suggested a few times already.

She sighed. It was tempting, but there was so much she could not forget, and the county had already indicated it would not accept him as a substitute parent. "Sorry, Dad," she said. "I love you, but even if I wanted to, I don't think they would go for it."

The nurses retrieved Jesse for his afternoon nap. Tiffany dozed until another shift of cameras arrived, sent by news directors who had seen an afternoon wire story and wanted something for the eleven o'clock news. Jesse, more accustomed to bright lights and stardom, performed once again, squinting and squirming and nestling against his mother's chest. He nursed greedily, sending a warm surge of hormones through Tiffany until she fell into a half-sleep, her headache and raw nerves yielding briefly to the serene comfort of a small mouth on her nipple.

When would they come? When would be the moment? Silvani, the social worker, had said she wanted to drop by to say hello. Tiffany sometimes enjoyed the challenge of summit conferences with the chief enemy envoy, but when Bedford mentioned Silvani's request this time, Tiffany felt her stomach churn. She realized what she was about to go through again.

She also recalled, as she watched Jesse nuzzle and turn small moving lips in her direction, her hollow feeling when Silvani suggested a few weeks after his conception that she consider an abortion.

"Tell her I will tear her head off," she said to Bedford. "Keep her away from me."

By 8 P.M., as Jesse returned to the nursery, Tiffany teetered on the edge of nervous sleep. But for brief catnaps, she had been up since Jesse's birth early that morning. Her family and friends had drifted away to home and dinner.

Yet sleep eluded her. The comforting ice-skating dream would not come. At 11 P.M. she switched on the television news, curious again about how she and Jesse would appear to the world. The glowing screen provided the last best hope of delaying their parting.

She stared at the ceiling. She sought comfort and insight in its shadowy blankness. What was tomorrow going to be like? The thought chased its tail through her imagination. That part of her brain never failed her, unlike the damaged gray matter that struggled to send proper signals to her muscles. Her old insomnia toyed with her battered nervous system for a while, and then let her go.

A nurse brought a breakfast tray at 7 A.M. Tiffany recoiled at the sickly aroma. Harsh sunlight through the thin green-and-blue plaid curtains brought her nerves back to jangled consciousness.

She thought to herself: I've got to feed my boy. I've got to eat some of this dire stuff.

She was allergic to milk, but she drank it anyway. She drank the coffee and the orange juice. She ate the cinnamon roll that wallowed in a pool of grease.

The nurse returned to find her staring at the remains of the meal. Tiffany held every muscle and nerve as still as possible in hopes that the breakfast roll would slide down into her intestine with no permanent damage.

Jesse, delightfully ravenous, was brought in. For a minute or two his unquestioned acceptance of her allowed her to hope that they might not take him that day. Maybe someone wanted to make a deal.

It was a quiet time. The television cameras did not reappear. Her father arrived and sat beside the bed as if it was an ordinary Saturday visit to his daughter, the new mother. No social workers arrived to spoil the mood. The baby took his fill and dozed off. A nurse retrieved him.

At noon, when another nurse appeared with news of what was to happen, it seemed smooth and unhurried, in keeping with the leisurely pace of the day. "Tiffany," said the nurse cheerfully. "The doctor said we're going to let you go home about one o'clock."

Tiffany found it hard to summon the ire she had resolved to hurl at whoever tried to take Jesse. They had decided on an indirect approach. They would remove her, not Jesse, from the hospital.

It took her a moment to absorb this. The nurse's smile had confused her. Tiffany frowned and grimaced, and the nurse looked puzzled. "Something the matter?" she said.

"You don't understand," Tiffany said. "As soon as I leave the hospital, they'll take my baby to a foster home and that's the last I'll see of him, except maybe once-a-week visits."

"Oh," the nurse said, helpless and still confused.

Tiffany blinked several times and felt her face grow hot. So smart. So incredibly smart. They knew she liked the nurses. She wouldn't open fire on the nurses.

They can't stand all these cameras coming in anymore, Tiffany," Bedford told her. "They can't stand the publicity. They figure with you gone, it will stop."

Large tears ran slowly down her cheeks as she struggled to pull on her street clothes. She had been pregnant for eighteen of the last nineteen months. She felt she had lived forever in maternity clothes, sprawled like a beached whale in her wheelchair. In the long-forgotten era before her pregnancies, she had pulled herself up on her wheelchair occasionally and gone out, eating whatever she wanted and dressing like all the other nineteen-year-olds she knew cruising First Street. She had told Patty to bring over her acid-washed jeans and purple sweater, a celebration of her body's return to normalcy. She had not considered how much her favorite costume would add to her gloom over losing Jesse because she had tried not to think about losing Jesse.

Her mind was spinning out a painful mantra: I am not ready. I am not ready. I cannot sit up. I hurt. I am not ready. I hurt. I am not ready.

Bedford said there was nothing she could do but fight in court.

She had to go home, rest, collect her energies. Her entourage helped her transfer to her motorized chair. She flicked the left-hand control and whirred out the door, turning right to pass by the nursery.

Her anger was beginning to burn away the tears. She thought: What the hell have I been in the hospital *for*? I just had a baby. I should be happy. I should be happy and I'm not. I'm miserable. *Where is my baby?*

The nursery staff had closed the shades on the viewing windows, too high anyway for someone using a wheelchair to peer through. The nursery was a tall castle, a Bastille, where her son was being held against his will.

She pushed the lever and the motor moved the chair up to the nursery door. A young doctor and a nurse stood there. A Channel 7 news crew, the only one to come the second day, hovered behind her, their camera silently recording. Tiffany thought the doctor and nurse looked as if they feared she would scoop up the baby and run. This image pleased her, and she smiled to herself.

"Excuse me," she said, letting her left hand hover menacingly over the motor lever on the chair. "You have two choices. You either move or I will bodily move you."

Two sets of eyebrows arched in surprise. This was not what they expected from a dimpled, somewhat older version of the March of Dimes poster child. They stepped back. Tiffany rolled in. The Channel 7 camera operator leaned close to tape one last moment with Jesse and Tiffany Callo.

He was just waking up, and very hungry. "He hasn't eaten yet," said a nurse as she placed him in his mother's lap. "Do you want to give him a bottle?"

"Excuse me! I don't want to give him that stuff," she said, lifting her sweater. "He wants Mommy's milk."

The nurse had instructions to move the child to bottles. She had been told it was unlikely he would ever see his mother again more than once a week. The nurse hesitated. "I don't think you can . . ."

"Want to bet?" Tiffany said.

She watched triumphantly as the sleepy infant arched his back to the side and attached himself to her breast. All the camera operator could see through his lens were two small feet and part of a small, fuzzy head protruding from the bottom of her sweater.

He sucked for fifteen minutes, off and on, as his mother planned their escape. The door was still open. The chair battery had a ten-hour charge. She could take him out the open door. They let her *in* without a protest. Maybe she could bully her way out. No, that was silly.

But how could she leave Jesse? He still seemed hungry after nursing. She took a small bottle from the nurse and, with a frown of resignation, advanced the cause of the enemy by accelerating his alienation from the breast.

When she left him, it had to be fast. She could not waste any motion. Boop, boop, boop. He would finish the bottle. Boom! That was the starting gun. She would hand him to the nurse. She would give him a kiss, give him some lovies, give him a hug, tell him Mama loved him. When the nurse took him, she would push the chair lever forward. She would not turn around or look back.

The last ounce of milk collected at the end of the plastic nipple. Tiffany gathered her strength, but the process of giving the baby back was awkward and painfully slow. The nurse stood for a second with the child, blocking Tiffany's way. She could knock the nurse down. The baby would drop into her arms and she could run—or roll. The language was not well equipped to describe the way she traveled. She would glide over the ice with her new partner.

She pushed the lever and the motor emitted a soft growl. She heard herself sob as she abandoned the fantasy and left her baby. She turned right down the hall, and then left past the reception desk. She concentrated on a new chant: Don't turn around, don't turn around, don't turn around.

Two of the younger nurses walked out with her, not quite certain what to say but determined to demonstrate that they had no connection with what was being done. The small group walked through the huge door to the pediatrics section, full of wall decals of Huey, Dewey, and Louie Duck. Tiffany saw four-year-olds caged in beds with high railings. At least their mothers could come see them, and someday maybe take them home.

They arrived at the elevators. Tiffany ceased her silent chant. Jesse seemed far away. The two nurses leaned down and hugged her.

"Be sure and come back and see us," one said as she straightened up, searching for some way to ease the strain. "If you get the kids, if you win this case, you bring those kids back and you show us how good they've grown up and how handsome they are."

Without returning to her room, Tiffany descended in the elevator and guided the chair through the crowded main lobby to the narrow front door. She rolled outside and then finally flipped the switch to the right and turned the chair so she could give the hospital a last look.

It was as tall and cold and implacable as ever. As a child, she had gone in with hopes that it could at least soothe her physical and emotional aches, but it never did. This time it had not only failed to give her anything, but had taken a part of her away.

She dispatched a silent thought to the people she assumed were up in some third-floor office filling out forms with her name on them: those wretched, sorry excuses for humanity. How could they do it to her again?

2

The first time Clay Bedford, Tiffany's attorney, saw her was in April 1987, nine months before Jesse's birth. Tiffany was sitting in Courtroom No. 1 of the Santa Clara County Juvenile Center waiting for a preliminary hearing on Dependency Petition 94106, the piece of paper that had taken her son David away.

Bedford, a round-faced man with curly, thinning hair, took one look at his new client and decided the case was hopeless. She could not walk. Her arms and hands were weak and quivered unpredictably. Sometimes he could not understand what she was saying.

He concluded that there was no way she was ever going to be able to take care of a baby. He could not imagine how she could change a diaper or do anything else that fit his vague bachelor's notion of a parent's duties.

That the case was a loser was no surprise to Bedford. He was accustomed to losing cases. He was only thirty-three, practicing law by himself and taking whatever court-appointed work came his way. All he had been told about *In the Matter of Antonio David Rios, Case No. 94106* was that he was representing a young mother with a handicap whose baby was now at the Children's Shelter.

He began to read the file and talk to Tiffany, and, gradually, the picture changed. It was the start of what he would later call a very expensive and adventure-filled education.

From the beginning he learned that Tiffany loved people, individually and collectively. Some disabled people became annoyed with crowds—the stares, the stiff smiles, the innocent but insulting questions. Tiffany, on the contrary, enjoyed the effect she had on people. Whenever she rolled into an elevator or drove her softly whirring motorized chair into a supermarket, she felt a change in the atmosphere. Her friends and attendants waited for her cue, knowing she had a talent for leadership. She thought this would help make her a good mother.

There were more than forty-two million disabled people in the United States in 1987, outnumbering blacks, Hispanics, and any other disadvantaged minority group. The total was expected to grow. They lacked the power of their numbers because they had no ghetto—no handicapped street gangs, no disabled electoral districts, no wheelchair caucus in Congress. There were no disabled Jesse Jacksons or Gloria Steinems, with national influence and celebrity, to unite and inspire them. Most disabled people lived in individual families, often hidden from public view, barred from public life and burdened by widespread, unquestioned bias against them. Each disabled person had to reach out for worth and recognition as an individual, surrounded by relatives and friends who, although often well-meaning, could not always understand what they needed or did not need.

Disability history was an infant field, but its few practitioners wondered if handicapped people might have been better integrated into society before medical science began to name their conditions and look for cures. People with minor, if then untreatable, conditions like dislocated hips seemed to be part of daily human life before the arrival of modern medicine. Some achieved prominence in politics and religion.

By the nineteenth century, however, disabled people had moved into the category of the sick, and even worse, the incurable, what historian Paul K. Longmore calls the "medicalization" of disability. They were put away in hospitals and institutions.

Those who wished to live normal lives were urged to act as much like nondisabled people as possible. Franklin Delano Roosevelt's excruciating efforts to obscure the effects of his polio—banning photographs below the waist, having aides prop him up, designing his wheelchair to look like ordinary desk furniture—added to the common assumption that handicapped people had to rise above their afflictions or stay out of sight.

An early-twentieth-century Chicago city ordinance said: "No person who is diseased, maimed, mutilated, or in any way deformed so as to be an unsightly or disgusting object or improper person to be allowed in or on the public ways or other public places in this city, shall therein or thereon expose himself to public view." An academically accomplished boy with cerebral palsy was expelled from a Wisconsin public school in 1919 because his presence was felt to be "depressing and nauseating." The eugenics movement that would be twisted into the Holocaust by the Nazis had great support in the United States among people who wanted to wipe out disabilities. Sixteen states had laws requiring sterilization of people with certain handicaps. Otherwise qualified applicants disabled by polio and cerebral palsy found that their Depression-era job requests to the Works Progress Administration (WPA) were stamped "PH" for physically handicapped and rejected.

A few groups, such as the three-hundred-member League for the Physically Handicapped, protested such attitudes as early as the 1930s. But it was not until the 1960s and 1970s that disabled people began to organize in large numbers against social and political bias. An unusually aggressive organization called ADAPT, American Disabled for Accessible Public Transit (later changed to American Disabled for Attendant Programs Today), locked their wheelchairs in front of buses and forced several cities to move toward providing more lifts on public transportation. Disabled people rebelled against demeaning terms like "crippled" and "wheelchair bound" and pushed for new laws to ease their access to offices, markets, libraries, sporting events, and the dozens of other places wheelchairs could not go.

But the movement was so new, and feelings about handicaps

so ingrained, that the activity had little impact on popular attitudes, particularly when it came to sex, family, and children. By having two children and insisting on her right to keep them, by lacking the private financial resources that kept most disabled parents out of the reach of the juvenile courts, Tiffany Callo was about to thrust the disability rights movement deeper into American life than it had ever gone.

Bedford slowly absorbed all this, each step taking him further into a culture and attitude toward life he found alien, but comforting in its way—a sense that human beings could live productive lives at a slower rhythm, with severe limits, and yet do all the important things, loving and caring and creating, that people ought to do.

Bedford had had little personal experience with disabled people. A law school classmate at Syracuse who lived in the next room had had polio and used a wheelchair. Bedford remembered that the classmate had fought the school administration over poor wheelchair access to some buildings and would sometimes honk for help if snowdrifts in their apartment house parking lot made it too difficult for him to get out of his car.

Bedford's seven-year marriage had ended in 1982, and he had no children. He specialized in taxes and accounting at Syracuse and intended to practice real-estate law until he discovered he was more eager to get out of bed on days he had some tawdry little criminal case to argue.

He decided to be happy, not rich. He discarded real-estate work in favor of helping people in real trouble, like Tiffany.

Bedford found, after he became accustomed to Tiffany's speech patterns and the extent of her disability, that she had a remarkable talent for coping with what had been a difficult childhood and a disjointed introduction to the adult world. Tiffany was funny, warm, stubborn, and yet always considerate of his time and understanding about his ignorance.

She let him taste some of the bitter by-products of her life. They had to meet in the lobby of a nearby bank when street construction made the way into his office impassable for a wheelchair. He watched one day as three buses stopped and departed before she found one with a wheelchair lift that worked. His client, he concluded, was far more tolerant of the administrative and political callousness that warped her existence than he ever would have been.

It appalled him that DSS, like nearly every other child-protective agency in the country, paid more than five hundred dollars a month to keep a single child in a foster home but could not spend that same amount on an attendant to help a disabled mother raise her child in her own home. It offended him that Tiffany was in court only because her children were healthy and nondisabled. If they had been born disabled, they would have immediately qualified for attendant care and could have been raised by Tiffany. Of course, if they had been disabled, probably no one but their mother would have wanted them anyway.

Bedford sought outside help. He informed the United Cerebral Palsy Association that the county had alleged Tiffany suffered from a "physical disability rendering her incapable of providing appropriate nurturance, stimulation, and care to said infant minor." He said, "I believe that the entire juvenile system is being extremely insensitive to the needs and humanity of my client in this matter. I assume that this insensitivity is not limited to my client."

Several experts, surprised and delighted that a young disabled mother was taking such a stand, sent Bedford the latest research. There was much there about how Tiffany could raise her own children, and how irrelevant her physical limits were. At that point, the county began to change its tactics in the case, and the real fight began.

DSS's legal approach to the sticky problem of Tiffany and her babies did not become completely clear until June 28, 1988, a hot Tuesday afternoon marking the beginning of what the court called a permanency planning hearing for David and a dependency proceeding for Jesse. The court would decide if Tiffany could regain custody of either child. DSS would do its best to stop her.

Before the hearing, Tiffany rolled restlessly up and down the worn linoleum of the Juvenile Center's outer lobby. Pushing the control button on her power chair, a black Everest & Jennings Marathon with two twelve-volt deep-cycle gel-cell batteries, she surveyed the dirty windows, stained square pillars, and empty plastic chairs. She felt surrounded by friendly enemies. She saw the county attorneys and social workers who, with smiles and regrets, had lured her into a regulatory purgatory. Everything she wanted—her children, a home, a career—dangled just out of reach because these nice people said she was not ready for them.

She saw Shirley Silvani, her tall, angular social worker, stride into the court foyer beyond the security checkpoint. She saw the deputy county counsel, Michael Clark, thin and quiet, follow behind. She spied the two psychologists who had given her an assortment of tests and condensed her persona into typewritten pages full of jargon.

With Bedford leading the way, she rolled through the security door to the court foyer, and then into Courtroom No. 1, the domain of Judge Leonard P. Edwards.

Edwards was a youthful, lean thirty-nine-year-old with thin brown hair who seemed very intense as he eyed each witness and mouthed the end of his ballpoint pen. The courthouse regulars thought he was smart and scrupulously fair, the sort who would be quick to block any county action that might interfere with Tiffany's right to due process. His father was U.S. Representative Don Edwards, a staunch liberal who had been in Congress longer than any other Californian. While a law student, Leonard Edwards had done civil rights work in Mississippi in 1964, and while a private attorney had been chairperson of the Mid-Peninsula chapter of the American Civil Liberties Union.

Tiffany liked the way Edwards looked and spoke. He had presided briefly over her troubled dealings with her father when she was a juvenile ward of the same court. But the judge, as nice as he seemed, could act only on what he knew and heard, and she did not like the looks of the experts the county had assembled against her. Most of her friends in the courthouse said they thought Edwards would eventually rule against her.

For a psychological boost, she had gone to a beauty college in

Fremont and had them give her one of those new short cuts with frosted highlights. It made her feel different, vibrant, a little stronger.

On behalf of the petitioner, I would call Dr. Amal Barkouki to the witness stand," Clark said.

Tiffany shuddered, unable to control her distaste for the attractive, olive-skinned woman with the short, curly black hair.

"Dr. Barkouki, what is your occupation?"

"I am a clinical psychologist."

In better circumstances, Tiffany and Barkouki might have found they had much in common. Barkouki herself had been a teenage mother. Her first daughter had been born when she was a seventeen-year-old undergraduate at Stanford University. She had grown up in an academically oriented family in Alexandria, Egypt, married an engineering student when she was fifteen, and followed him to California. She excelled as a psychologist and became a noted expert on child abuse and neglect, as well as an activist in Arab-American affairs.

Barkouki often argued against county attempts to remove children from difficult homes, but she had not been swayed by Tiffany's youthful persistence and charm. She had helped put Tiffany through the analyst's obstacle course: the Millon Co-Axial Multivariate Inventory (MCMI), the Minnesota Multiphasic Inventory (MMPI), the Rorschach, and the Bender. In all, she had seen Tiffany for about four and a half hours, which included an hour during which she watched her with David, and then had written a report.

"And following your analysis of the testing, and following your interviews with Tiffany, did you arrive at a clinical diagnosis concerning Tiffany?" Clark asked.

"Yes."

"And is that clinical diagnosis contained in your report dated June 7, 1988?"

"That is correct."

"And referring specifically to the top of page eight of your report, was your diagnosis that Tiffany suffers from generalized anxiety, a borderline personality disorder with narcissistic histrionics and paranoid traits?"

Tiffany let the long, Latinate terms flow over and through her, hoping the judge would not see her dark look. That was not her, she thought.

Barkouki answered Clark's question. "That is correct," she said.

Bedford jumped to his feet. "I would object," he said, "and I base that on the fact that there has been no showing that any of these tests are scientifically accepted, especially as they relate to disabled persons, and in particular as they relate to people who have cerebral palsy."

Edwards looked interested. This was a crucial issue. "I will let you develop that in cross-examination," he said.

Clark asked Barkouki to explain her diagnosis. She fumbled for a moment with her files and inspected her notes through large, square-framed glasses.

"Okay, here we go. With generalized anxiety, it has to do with how she responds to stress, everyday stress, the need that she has to always be doing something, and having many things going on at once; her own self-report of not being able to sleep without thoughts or ideas bothering her . . ."

Tiffany glowered. Bothering me!?! I think, therefore I am.

". . . or being afraid of losing her mind; feeling anxious about something or somebody almost all of the time; feeling as if she can't sleep, afraid of dying, afraid to be alone."

Tiffany remembered two questions that, Bedford explained to her, had been taken as proof of her paranoia. Barkouki had read to Tiffany a question, "Are you being followed?" She had said yes, for she was certain that her soon-to-be ex-husband was checking her movements, something he had done in the past.

Barkouki had read another question, "Are you being poisoned?" Tiffany said yes again. "DSS is poisoning me," she remembered telling the psychologist. "They're trying to poison my whole life with this case."

Barkouki later said the test rules prohibited her from recording Tiffany's explanations of her answers. The psychologist could mark only yes or no, but could factor the explanations into her evaluation later. A friend cautioned Tiffany never again to speak metaphorically while taking a psychological test.

Barkouki told the court that Tiffany's Rorschach test "had a lot of indicators of borderline disorder."

Tiffany waited to hear the tale of the bats.

Barkouki shifted in the chair, studying her notes. "For example," she said, "to name one, the first card that most people see as one bat, she sees as a family of bats all connecting with one another. She has many indications in the Rorschach of this kind of merger, seeing more than one connected with each other. In terms of child rearing, that would be very difficult for a person with this."

One of the attorneys objected to this as irrelevant, and the judge agreed. Clark asked: "What other observations did you make with regard to—"

Barkouki did not wait for him to finish the question. "She has a tendency toward what we call overidealization, and then devaluation. That is overidealizing somebody, falling madly in love with them, being very close to them, and then turning quickly against that same person and feeling angered and betrayed by that person." She could not handle, Barkouki said, "what the rest of us would believe are somewhat day-to-day levels of disappointment."

The hearing was less than half an hour old, and Tiffany already felt weary. There were moments when it seemed as if she lived on another planet, a place that people never came close enough to see clearly. This eminent psychologist had produced this portrait after spending less time with her than it takes for an average outing to the beach.

Viewed through the lens of modern psychology, her vanity had become narcissism, her flares of temper histrionics, and her sour view of Shirley Silvani and Michael Clark raging paranoia.

Even her struggle for her children became part of her psychosis. "In my interviews with her," Barkouki said, "she speaks of being chosen by God and having a special relationship with God, in a sense of having some sort of special destiny about bearing children, and having a special destiny to lead in some way."

The psychologist seemed to be saying, Tiffany thought, that even clinging to hope could be held against her.

"Now, I realize that not having your kids is a stressful situation, don't get me wrong," Barkouki said. "But my concern is that her neediness, internal neediness, is so great that the children will have to mold themselves toward that neediness."

As Clark paused to frame a final question, Tiffany saw that the psychologist had painted a ghastly picture of her. Still, it seemed unreal, artificial—a portrait by an artist who had hardly looked at all.

"Now, in your opinion," Clark said, "does Tiffany have the ability to even form a stimulating or nurturing relationship with the child?"

Barkouki considered this. "That she can form? I think it is possible. That she can maintain that? I don't think it is likely. And by that I mean form for a short period of time.

"In observing her with children, and I realize that, you know, I only saw one hour of observation"—Tiffany nodded in surprise at the psychologist's honesty—"but I saw something that really works against being able to form and maintain a relationship with a child."

Barkouki had closed the door, Tiffany thought, but she had thankfully left it unlocked. She had not seen David coo and giggle as they wrestled on the floor. She had not seen the baby she nursed or the toddler who hugged her neck.

Clark attempted to nail his case shut without returning to the psychologist's admission of fallibility. "In your opinion, do you believe that Tiffany could benefit from reunification services within the next twelve to eighteen months?"

"No."

"Now, in your opinion, does Tiffany have the ability to form stable, long-lasting relationships with other adults?"

"No, she has that overidealization devaluation, and it is a real problem for anybody that gets really close to Tiffany. She is charming on the outside, she is very engaging, she is articulate, she is pretty"—I am the wicked queen in *Snow White*, Tiffany thought, beautiful but rotten to the core—"she knows how to speak in an engaging way, she is somewhat seductive. She is somewhat theatrical. She is very charming, but when you get really close emotionally"—as I'm *sure* you did during our four and a half hours together, Tiffany thought—"all the turmoil of her ambivalence about dependency comes up."

Tiffany sighed. Bedford had said it was not going to be easy.

Bedford began his cross-examination with a discussion of the Department of Social Services Auditorium at 55 Younger Street. It was a crowded, noisy, poorly organized torture chamber that many visitors and DSS staff had come to call the Zoo.

"Now," Bedford asked, "who decided that the evaluation with Tiffany and the two children would occur at the DSS auditorium?"

"I called to find out if we were going to do that," Barkouki said, "and how we were going to do that, and Ms. Silvani said there was an appointment already scheduled for Tiffany to visit with her kids at the auditorium, and would I want to go there."

"At any point did you suggest to Ms. Silvani the auditorium was not an appropriate place for this observation?"

"It wasn't my favorite, but I am sure it wasn't anyone's favorite."

Edwards looked over at her: "You didn't answer the question."

"Did I say to her, 'No, it wasn't appropriate'?"

"Yes," Bedford prompted.

"No. I took into account the limitations of the space and the place."

"So you think that your observations in the auditorium were satisfactory for the hours you spent with Tiffany and the two children for the purpose you have?"

"Adequate," Barkouki said, her expression neutral. Barkouki would later draft a damning indictment of the Zoo that would help persuade DSS to move out of 55 Younger Street and find a more congenial setting for reunions of parent and child.

Bedford asked about Barkouki's professional background. She had received her Ph.D. in 1975, she said.

"Since 'seventy-five," he said, "what percentage of your practice deals with disabled people?"

"I would say about ten percent."

"Of that ten percent, what percentage deals with people with
cerebral palsy?"

"I think I have seen two people with cerebral palsy, one seriously cerebral palsied, and one more mildly."

"What would you say Tiffany is? Severe, mild, moderate?"

"Moderate."

"Do you know what her exact diagnosis is? What the exact
terminology for her brand of cerebral palsy is?"

"No, I would have to look it up in the records. Something
spasticity."

"Do you have any knowledge as to whether or not Tiffany's
cerebral palsy is either going to improve, regress, or remain the
same over the next period of years?"

"I think somewhere in the record it said it might get worse,
but I don't—I have no knowledge."

"So in that sense you don't know what the prognosis is for
people with CP in general?"

"I don't know if I would say that."

"Okay," Bedford said. He thought he had made the point that
despite Barkouki's expertise in child abuse, her knowledge of cerebral palsy was rudimentary. "Well, in general, is CP, first of all,
a disease, a condition, or what?"

"Generally, it doesn't deteriorate as badly as people may think
it does."

"What is the life expectancy of someone with CP?"

"I suppose it may depend on the complications that may come
with it. It depends what parts of their bodies are mostly affected,
otherwise it would be normal."

"Can you tell me what the most common cause of CP is?"

"I believe that it may either be something—it is certainly
something intrauterine or maybe something at birth in terms of it
is considered a birth defect."

Well, Tiffany thought, she got that right.

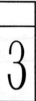

3

Through the winter and spring of 1967, Nancy Joy Callo had experienced nothing unusual during her first pregnancy. She was only seventeen and felt comfortable enough in her sixth month to go dancing.

She had married Bob Callo, a dazzlingly blond twenty-two-year-old Army veteran, on February 17, 1967. The ceremony in a municipal judge's chamber had occurred five months after she met Callo at Sal and Luigi's Pizza Parlor on First Street in San Jose and four months after they conceived a child in the cramped backseat of a Nash Rambler parked down the street from her mother's apartment.

It was a difficult marriage from the beginning. They fought often and suspected each other of infidelities. Nancy's parents had divorced when she was four, and though she was intelligent and received B's in high school without much effort, she had spent her teenage years mostly unsupervised. She dated men in motorcycle clubs and flaunted an unsavory reputation.

Bob Callo had a drinking problem from his Army days in Germany and Vietnam. He did not seem able to hold a job very long, except when employed by his mother and stepfather in the family business, the Callo Sign Company. He had what later would be called a learning disability. He could not read and was bitter about what he considered his lifelong fate to be ignored or abused by others.

The couple had little money. Often food stamps were the only thing that carried them from one week to the next. Nancy had been expelled from high school because the dean said her pregnancy set a bad example for other girls. She spent her days in Sal and Luigi's, gossiping with friends.

Nancy and Bob still loved each other. They enjoyed driving in his immaculate 1957 Chrysler Windsor sedan, painted peach with a cream top. They looked forward to having the baby. Bob announced months before the birth that if it was a girl he wanted to name her Tiffany, a tribute to the gentle, loony sophistication he had found so absorbing in the film *Breakfast at Tiffany's*.

Nancy saw a doctor at El Camino Hospital in Mountain View once each month. All signs pointed to a normal delivery.

On Tuesday morning, April 18, she was ironing shirts in the kitchen of the one-bedroom apartment over a garage that her mother-in-law had found for them in Mountain View. She felt a wet trickle down her leg. Water was soaking her pants leg and forming a puddle on the linoleum floor. She swore and rushed to the linen drawer, pulling out towels to dry up the mess. Then she called her doctor and at his urging drove to the hospital.

After a quick examination, her doctor confirmed that the amniotic sac had ruptured, a bad sign with a fetus barely six months old. "Go home, drink a lot of water, stay off your feet, and we'll see what happens," he said. Labor would come soon, but each additional day in the womb added to the baby's chances of survival.

Thursday night she began to feel cramps in her lower back. By 6 A.M. Friday she was in labor. Bob rushed her to the hospital, where labor proceeded rapidly.

At ten minutes after noon, a red-skinned, tiny baby girl was born. She was only three pounds, one ounce, and nearly three months premature, but she sucked in air and cried lustily within seconds, easing the tension in the room. A nurse weighed her, measured her, and cleaned the birth canal debris off her raw skin. Unexpectedly, the infant stopped breathing.

"Get her out of here!" someone shouted. The nurse picked the infant up, still wrapped in a pink blanket, and walked quickly toward the nursery to place her in an oxygen-fed incubator to ease her breathing.

Nancy was later told by a nurse that it took about three minutes for the child's breathing to resume. Such incidents often lead to lawsuits in today's hospitals, but Bob and Nancy were young parents who had neither the inclination nor the money to sue for malpractice. It would be almost two years before either of them even knew something was wrong.

Cerebral palsy had been with the human race much longer than the medical profession. For centuries the distorted speech, loss of muscle control, and apparent mental retardation were viewed simply as an act of God. After doctors began attempting to explain such conditions in scientific terms, research focused on some basic deficiency of the nervous system brought on by disease or genetic factors.

No clear explanations emerged. Doctors discovered that cerebral palsy had multiple symptoms—spasms, involuntary muscle movement, unsteadiness, seizures, abnormal sensation and perception, impairment of sight, hearing, or speech, mental retardation—which did not all appear at once. It could arise from several causes, including defective development in premature infants, injury, or disease. Cerebral palsy—"cerebral" referring to the brain and "palsy" to a disorder of movement or posture—became a convenient, collective, and somewhat misleading term for a host of conditions that had no single cause or set of symptoms.

Yet the consequences of cerebral palsy were enormous, particularly as medical technology increased the chances that premature infants—those most likely to develop the condition—would survive into childhood and beyond. In 1967 Tiffany Callo and approximately seven thousand other infants were born with the condition in the United States. By 1990 a total of at least half a million American children and adults displayed one or more of the characteristics of cerebral palsy.

The cause of Tiffany's disability remains unknown. Researchers have concluded that a principal factor in cerebral palsy is not enough oxygen reaching the brain of an unborn or newborn baby. The oxygen supply may be dangerously reduced if the placenta separates too soon from the wall of the uterus, or if the child is in a difficult birth position, has too long or too sudden a labor, or has a tangled umbilical cord. Jaundice, caused by liver malfunction, is almost always found in premature infants with immature livers, as it was in the Callo case. If severe, jaundice can also damage the brain. German measles or incompatible Rh factor or blood type between parents can have an impact. Mistakes in the delivery room, such as failure to force oxygen quickly into an infant who has stopped breathing, can also cause cerebral palsy.

But research at the National Institutes of Health indicates that the vast majority of cases of cerebral palsy in premature infants are the unavoidable result of immature development of the nervous system. The three minutes the newborn Tiffany Callo reportedly spent without oxygen would not have been enough to cause severe brain damage. Even if Nancy had been taking drugs during the pregnancy, something Bob suspected but she denied, it was unlikely it would have led to their daughter's condition, particularly since she was checked monthly by a doctor prior to the birth.

Like the vast majority of disabled people in the United States, Tiffany was the victim not of malpractice, conspiracy, or immorality but of chance. The rate of births of infants with her condition is thought to have declined somewhat since 1967 because of better equipment and more sophisticated techniques for dealing with prematurity, but the birthing process remains unpredictable. There has yet to be discovered a way of keeping some children from arriving too soon.

Bob Callo expected a long wait, but shortly after noon, Nancy's doctor strolled into the waiting room and motioned him into a corner for a talk.

"You have a daughter, Mr. Callo, although she's very small. We're going to have to put her in the incubator since she's premature. She also has yellow jaundice. That's quite common in these cases. We will need to give her some blood." Bob Callo appreciated the man's quiet tone of voice and his willingness to provide some sense of the danger. "I'm not sure how it's going to go with the baby yet," the doctor said. "But your wife is fine. It wasn't too hard for her."

Bob Callo decided not to be alarmed. Kids were born premature every day. "What are the baby's chances?" he asked.

"She's fifty-fifty," the doctor said. "One thing in her favor is she came out fighting. I didn't have to spank her. She yelled very loud."

The baby remained in the hospital for a month and four days. Nancy was released after three days, returning to the apartment with the unearthly feeling that nothing had happened. She had given birth, and yet had no baby. That same afternoon a hospital clerk called to ask both parents to return to give the blood Tiffany would need to fight the jaundice. The doctors gave the infant three transfusions, probing for veins at the bottoms of her feet.

The Callos came to the hospital nearly every day and were allowed into the nursery to peer at their daughter. It was like entering a nuclear laboratory to handle a rare and precious isotope. They put on hospital pants, shirt, mask, and cap before they could peer into their daughter's small glass home. She looked raw and red, but well formed, with her fine cheekbones already in evidence. Bob Callo marveled at her perfect tininess. She could fit in a shoe box.

On May 25, a hot, smoggy day, Bob and Nancy, with help from his mother, Elnora, brought the child home. She was delicate and pretty, with large, electric blue eyes, but still small at five pounds and two ounces. Even the smallest baby clothes were too big.

They placed the bassinet beside their bed and watched in relief as the child consumed baby formula with tight-lipped concentration. She slept well, rarely waking more than once a night. She loved to cuddle in their arms.

Their concern about the baby's health and their relief at her return had brought a truce in what Nancy and Bob realized was an increasingly troubled relationship. They both had bad habits they found difficult to break. Tiffany's presence failed to provide the salve they halfway hoped might heal several emotional sore spots.

The deterioration of their marriage accelerated after Bob was arrested for speeding and drunk driving, and, because of previous traffic violations, sentenced to three months at the Elmwood work farm.

Since Bob had a job at a steel galvanizing plant in Santa Clara, the judge let him leave the farm during the day and return at night. That required Nancy's love and cooperation, a rapidly diminishing commodity. She rarely drove him to work, forcing him to walk the ten miles. If she did not appear at quitting time, he begged coworkers to give him a lift back to the farm to avoid extra time added to his sentence.

A man at work needled him: "Hey, I saw your old lady out cruising the streets the other night." Bob ignored him. "Yeah, she's out there driving your car. Picked me up over on First, and we went out. She's a real sweet lady."

Bob had wondered about Nancy's nights. There were second-hand accounts of her driving around at 5 A.M. with Tiffany in the baby seat and the windows wide open.

"Oh, that lady of yours, she's real sweet, Bobby," the taunting coworker went on. "Tell you what, it's too bad you're not around nights to see that." Bob's intestines quivered and his face became hot. He walked over to his tormentor, bent low, and slammed his shoulder into the man's stomach. He hoisted his screaming victim aloft and walked up the stairs to the catwalk above the molten lead tank. While the man shouted and struggled, Bob hovered on the edge, feeling his fatigue, and gladly gave up his victim to three men who had run up the stairs after him.

It was a sweltering August, yet Nancy had taken to wearing long-sleeved shirts. One day he cornered her, grabbed one sleeve, and yanked it up. There they were, the little puncture marks of a speed addict.

"What is this bullshit?" he said.

She snarled at him. "What are you talking about? Get your hands off me. I went to the blood bank, all right? Somebody's got to make some money doing something around here."

"Try again, Nancy. Those needle marks are too big."

"Go to hell, Bobby," she said.

When she failed to show up the next evening at work, he went back to the apartment and found her there with a man he did not know. The next morning he returned with his mother. They picked up Tiffany, a few of his clothes, and left.

"Suit yourself, Bobby," she said. "I got other plans."

Tiffany Callo's parents parted, more in relief than anger, when she was three months old.

The collapse of Bob's marriage and his return home did not suit either him or his parents. Bob did not get along well with his stepfather, Jesse Callo, a Philippine-born Navy veteran his mother, Elnora, had married when Bob was seven. Still, Elnora, a slim and energetic woman, was happy to have more contact with Tiffany.

She was a sweet, easy baby. Bob became concerned, however, when at six months she still could not sit up. In the high chair she had to be strapped in and watched to make sure she did not slide onto the floor like rag doll. He was patient; the doctors had said to expect late development in premature infants.

Bob decided to begin a program of exercises. Because of his learning disability, he could not read the books that offered advice on baby development, but he had seen babies being handled on television. He had a few ideas of his own.

He lay on the couch and put her on his chest. The contact was warm, soft, and sticky. She seemed to thrill at the sound of his voice and the feel of his muscles supporting and cradling her. He rotated and pumped her arms and legs, creating the image of a weight-lifting elf. He put her on her back on the rug and held her legs up in the air, turning them in a bicycling motion to stimulate the muscle tissue. He pulled her arms up and down to the rhythm of a Beach Boys song on the radio.

She showed no interest in crawling, but at eight months learned to roll over. That became her principal means of propulsion. She was the family tumbleweed, rolling across the floor in search of a favorite toy. At least once a day Bob put her on her stomach, placed his hand underneath her, and lifted her slightly to demonstrate the crawling position. Each time she flopped down happily and rolled away.

Bob divorced Nancy but promised she could see Tiffany on two conditions. She had to be sober and she had to be decently dressed and combed. When Tiffany was nine months old, Nancy arrived for an evening visit, walking and speaking unsteadily. Bob could smell the alcohol but decided to ignore it. She seemed to be on her way to another party and probably would not stay long.

"Oh, baby, baby," she said loudly, hugging Tiffany with unusual ferocity. The child, terrified at the painful squeezing, began to cry. Elnora touched Nancy's arm. "Maybe I should take her for a little while," she said.

The mother snarled at the grandmother. "Get *away!*" she shouted. "This is *my* kid. I don't get to see her too often. *Let me hold her!*"

Elnora persisted. Nancy held Tiffany with one arm and shoved the older woman away with the other. Elnora slipped on the rug and landed hard on her hip. Bob and Jesse, in rare unanimity, exploded in anger. Bob dragged Tiffany away from Nancy; Jesse pushed her out the door.

Later that night Nancy was arrested during a police drug stakeout. She slammed a squad car door on a police captain's foot and broke a bone. She was sent to the Elmwood farm, her ex-husband's former residence, for six months. After her release, she did not try to see Tiffany again.

By her first birthday Tiffany could sit up with some help, but her neck wobbled and her legs could not brace her well. While other one-year-olds were walking, she could not even pull herself up to stand. She gurgled and smiled and flashed her dimple, delighting strangers. But she could not say a single discernible word.

The doctors did not seem alarmed. "When it will happen, it will happen," one said.

Elnora defended her granddaughter. She said Tiffany had been born premature and would take life a little more slowly than others. She established a tight bond with the child and seemed to be the only adult able to read Tiffany's signals and produce the drink or the cookie or the comfort she wanted.

"You know, Mom," Bob said, "if you weren't at her beck and call all day, she might learn to say something, you know, ask for what she wants."

Elnora frowned. He persisted. "Look, she's got to start. You just anticipate everything she wants. She's got to start communicating."

Elnora would fetch water or milk, depending on Tiffany's mood, without the child's saying a word. This telepathic communication became so sophisticated that the grandmother could eventually tell if her small customer wanted chocolate or strawberry flavoring in the milk. Much to her father's distress, Tiffany eventually refused to drink anything but milk flavored by Elnora. She ate heartily, but demanded to be spoon-fed. Bob lectured his mother, with little effect, on the need to force Tiffany to handle utensils.

Bob thought one way to lure Tiffany out of his mother's comfortable cocoon and into speech was to read to her. He called it reading, although he was incapable of deciphering more than a few words from even the simplest book. Instead, he made up stories, a different one each night. He turned off the lights in Tiffany's bedroom and lit a single candle to focus her attention on the words and the mysteries that surrounded them. The candle stories were full of ghost ships and lighthouses, with the single flickering light a perfect prop. Some were frightening; some were not.

"So the sailor ran to the lighthouse, Tiffany," he said, shielding the candle with his hand. "First he turned the light on"—he uncovered the flame—"and then looked out to sea and waited for his ship."

Before going to work each morning, Bob put Tiffany on his chest, did their exercises, and talked to her about his plans for the day. He refused to use baby talk and tried to persuade others, particularly his mother, to speak normally to her. "I can't do that goo-chee, goo-chee, woo, woo, woo, Mom," he said. "I don't think you should do it. She's got to learn. If you keep talking baby talk, that's all the kid is going to know."

Almost from the beginning his daughter was a personality to him, someone he expected to be talking to the rest of his life. The nightly tide of stories and conversation and the child's own innate intelligence eventually had an effect. By the time Tiffany was two years old, she could say several words.

But her first word, Bob admitted, was "Gran-ma."

When Tiffany was eighteen months old, her pediatrician sent her to a specialist in developmental problems. He tested her reactions, her muscle tone, her eyesight, and every motor function imaginable. He took a lot of blood, something that for Tiffany would become as commonplace as putting coins in a church collection plate. Her blood type was A positive. When she enrolled in school and learned about grades, she called it her A+ blood.

The diagnosis took several visits and a long wait for results. It was not until March 1969, nearly Tiffany's second birthday, that Elnora Callo answered the telephone in her kitchen and listened quietly while a doctor told her her granddaughter had cerebral palsy. "It's a motor disorder, Mrs. Callo," the doctor said. "If your son will come see me, I'll try to explain."

Bob did not completely understand what cerebral palsy was, but he knew it was bad. He tried a small prayer. Why her, Lord? Why not me? It seemed wrong for a life with as much promise as hers to be dealt such a blow when his own was already so hopeless.

In the doctor's office he listened carefully, but the meaning did not become much clearer. The patient was strapped into her baby carrier, smiling at the physician's familiar face and soft fingers. "It's a brain disorder, affecting this rear portion of the brain," the doctor said, tapping the child's small skull. "That part of the brain is not fully developed in Tiffany, but it is what controls the muscles. The signals aren't getting through to the body. The signals are dead."

Bob looked at his daughter, happy with a toy, and tried to frame a question. "Is there some way to stimulate it?" he asked. He had heard something about experiments with monkeys, about running electrodes into motor nerves. "Is there any way to stimulate it with shock therapy or something, and maybe to wake it up?"

The doctor scratched his head. He had a look Bob had seen often on the faces of schoolteachers and personnel managers and others put on the earth to make him feel inadequate. "I don't think I know of any treatment like that that has ever been successful," the doctor said.

Bob sighed. "Well," he said, "what can we expect?"

"She may improve a bit. It is hard to predict. You are going to have to let her go at her own pace. She will never walk or sit up. She may never talk. You just have to be grateful for whatever progress you make."

This annoyed Bob. Couldn't the experts give him some sense of what her limits might be, some benchmark he could use? No, the doctor said, each case of cerebral palsy was different.

Bob picked up Tiffany in her carrier and walked out of the office in a daze. He felt, not for the first time, as if he was stranded in midair, strung up by his thumbs.

Jesse Callo, full of immigrant energy, had established a successful sign-painting business. His three-bedroom light brown stucco house in Sunnyvale, a west northwest suburb of San Jose, was spacious and comfortable. But Bob felt cramped there. Tiffany grew up loving her grandfather's lean, quiet strength, but Bob thought Jesse was cold and hard, and unwilling to give him the opportunities he deserved.

Eager to move out, Bob found a small apartment in Santa

Clara, another San Jose suburb, and began to plan the rest of his life. He had to find a job that offered medical benefits. If there was ever a cure for what Tiffany had, he wanted access to it.

It was becoming clear to him that he had missed whatever boat might have taken him to wealth and happiness. His life, at least for the foreseeable future, was to be this small, squirming, puzzling child and a succession of frustrating and backbreaking jobs with little chance for advancement. He loved the child, so he set out to suffer the jobs and be the best father he could be.

He hired baby-sitters at first, usually neighborhood women willing to take Tiffany into their apartments for the day. Her long days inside while he was at work made the outside world alien and somewhat frightening to her. He tried to coax her out on weekends with the promise of a picnic. "We won't go far, Tiff," he told her, sitting on the couch and cradling her in his arms. "We'll just get a blanket and go out and eat on the grass."

She resisted, shaking her head in that wild, uncontrolled way. The doctor had greatly underestimated her ability to communicate. She was talking by age three, and loudly expressed her views about being coaxed out onto the lawn. She examined the grass suspiciously and looked around. "There's nobody out here, Daddy," she said.

"Well, first off you've been cooped up in the house all this time. Nobody knows you're even living here. They never see you. So let's get you out here and maybe you'll meet some friends."

Like the candle stories, he improvised. He bought a toy bowling set which he placed on the small lawn to lure her out on Saturday afternoons. He provided sandwiches and juice and showed her how to roll the ball toward the pins. They kept score—she was good with numbers—and made side bets in potato chips.

At low moments Bob brooded on the breakup of his marriage and the lack of a mother in his daughter's life. How would she learn to cook and dress and sew? He decided to build a scaled-down, accessible toy kitchen. He drew a plan in meticulous detail: a table here, a stove over there, cupboards here, cupboards over there, a small refrigerator, a special chair where she could sit and another to help her keep her balance and do stretching exercises. His mother added a working toy oven.

Tiffany loved the arrangement. For several months it was difficult to persuade her to play with anything else. The kitchen set was one of the few things Tiffany's father gave her that she never forgot. Other children in the neighborhood, invited in to see the new kitchen, told their parents. Bob was asked by two other families if he could do the same for them.

His daughter, Bob told himself, was not going to succumb to his terror of letters and words. He bought her books and found she particularly enjoyed the exciting surprise of those that produced pop-up pictures in three dimensions. He bought her a toy typewriter, which he hoped would help her compensate for her clumsiness with a pen or pencil. He bought wooden puzzles with large pieces that would not be too difficult. She loved to inspect each part and slowly, painstakingly, fit them in.

He took each day as it came, enjoying the little girl's company and the sense of responsibility she gave him. For a while he thought it was going to work out fine.

When Tiffany was four, she began to attend the Fremont Older School in Cupertino, a suburb on San Jose's western edge not far from Elnora's house. The school was a collection of one-story redwood-paneled buildings surrounded by grass and maple trees.

Tiffany loved Fremont Older. The school was full of lively children with nearly every disability and condition imaginable, from cerebral palsy to muscular dystrophy, from leukemia to ulcers. She met Liz Balcom, a short, sassy girl whose cerebral palsy was less severe than hers, and Denise Hicks, whose spina bifida, an opening in the vertebrae affecting the spinal cord, made it difficult for her to walk. They called themselves the Three Musketeers and became inseparable.

Despite Bob Callo's fear that Tiffany might inherit his learning problems, she worked hard and absorbed her lessons well. Tiffany's teachers discussed moving her over to a mainstream class of nondisabled children, but an operation pulled her out of class for six weeks and set back the timetable. The surgeon wanted to extend the muscles in her thighs to try to strengthen her limbs and increase her mobility. It was part of an ultimately unsuccessful effort to straighten her legs so her ankles would not cross when she tried to stand.

When she returned to school, she was on medication that made her drowsy and forced long naps in the middle of the school day. Her progress slowed. In the third grade, she was transferred to the Chandler Tripp School, just west of the sprawling Valley Medical Center. This was considered a promotion, but she was put in a class that seemed to be reviewing work she had mastered in the first grade.

Bob Callo feared she was being parked and forgotten. Chandler Tripp was a modern institution with beige brick and stucco buildings set among pleasant courtyards. There was plenty of new equipment, but Bob thought the program lacked the academic emphasis of Fremont Older. The Chandler Tripp teachers did not talk about putting Tiffany in a mainstream class.

Bob visited a few classes and saw pupils coloring pieces of paper and listening to a teacher read. Tiffany was not encouraged to read on her own, or tell stories to the rest of the class. The school seemed to him a glorified babysitting operation.

He tried to supplement the intellectual diet at home. He gave Tiffany story books to read. They worked with flash cards on addition and multiplication.

A year before Tiffany began school, Bob had married a woman I shall call Lucy, who seemed to accept Tiffany and her disability. He was delighted to end his reliance on baby-sitters, who either paid little attention to Tiffany or treated her like a troublesome pet with an annoying habit of picking up dirt as she dragged herself across the floor.

Eventually, however, the demands of a small, often helpless and sometimes irascible child began to wear on Lucy. She became convinced that Tiffany's endless play with her food was simple dawdling, unrelated to her disability. She insisted that the child eat everything on her plate, and put a kitchen timer on the table. "If you don't eat this before this timer runs out," she said, "something bad's gonna happen to you."

Tiffany still insisted on her own measured pace, the rhythm

that had fit her life since birth. Her father did not push her, at least not when he was in a good mood. He knew how painful and confusing it was to be forced beyond one's limits. If Tiffany cleaned her room and put away her toys, he did not care how long it took. In some important ways, both father and daughter played their lives at 33⅓ while the rest of the world whirled ahead at 78. They wanted food and shelter and some love in their lives, but they did not see any reason to hurry.

Bob would discover his only professional success in the painstaking construction of models and prototypes, where care and patience always produced the best results. He thought one of the best things he ever did was to slow down the war in Vietnam a tiny bit by keeping a faulty helicopter off the line, even though he was demoted for it. He assumed he had saved a few lives that day, and could count dozens of times—such as his marriage to Nancy—when impulsive haste had brought disaster.

All this was lost on Lucy. When Bob was not there to provide a buffer, Tiffany's stubbornly slow pace, her insistence on a different scale of time, grated on her stepmother.

At age five Tiffany began to use a manual wheelchair, a light, gray-and-blue Rolls-Royce model. It increased her mobility but also added to Lucy's annoyance, for now there were wheelchair marks on the floor and the baseboards.

Several times when Tiffany defied Lucy's time limit for meals, the woman pulled the child over her knee and spanked her. One day Lucy's rage overcame her so completely that she stripped Tiffany naked and dragged her, leg braces and all, into the bathroom. She turned on the cold water in the tub and switched on the shower. "God will get you!" she shouted at the child. "The Devil is going to get you, you little goddamned brat." She dumped Tiffany in, leaving her soaked and helpless on the slick porcelain bottom.

Bob knew Lucy was not the mother to Tiffany he had hoped she would be, and his own feelings toward Lucy were changing. Eventually, both began to consider divorce. Bob took Tiffany to his parents' house, where Elnora welcomed the two wounded spirits back into her tidy nest.

Bob did not want to stay there long. His stepfather interpreted his return as another sign of his essential worthlessness. His mother catered to Tiffany's every desire. Since the child was in school now, he thought she needed to develop a sense of independence and initiative. How could that happen with Elnora jumping up every minute to get her a glass of chocolate milk?

Tiffany saw her grandmother in an entirely different light. Elnora was the fighter in the family. She had been left pregnant at sixteen by a man who would not marry her. Yet she had carved out a good life. Her husband Jesse's success was in part a measure of her discipline and her appreciation of the worth of time and money. And she still had time to be kind to people.

The older Tiffany became, the more the child understood the world's view of her limits. When she was in her wheelchair, people refused to make eye contact and seemed reluctant to speak to her directly. Every time she heard people talk about her future, there was an underlying assumption that she would be dependent on her family all her life. She was advised to pursue her interest in cooking, but few people suggested she could ever have a family or a career.

Even her father, as loyal and protective as he was, undermined her confidence in many ways. He was one of the few people who thought she could lead an independent life, but he believed that the only way to ensure this was to knock off her rough edges and whittle her down to a fine point. Nothing she did, it seemed to her, was ever quite good enough for him.

Even her beauty, a treasure for any father, brought only grudging comment. If Elnora took Tiffany out and bought her a new dress and necklace, Bob would praise the result, but with a sarcastic edge. "Oh, you do look nice," he said, "but did you brush your teeth?" It was a remark any father might make to a forgetful daughter, but Tiffany took it as a vote of no confidence, particularly in contrast to the warmth and comfort her grandmother bestowed without qualification.

When she turned ten, the therapist at school recommended she switch to a motorized wheelchair. Bob objected. "It's just going to make her lazy," he said. "She has to push those wheels, it helps her arm strength, but you want her just to flip this little switch."

The therapist gave her a power chair anyway. Tiffany brought it home and triumphantly ran it back and forth in front of her father. Bob called the school. "What is this?" he shouted into the telephone. "You don't even consult me?" He knew he had lost.

The doctors prescribed daily exercises to improve Tiffany's muscle tone and make her more self-sufficient, using braces, a walker, and sometimes crutches. She did the exercises, but little improvement resulted. She never learned to crawl, but she could do what she called "the lizard"—a slithering movement across the floor propelled mostly by her elbows. She looked, to her amusement, like John Wayne in one of those World War II movies, crawling low under barbed wire and tracer bullets.

A decade later, some experts in physical disabilities began to challenge the usefulness of strenuous exercises for polio, cerebral palsy, multiple sclerosis, and an assortment of other immobilizing conditions. Only a few of the many people with such conditions who courageously pushed themselves to the physical limits had actually enjoyed long-term benefits. Forcing such people to walk with braces was unnecessary torture, these experts said. They recommended that therapists stop trying to shame clients who found wheelchairs more convenient and less draining.

The writer Anne Finger said she wept when she read a 1981 article in *Rehabilitation Gazette* that informed her for the first time of something called the post-polio syndrome. "The article said that those who were the best patients fared the worst," she said. "Polio rehabilitation was aggressive—long hours devoted to physical therapy, straining to get damaged nerves to function again. It was the Protestant ethic gone wild: The more you worked, the better you would get. The more you suffered, the more you gained. Now the theory was that we had been 'over-rehabilitated'—that our weakened nerves broke down because they were forced to do too much."

By the 1990s, many disability rights activists would be arguing that their energies should be conserved for the work they did best—calculating, planning, organizing, imagining, and all the other tasks the brain could perform without any help from the arms and legs.

In time the only chores that continued to frustrate Tiffany were putting on shoes and socks, arranging her hair, and cleaning herself after the toilet. Getting in and out of the bathtub was also a challenge, but she could do it if given enough time. She began to develop a lifelong hatred for pieces of furniture that always seemed to impede her way when she rode her chair. She plotted to get rid of them.

She was thin but surprisingly strong. She wore large glasses to correct the weak vision that was one symptom of her cerebral palsy. She seemed thoughtful, and relentless, in almost everything she did.

The point was to keep trying, her father told her. It was her job, for instance, to keep the bathroom clean. "If you can't do everything, you give at least that effort, you try," he told her. He did not want to hear her say she could not do it. He would never say that to her. He had had enough of people telling him he could not do things.

"If you can't do it, Tiff, at least make the honest effort, then you can call me and I'll come in and help," he said.

The therapist had told Bob that he had to keep Tiffany busy. If she just sat, her muscles would atrophy and depression would set in. Callo devised small rewards for his daughter. If she remembered to brush her teeth for a week, he would take her to the flea market at an old drive-in theater south of San Jose. In the jumble of dusty tables and weedy concrete, her wheelchair did not seem so out of place. She bought costume jewelry from one of the booths and ate hot dogs with her father.

Bob found a studio apartment in Santa Clara where Tiffany and he could recapture some of their old independence while relying on his mother as a daytime baby-sitter. Several months later he rejoiced when he found another woman whom he could love, and who could care for Tiffany. But the results, once again, were different from those he intended.

Tiffany Callo was removed from her father's care at age eleven, one of approximately 180,000 American children consigned to some form of court protection in 1978. Her disability made her an unusual addition to the large and multicolored assembly of children in shelters, foster homes, and institutions, but her route there was not the least bit out of the ordinary.

When child protective services began to win the power to remove children from homes in the nineteenth century, the caseworker's watchword became: When in doubt, take the child. The increase in drug use, divorce, and female poverty had put an explosive strain on the American family in the 1960s and 1970s. Court officials in Santa Clara County worried in 1978, as they pondered what to do about Tiffany Callo, just how many more children they could handle. They had no idea they would look back on the 1970s as a time when the problem had been relatively manageable.

Bob Callo fell in love with a woman I shall call Lorna. She was slim, pretty, and barely five feet tall, with long brown hair falling to the small of her back. She was quick and bright and fun at a party. Unlike Lucy, she had experience with children. She had two daughters of her own, aged six and eight.

Tiffany, age nine, had developed a hard shell of doubt about strangers coming into her tight family circle. But her father seemed happy, and her own life revolved so much around school that the opportunities for conflict with Lorna were limited.

Bob Callo had found work on the warehouse staff of a large electronics firm. They seemed interested in some of his ideas and model-making talents. He left each day at 6:30 A.M. and depended on Lorna to help Tiffany prepare for the 8 A.M. school bus.

Tiffany had adopted her grandmother's approach to uncomfortable social situations. Those who irritated her, she enveloped with compliments, like an oyster coating an unwelcome grain of sand. She thanked Lorna for the smallest favor and praised the beauty and intelligence of Lorna's two daughters when they visited on weekends. But all Tiffany's efforts did not chase the problems away.

On Sunday mornings Lorna cooked scrambled eggs and bacon for her girls. The scent filled the small apartment with cozy warmth and made Tiffany famished. But it was the family rule that she rise and dress herself. Several times she hungrily reached the breakfast table after an interminable battle with snaps and buttons only to find all the bacon gone and only a few small clumps of eggs left. She ate cereal and felt sorry for herself.

Her tortuous morning routine on school days was made worse by bladder and bowel problems. Her father lectured her about fouling her sheets, pressing her to get out of bed when she felt the first urge. But when he took her to a specialist, the doctor said the problem was more complicated than that. This was one more signal that her clumsy nervous system often fumbled. She could not be expected to reach the toilet in time no matter how quickly she responded to the first bodily signal.

Bob adjusted. He stopped yelling at his daughter and let her take care of the problem herself. "Okay, Tiff, you're a big girl," he said. "You know how to change your bed. You just take the wet and dirty clothes, put a little soap with them in the sink, and then hang them over the bathtub to dry. When I do the wash, I'll just pick them up and throw them in with everything else. No problem."

While Tiffany and her father made peace, she and Lorna settled into a morning war of ambush and attrition. Bob left them to work it out. He told Lorna to let Tiffany get herself ready, but the pressure of the coming bus put Lorna on edge and led her to push the girl in spite of herself.

One day after school Lorna peeked into the child's room as Tiffany was making her bed. Wet sheets from an accident that morning were still on the floor. Lorna pronounced the room a pigsty. "You got to do better than that, Tiffany," she said. "Your dad is going to kill me if we let this go on."

Tiffany was tired of hearing this. She did not think Lorna ever lifted a finger to clean the rest of the house. The woman complained of migraine headaches the minute she came within ten feet of a broom or a vacuum cleaner. "Listen, Lorna, you just stay out of my room," she said. "I got everything under control. I don't have to take that kind of stuff and I'm not going to do it."

The woman became angry. "You little jerk. You expect me to run around and get you ready for school every day, don't you? I think it's time for some changes around here."

She went to the kitchen and returned to the child's room with a pizza paddle Bob had bought when he thought he might take up pizza making. Tiffany was wearing a school dress and her leg braces, a lattice of brown-painted steel that the child loathed. Lorna gripped the paddle handle tightly and approached the girl. "You're stupid, you know?" she said. "You're a lazy little brat. You don't do anything your father tells you."

She shoved Tiffany up against the bed, lifted the child's dress, pulled down her panties, and began to strike her rump with the flat side of the paddle. Lorna's muscles tightened and her breath came hard as she swung downward with a two-handed motion.

Tiffany howled and squirmed. Lorna struck again and again, cursing the child, consigning her to every pit in hell. The woman was very small and not very strong, but her fury gave each blow great force. The child tried not to cry, but felt the pain and humiliation. The bruises were going to show for a long time, she thought.

After one hard swat, the dried, little-used wood of the paddle split in two. Lorna continued the beating with the remaining half, but found it too light to have much effect. Tiffany was now flat on the floor on her back, holding her breath for the next blow and trying to suppress tears that might give the woman further satisfaction.

Lorna stood over her, took a few quick breaths, and cursed. "You little bitch," she said. "You don't think anybody can get to you, do you?" She rolled the child over into the pile of wet sheets and clothes and began pushing wadded hunks of linen into her face as if to smother her.

As she squirmed under the woman's weight, looking for something to grasp, some of Lorna's long hair fell across her face. Tiffany clasped it in her hand, jerked back and simultaneously struck upward with her knee and braces, hoping to hit some soft spot that would at least surprise her tormentor.

Lorna groaned, swore, and rolled off the child to the floor. The woman looked dazed and somewhat ashamed. She rose up on her knees, absorbing what had happened, and spoke to Tiffany in a quiet, intense tone. "You little bitch. You think you really run this place, don't you? You think you've got me now, right? Listen, you so much as tell your father anything about this happening, I'm going to get a gun and shoot both of you."

"You bitch," the little girl said, still sprawled on the floor and crying. "Get out of my house. This is my dad's place. If you don't like it, that's too damn bad."

Lorna seemed stunned at the child's response and walked off unsteadily to the kitchen, apparently seeking a quiet moment to ponder just what she had done.

Tiffany did not tell her father. The next morning she felt bruised from her neck to her thighs, but took the bus to Chandler Tripp and hid her injuries. She did not know how her father would react if she told him. He was usually on her side in the war against Lorna, but his crumbling relationship with the woman had worsened his drinking problem, and she could never tell what kind of mood he was in.

She had sounded like a wounded, enraged adult when she fought with Lorna, but she was still only eleven. She thought the woman might be capable of killing Bob, Elnora, or others she loved if she reported the assault.

The thought curled about her innards like a parasite. Stomach upsets flared. The second day after the beating, she excused herself from a test and remained in the restroom stall for a long time.

"Are you okay, Tiffy?" asked a teacher's aide.

"I really don't feel good," Tiffany said. "Something is going on today, and I really am sick. I don't know what it is."

The aide wheeled her over to the nurse's office. The nurse felt her forehead and was about to speculate on the flu when Tiffany felt her stomach heave and begged them to lift her over to the toilet.

She spent the next half hour emptying her stomach. She rested between heaves by sitting back in her chair with a wet washcloth on her forehead. The nurse had many questions. What had she had for breakfast? How were things at home? Was her father at work a lot? What had she had for dinner? Who was taking care of her after school?

There was a mark on the child's arm the nurse did not like. The questions became more pointed. Had her dad hurt her? Had anybody in the house hurt her? The school staff members were aware of an underreported statistic: Children with disabilities could be as much as eight times more likely to suffer abuse.

Tiffany felt at a dead end. She saw darkness closing in. Her mouth was dry, full of bitter residue from the vomit. Her heart beat loudly. She began to cry.

"I don't . . . I don't want my *daddy to be hurt!*" she said. "I don't want my daddy to get hurt 'cause it wasn't his fault. He has been sick. It's been really hard for us. He has been working a lot of hours, coming home and going to bed. . . . The lady who takes care of me, the lady who . . ." She could not seem to get it out, so she reached down unsteadily with her left hand and pulled up her blouse.

The nurse saw many bruises. There was also a mark that looked like a handprint. There were marks on the child's back, shoulders, and rump. She hugged Tiffany and eased her into her chair, then sent the aide to get the principal.

When at 5 P.M. the school bus still had not appeared, Bob unleashed another of his frequent curses at the wayward driver and called the school transportation office. "Listen," he said, "the bus is even later than usual. Do you know what's going on?"

The secretary on the other end of the line seemed puzzled. "I think everything was on schedule today," she said. "Maybe he just got held up in traffic."

Bob hung up and waited another half hour. Still no Tiffany. He called the school principal's office this time. "You have *any* idea what's going on?" he asked. The secretary asked him to hold on while she checked. The next voice on the line was the principal's: "Mr. Callo, Tiffany's been taken to the county children's shelter."

Bob paused, groping for some understanding of what this meant. "You didn't send her home? What's the problem? What's happened?"

"It's a county matter now, Mr. Callo," he said. "I'm not allowed to tell you anything more. You'll have to get in touch with the county authorities."

"What?" he said. "It's five-thirty on Friday. How'm I gonna find anybody?"

"I'm sorry. That's all I can say." He hung up.

Bob found a number for the shelter, but the officer who answered the telephone said he could not handle inquiries on evenings and weekends. If the school said his daughter was there, then he should know she was in good hands. Call Monday and make an appointment.

When Bob told Lorna what had happened, she seemed surprised but said little. He took Monday off and, with Lorna and Elnora, went to Chandler Tripp for an explanation. Again the principal refused to provide any details and suggested they visit the shelter.

They parked near the flag pole outside the rambling collection of off-white buildings across from Kelley Park. A police officer and a social worker brought them into an office and gave them a terse account of the investigation so far. They said Tiffany was being held under protective custody because she had black-and-blue marks on her buttocks. They had talked to Tiffany and would want to talk to Bob eventually, but felt it best to keep her in the shelter while the investigation continued.

Bob felt even more confused and frustrated. Tiffany had had problems keeping her bottom clean. She vigorously washed her feet, her legs, her arms, and even her back, but it was difficult for her to wipe her rump after using the toilet and it became a point of contention. He would often find brown streaks in her panties and remind her to try a little harder, which she invariably promised to do.

Bruises, however, were an entirely different thing. Had she had a fight at school? Had she fallen? The police officer would not say.

Lorna listened to the officer without comment. Bob had been aware of vague charges by Lorna's ex-husband that she had abused her two daughters. He knew she and Tiffany did not get along, but he had seen no signs of physical cruelty. He told the police officer he was baffled. They scheduled separate interviews with him and with Lorna the next day.

They went to the county Juvenile Center building on Guadalupe Parkway and were ushered separately into small rooms. For an hour Bob answered questions he found increasingly annoying. "Have you ever hit your daughter, Mr. Callo? Do you ever get angry at her? Have you ever abused her in any way?"

He looked at the juvenile officer. "Man, I love my daughter. I would never, never, ever do anything like that. Why don't you tell me what *she* said? I can't believe she won't tell you how this happened."

The officer nodded. "As I say, Mr. Callo, we've talked to her, but the investigation isn't complete."

Lorna was questioned in another room. Driving home, she

said they asked the same questions. She denied doing anything to Tiffany.

Bob was not allowed to see his daughter at the shelter. He and his mother packed some of her favorite clothes, books, and toys and left them for her. After a week, an assistant district attorney called him in and told him that the investigation was inconclusive, but what information they had seemed to point not at him but at Lorna.

He did not say much to the officer. He was too angry to be coherent. He vowed to break it off with Lorna and remove her from the apartment that night. When would Tiffany get to come home? he asked.

The attorney frowned and hesitated. "She is now in custody of the county," he said. "The court is supervising the case. The law says in these cases we have to investigate the home, talk to the parents and the child about the cause of the problem, and outline remedial measures. We have to satisfy the court that the problems have been solved before she goes home. We might send her home fairly soon on a trial basis, but you're going to have to help us on this, Mr. Callo."

The initial hearing a week later left Bob with a distaste for the juvenile court system that would remain with him long after his daughter reached adulthood. In listing the investigators' concerns, the county attorney noted that Tiffany's teacher said she had dried egg on her face some mornings when she came off the bus.

"Sure, that happened sometimes," Bob said. "The bus came so early. Whenever my daughter sat at that table, there was a napkin or a wash rag to clean up her face, or if she couldn't do it, I would get it, but occasionally she'd drop some egg on her shirt or something like this and it was too late to change it because the bus was out there honking."

The social worker who inspected the apartment complained of a large bag of beer cans on the front porch. "We were *collecting* them from all over the neighborhood," Bob said. "Tiffany used to organize the neighborhood kids to do it." The judge nodded. "Collect them myself," he said.

It made no difference. They were not going to return her soon.

Even his efforts to coax Tiffany toward self-sufficiency were used against him. The social worker complained of finding wet sheets and clothes on the floor, items that had been on Tiffany's list of chores.

With dozens of cases to handle and few financial resources, social workers and judges had to make decisions every day based on incomplete, poorly understood information. In 1978 nearly one million reports of child abuse and neglect were filed in the United States. Every social worker and police officer knew a colleague who still had nightmares about a child not removed from an abusive home soon enough.

The best policy, most professionals thought, was to play it safe and try to solve the parents' problems while the child was kept in a separate place. They did not know that the disintegration of the American family structure, accelerated by the crack cocaine epidemic beginning in 1986, would overwhelm the shelter and foster-homes system designed to care for such children.

By 1990 reports of child abuse and neglect would have more than doubled to 2.4 million a year. Child welfare agencies and their shelters and foster-care programs would be so overextended and understaffed that more than a dozen class-action suits would be filed against them throughout the country. Connecticut's state system would be put under court supervision.

Removing the child from the home as an automatic first step in any abuse case would no longer seem such a good idea. Many sociologists, judges, social workers, and psychologists would begin to wonder if there were ways of helping frustrated parents deal with their problems while keeping their children at home.

It was an idea with some promise. If Bob Callo had had expert counseling about his style of parenting, his career goals, and his drinking habits, if a judge had agreed to return Tiffany in exchange for the removal of Lorna and a reasonable plan to increase the number of hours he spent at home, his relationship with his daughter might have developed differently. But in 1978, Bob had no choice but to work out his problems on his own, with his daughter removed from his life and no easy way to get her back permanently.

When Tiffany turned twelve, the court agreed to let her return to her father for ninety days to see how they got along. Lorna was gone, her goods tossed into a suitcase and several paper bags and placed on the front porch. Bob promised to try to stop drinking. But Tiffany could not shake an uneasiness about her father and their life.

Lorna returned to the apartment once. This frightened the child even though Bob quickly ejected the woman. He was working even longer hours than usual to pay the legal bills and employ baby-sitters for Tiffany. He did not want any creditors to be able to tell the court he could not pay his bills and provide for his daughter. A business slump had cost him his steady job at the electronics warehouse. He began a long series of computer industry assembly jobs, with few fringe benefits and work often tailing off after a few months. He also tended bar and worked as a fry cook, but that only added to his baby-sitting bills and his daughter's sense of being abandoned.

He still insisted that she do her chores. He prepared a list each morning and asked how many she had done each night. He believed she could eventually live a life independent of him, but she had to become accustomed to daily labor and finishing what she started. She could not survive on charm and quick wits, even if she had them in abundance.

At the end of the ninety days, Tiffany felt wrung out. She did not like being left with baby-sitters. Who could tell what they might turn out to be? Maybe Lorna was waiting to make another visit. She missed her father, but she resented, like any adolescent, his emphasis on housework and homework. There was no one in the juvenile court system with enough time to assess the depth of her feelings about her father and get at their roots.

The strain of pleasing the court and earning enough to pay the rent and the baby-sitters had done nothing to ease Bob Callo's alcoholism. Although he suppressed his rages, it was clear to both of them that he was not getting any better. When the ninety days were up, the social worker recommended that Tiffany be placed in a foster home. Tiffany did not object. She began a journey into adulthood that would only occasionally take her into her father's house again.

Almost twelve, Tiffany was placed with the Howletts, a Mormon couple with three children whose love and compassion and ease with all the intricacies of family life she found irresistible.

The noise and aimless wanderings and hair-pulling fights at the shelter had worn her down. The solid plainness of the Howletts intrigued her. Here was a mother and a father and a brother and two sisters made to order, easy as telephoning for a pizza. All she had to do was make them like her. It was the kind of thing she lived for, fresh targets for her high-velocity charm.

She wheeled into the small Howlett home, with its dangerously sunken living room and narrow halls, and pronounced it a palace. She insisted on helping set the table. She pulled the plates off a low shelf, placed them carefully on her lap, and wheeled them over to the table. She tended to her own toileting, scolding herself viciously whenever she waited too long before heading for the bathroom.

Glenn Howlett, a husky machine operator, and his wife, Mary, had often rearranged rooms to accommodate more children and guests during their seventeen years in their San Jose house. Tiffany moved in with Terry, the thirteen-year-old Howlett daughter. They installed bunk beds and put Tiffany on the bottom bunk, where she enjoyed talking to Terry late into the night.

If the family gathered in the living room to watch television, Tiffany had to be lifted down the two small steps. She was rail-thin, barely eighty pounds even with leg braces, but no one thought of her as fragile. She was a friendly, bubbly presence, her desire to please almost overwhelming. She lived for the sisterly camaraderie with Terry and Leslie, then sixteen, and developed a crush on Glenn Jr., then twelve.

Mary Howlett had her own disability, a disease of the retina that had left her legally blind. She had not let it get in the way of raising her family, though. It was easy for her to resist the temptation to fawn over the disabled child. Tiffany, practiced at directing the world about her, liked the sense of independence the Howletts gave her and became even more wedded to their lifestyle and love of children.

The Howletts always took Tiffany with them when they visited friends, and going to church seemed an extension of that. The child enjoyed the beauty of the local Church of Jesus Christ of Latter-Day Saints. The Bible studies and outspoken commitment to family values gave her a sense of a larger purpose to life. This was something she thought she had missed in Bob Callo's earnest attempts to make ends meet and prepare her for adult responsibilities.

The Howletts were no more pleased with the curriculum at Chandler Tripp than Bob had been. They encouraged Tiffany's interest in mathematics and helped her increase her typing speed. She began to acquire a knack for one-finger typing, and enjoyed the new sense of control over schoolwork.

Bob came to see her on weekends and would take her to a park or the beach, an effort to recapture the memories of their picnics on the apartment complex lawn years before. They tried to sort each other out, the tall, muscular, and now increasingly heavy man, determined that his daughter be better prepared than he for an indifferent world, and the effusive but emotionally brittle girl who wanted steadiness and warmth.

Tiffany preferred her foster father's calmer approach to life. Glenn Howlett enjoyed sitting on the couch and chatting with her about the course of the world, about God and family and the future. "You're the best daddy in the world," she said to him once. He looked embarrassed but pleased.

Bob refused to give up. The system had taken nearly everything else from him, but he was not going to give up fatherhood without a fight. The judge and social workers noted his diligence. Tiffany found her memories of Lorna and fears of her father's old black rages melting in the warmth of the Howlett circle.

When Mary Howlett mentioned that the county had contacted them about two small boys who needed a home, Tiffany took this as a sign that she should leave the Howletts and return to her father. She would be helping the boys, spreading the Howlett magic around, and making her father happy at the same time.

But she was fourteen and began to understand that the system, if she wanted, would let her be part of her father's life without ever again being under his control. She harbored lingering doubts about his temper and did not like the way the seventeen-year-old son of his new girlfriend had been looking at her. She developed a habit of staying with him for a few months and then seeking other arrangements.

When she was sixteen, she tried living in a group home with other disabled youths. She loved entering a new world where she could share experiences with people whose perspective was so much like her own. The director even took her to a Planned Parenthood clinic and had her fit with an intrauterine device, a rite of adulthood that Tiffany found pleasing, even if somewhat cold and clinical.

Then one evening when she was alone, the director's fiancé and one of the young male staff members found her and raped her. They told her that pressing charges would be futile, and that they would hurt her if she tried.

Such incidents were common. Disabled women had a fifty percent higher chance of being raped. Her decision to report the incident to the county sheriff's office eventually aided an investigation of other incidents in the same home four years later. But at the time her accusations were met with cold silence.

The group home director refused to believe she had been forced, despite her obvious inability to fend off such an attack. A sheriff's deputy took her statement, but nothing came of it for a long time. She missed three periods but found herself too numb with terror and despair to see a doctor. Apparently the IUD had not worked. One morning at school she felt a painful cramp and excused herself to the restroom. There she miscarried, a bloody mess. She was cold and sick and beyond pain. She felt dead.

The terror stayed with her for years, making it very difficult for her to consider any living arrangement that left her alone for more than a few minutes. She resumed living with foster families, and clung to their order and warmth, so different from the chilly underside of life she had discovered at the group home. She honed her talent for fitting into any family and thought often about how to balance her need for both security and independence.

When she turned eighteen, she began to think about what kind of a family she was going to make for herself.

N ancy Joy Callo Naval remembered walking into the 49er Cocktail Lounge in January 1985 with a friend who was looking for bartender work. While her friend filled out the application, Nancy ordered a drink and glanced at a husky, blond man sitting a few stools away. He looked familiar.

She had no qualms about starting conversations in bars. "What's your name?" she said.

"Bob," he said. He seemed to be inspecting her also.

"Bob what?"

"Bob Callo."

"You remember me?" she said. The man looked uncertain. She laughed. "I was your first wife."

True to the nature of their relationship, Bob later told a very different story, in which he recognized Nancy and *she* seemed befuddled. Both agreed that their first reunion in seventeen years was friendly, if a little stiff. They talked about their families. Bob left the bar briefly to drive the half-mile to his house and fetch Nancy a picture of Tiffany.

Nancy's hair had turned gray and she had put on some weight, although not as much as he had. She was on welfare, living at her mother's house and raising a son from her second, failed marriage.

She wrote down Bob's address. A few days before her daughter's eighteenth birthday, she dropped by to give Bob something to give to Tiffany.

Bob drove to Chandler Tripp. He kissed Tiffany and handed her a sealed envelope with no return address. "I love you," he said. "If you need anything, call me later. I don't know exactly what this is, but I have a feeling."

She ripped open the envelope to find a pretty, if somewhat somber, birthday card. Someone writing very carefully had added a note at the bottom: "I've been wanting to write you for such a long time," it said. "I thought I'd never have the opportunity to talk to you, but now that you are finally an adult and allowed to make your own decisions, here is my name and address.

"I am your natural mother, Nancy Joy Naval."

Tiffany stared at the words for several seconds. Her father had always claimed that her mother was dead. If she pressed the issue, he said, "If she's not dead yet, by the time you meet her, if you're unlucky enough to meet her, she'll probably be skin and bones and dying on the amount of narcotics she uses."

Tiffany did not believe it. She dreamed of what the woman looked and sounded like. She had no memories of her and until then no evidence—not even a postcard—that she was alive or had any interest in her daughter.

Yet Elnora had said once that her mother's name was Nancy, and here was that name on the card. The message had the terse, heavy feel of emotions kept in check. She had habitually called her foster mothers "Mom," for she loved the word. Now she might be able to use it without stretching the truth.

She shared the mystery card with her teacher and took it home to Jackie and Keith Haldeman, her latest foster parents. "What do you guys think?" she asked, breathless. "Do you think it would be okay if I saw her? Or do you think I should stay away? Do you think it would hurt me?"

They gave her the answer she wanted. That night after dinner she rolled into the kitchen and called the number. A woman answered. Tiffany assumed her most formal intonation.

"Is Nancy there? This is Tiffany."

The woman gasped. "Oh, my God, Tiffany," she said. "This can't be our little Tiffy."

"Yes, it is," she said, delighted to have created such excitement. "Who's this?"

"This is your grandma, Jean Jackson, your mom's mom," the woman said. She was speaking quickly, her voice trembling with agitation. "Your mom lives with me, along with your brother."

Tiffany felt her poise crumbling under this onslaught of information. "Aaah, oh, my God, I've got a brother that I never knew? Oh, I want to hear more. Is my mom there?"

The older woman began to cry. She seemed both happy and irritated. "Darn it," she said. "You call for the first time and your mother's not home. She's running around doing some errands." She asked Tiffany to call again at 9:30 P.M.

When she did, Jean Jackson answered the phone again but immediately shouted "Nan!" and handed over the receiver.

"Oh, God, Tiffany, this is your mom," Nancy said. "I've been waiting so long, I hardly know what to say." She vibrated like a violin string, her emotions making it difficult for her to complete a sentence. She wept. "I didn't think you would want to talk to me," she said. "I bet your dad told you lots of horrible things, about how awful I was and all that."

Tiffany ignored this. She wasn't going to spoil the moment with a discussion of her father. "Can I see you sometime?" she said.

"Sure," the woman said, pleased and a little calmer. "How about next week?"

"What's good for you?" Tiffany asked. "Weekday or weekend?"

"Well, on the weekend your brother will be home, so I can bring him too."

The idea of having a sibling thrilled Tiffany. She wanted to ask several questions, but first she had to make sure this woman knew exactly what she was dealing with.

"Mom," she said, savoring the word, "Mom, there is one thing I've got to tell you. When you meet me, I don't know if you were notified, I went into foster care. . . ."

"Yeah, I did get some notice from the court when you first went in," she said.

"Well," Tiffany continued, determined to get this over with, "I don't know if you received any pictures before then, but I want you to be prepared. I'm permanently disabled and I've been in a chair, a wheelchair, since I was five."

"Yeah," the woman said very softly, "I knew something about that."

"You knew I had cerebral palsy?"

"I knew you had something that wasn't normal, but I didn't know what they called it."

Nancy came to the Haldeman house to see her daughter that Saturday. Tiffany had imagined someone modeled on the design of many of her friends' mothers—skinny and wrinkled with age. The woman she saw was only thirty-five, and seemed lively and pretty. Nancy's long hair was full of gray, with some white streaks.

With her came a lean, sharply angled, dark-haired boy of fourteen, Tiffany's half brother Sam. Tiffany thought he was achingly cute, but so tall, looming over her in her chair, that she felt like shouting to make herself heard.

She enthusiastically played the role of hostess, offering drinks and taking them on a tour of the Haldemans' backyard. She showed off the Haldeman turtle and the huge, mooselike Haldeman dog. Mother and daughter appeared to be about the same height, five feet one. When Nancy removed her glasses, everyone decided, she and Tiffany looked like sisters, with their small noses and widely spaced eyes.

Nancy did not say much about her life, but Tiffany thought she sensed a reluctance to relive too many hard moments. That seemed to be something they shared.

Perhaps they had missed a great many years together, Tiffany thought, but that did not mean they could not become friends. Nancy seemed to take the wheelchair in stride. She had her own handicaps, invisible ones.

They began to see each other regularly. When Tiffany's date for the high-school prom did not appear as promised, her mother persuaded Sam to take her.

Tiffany had her doubts. "Mom, what am I going to do if they ask me who he is? You know, it's not going to look good."

"Don't worry," she said. "Just say he's your brother. He's not going to embarrass you. He may look like he doesn't know what he's doing, but he's actually pretty good at occasions like this. He's nice and tall, at least."

"All right, Mom," Tiffany said. "I'll take the chance if you say it's okay."

"Life is full of chances, Tiffy," she said.

For all Nancy's faults, she provided Tiffany with an emotional anchor just when she needed one, for the woman most important to Tiffany's upbringing was no longer there.

Elnora Callo had died of a heart attack at age fifty-five when her granddaughter was sixteen. She had been Tiffany's best friend and protector. When Tiffany later made critical decisions in her own life, she tried to imagine what Elnora would have said.

Elnora had tried to keep her ill health a secret, not easy when dealing with a sharp-eyed teenager who knew a lot about hospitals. During their Saturday-morning ritual of doughnuts and solitaire in Elnora's kitchen, the older woman would sometimes lightly broach the subject of death and give Tiffany a chance to grow accustomed to the idea.

She had looked at her family and decided that her granddaughter had the most sense and gumption, and would be the one she could trust with a small assignment. "I'll try to leave something for you, Tiff," she said, "but you have to promise me that they will have a party for me when I am gone, and everybody will be happy and enjoy themselves, and think of all the good things that happened in my life."

At her grandmother's funeral, Tiffany buzzed her chair up to the casket and took a last look. Elnora seemed peaceful, but Tiffany felt nauseated. She had been set adrift, with no life line to

pull her back to the smell of chocolate chip cookies baking in Elnora's oven.

As Tiffany thought about her options, her plans for going to
law school or becoming a model, she realized what she really
wanted was her grandmother's life. She wanted to marry a sen-
sible, hard-working man. She wanted to keep house, raise children, and, like Elnora, involve herself as deeply as possible in the
lives of everyone she knew.

Instead, Tiffany found herself living the life of a young single
woman in the 1980s. For a while she was very close to an electronics assembly worker named Robert, someone her mother had introduced her to. He had a roving eye and a conviction for drunk
driving. She soon left him.

She joined friends her age in the clubs along San Carlos Street
near San Jose State. She tried liquor and marijuana and even a bit
of cocaine. None of it was very satisfying. She had seen what
drugs had done to her mother, and booze to her father.

People who met her for the first time were put at ease so
quickly that they often failed to see how much energy went into
her gaiety and conviviality. Many simple acts of her life were a
chore. Unless the proper equipment was installed, she could not
go to the toilet without help. The sidewalks on which she rode
her wheelchair were full of holes and high curbs. It was torture to
try on a dress at a store, and often she had to guess what would
fit her and what would not.

About the time she turned seventeen, the newspapers were full
of the story of Elizabeth Bouvia, a twenty-six-year-old Southern
California woman with cerebral palsy no more severe than Tiffany's. Bouvia said she was so depressed by the struggle to get
through each day that she sought court permission to starve herself to death with the help of painkillers. Some disabled observers
thought Bouvia was reacting not to her disability but to a series
of personal crises. Tiffany's bad moments never lasted that long.
She embraced people and music and sunny days with effusive enthusiasm, making it seem so natural that no one stopped to wonder how she did it or what that said about a disability's weak hold
on a vibrant personality.

Briefly, she moved into a room in her father's house and they began to argue about her friends and her social life, particularly her occasional drinking. By this time, Bob was attending Alcoholics Anonymous meetings, and he was worried that his daughter would become a drunken recluse, with even fewer outlets for her frustration and anger than he had.

Tiffany did not see a problem. She was still working toward a high-school degree. She had a large, farflung network of friends. She never experienced the blackouts and rages that afflicted her father when she was a child.

"Dad, it's my room. It's my life," she said. "Why can't you let me enjoy what I know? I'm not hurting anyone. I'm not hurting myself. What's the problem?"

At the end of one argument he hit her so hard that both she and the wheelchair fell over. She sputtered and swore and then screamed in pain. "I'm sorry, Tiff," he said, contrite. She ignored him. She straightened her clothes and looked straight at him.

"Don't you ever do that again," she said. She thought for a moment. "To make sure you don't, I'm leaving."

The $560-a-month Supplemental Security Income (SSI) check from the Social Security Administration, paid to her as a disabled adult with no other income, guaranteed a certain amount of independence. She sought out a living arrangement that would provide the balance of freedom and security she craved.

Tiffany called a friend who said she knew someone with an extra room. The man with the room was named Tony Rios. When he called, his voice sounded familiar. He said the same about her. "Which bank do you bank at?" he asked.

"Sears Savings Bank, down there on First."

"Bingo," he said. "That is exactly where I bank at." They laughed. Tony used a wheelchair too. They had noticed each other months before, rolling in the first day of the month to deposit their SSI checks. Some disabled people instinctively avoided contact with each other. They absorbed, almost subliminally, the bias in favor of becoming as much like nondisabled people as possible.

But Tiffany had not approached Tony before because she had been with Robert.

"So I hear you need a place to stay a couple of weeks," Tony said. He lived with his father in a three-bedroom apartment approached by a ramp. They made a quick bargain, three weeks' lodging for seventy-five dollars until she could find something more permanent. In the bank, Tiffany had thought Tony looked remote and angry, but on the telephone he exuded charm and a self-possessed, worldly sense of humor she found intriguing.

He was fourteen years older than she was, a veteran of San Jose street life who offered a strange mix of mystical religious intensity and offhand Bohemian warmth. Juvenile rheumatoid arthritis, a viral fever often followed by painful swelling of the joints, had transformed his life when he was six years old. Until then, he had been an active, cheerful boy, but after a year-long stay in the hospital, he emerged slower and weaker, no longer able to run about the neighborhood. He remained an intelligent and sometimes unusually perceptive student at school, but his life was haunted by the uncertainty of his medical condition, which, in a series of unpredictable crises, grew worse.

Tony started at Chandler Tripp, the same school for the disabled Tiffany would attend a decade later. At sixteen he had a serious relapse. Although he could still walk short distances, moving became so painful he was advised to use a wheelchair full time. The swelling retarded the growth of his arms and legs and left him small and thick-waisted, with a dark look that coolly appraised everyone he met.

When he was eighteen, Tony left home and school and spent his SSI benefits on rent for a San Jose apartment. Like Tiffany, he experimented with the city's youth culture, a string of bars and dance clubs frequented by San Jose State students and the thousands of young people drawn to the Silicon Valley by the electronics boom.

He roomed with a paraplegic who had become disabled in a hunting accident. Both young men learned that wheelchair users, particularly ones with wit and some money, could find young women and good times. But when another roommate was shot to death after a marijuana deal soured, Tony lost his taste for parties and street life. An attractive female evangelist he met at De Anza College persuaded him to embrace God and join a group home for young Christian men in Santa Cruz.

After a few years he tired of the monastic life and moved back to live with his widowed father in San Jose. He sought some purpose in his life, a career perhaps or a family. He was in his thirties, and felt ready, but he also found that he still liked life in the streets after all.

Tony's father welcomed Tiffany to the ground-floor apartment near San Jose State. Tony himself appeared that evening. The two young people inspected each other and began a long, rambling conversation that lasted until midnight.

Tiffany liked Tony's brown eyes and his edgy sense of humor. He had black hair and a mustache, and usually wore hooded sweatshirts and a blanket to cover his legs when he rode his chair. He was extremely self-confident, at least on the surface, and full of wisdom about sights and entertainments in the area. Tiffany had never been attracted to another disabled person before, but she knew how quickly she made up her mind about people, and she could sense where this was headed.

At thirty-three, Tony had far more experience with women than Tiffany had with men, but he too had never attempted a sexual relationship with someone who had a disability. Her stories about confronting child abuse and being tossed about by the court system awakened an interest in sheltering and protecting her. He found her bubbling enthusiasms enchanting, even if they signaled a real difference in age and temperament. He brooded more than she did about the stigma of disability and could clearly remember, as she could not, what life had been like without a wheelchair.

Their bedrooms shared a wall. Each could hear the whirr of the other's power chair. For a while they played sister and brother, rolling about town together visiting friends and relatives, then retiring to their separate rooms at night.

At a hastily planned picnic in a downtown park, Tiffany wore a revealing black-and-silver sleeveless halter and purple shorts, with a green sweatshirt pulled over for modesty. In the hot air of early spring she removed the sweatshirt, and the distance between them seemed to evaporate. Tony wondered what he ought to do.

"Miss Tiffany," he said, "I want to take you somewhere, but before we go there, we're going to have to go back to the house and get some things. I want you to pack like for a vacation, like you're leaving for a week."

Her heart fluttered. Most of the surprises in her life had been unpleasant ones. Her options were always so limited. This might turn out to be just a male sex thing, but she loved the way he packaged it, as a gauzy, romantic, mysterious adventure.

"Get everything you need," he said. "Don't miss a thing." He thought for another moment. "And don't forget the battery charger for your chair."

She groped for her lines in his little drama. "Tony, Tony, what are we *doing*? What insane idea do you have now?"

He grinned wickedly. "Never mind," he said. "You'll see when we get there."

With her small suitcase on her lap, she followed him north toward First Street and the airport. After forty minutes in the chair, absorbing the jolts from sidewalk cracks and poorly made curb cuts, he led her into the driveway of an older motel that, he knew from experience, provided excellent access for wheelchairs. The clerk recognized Tony. He gave them a room without raising an eyebrow.

Later that day they went out again to shop. Tony acted as if Tiffany had just won a contest. He insisted she buy anything that struck her fancy. In one clothing store she purchased four new outfits. She watched Tony ceremonially pull large bills from his sweatshirt sleeve. She wondered, not for the last time, where he got the money.

The week in the motel went well. They had become a couple, intent on taking the relationship seriously in the way they had seen other couples do. Living with Tony's father was no longer good enough. Their two monthly SSI checks totaled more than nine hundred dollars, enough for an inexpensive apartment Tony found on Eleventh Street. The county welfare department had money to build them a ramp up the short stairs to the tiny ground-floor, one-bedroom unit in a brown stucco building full of Vietnamese and Hispanic immigrants. They thought they had all they needed.

6

The apartment's previous tenants had not come close to Tiffany's standards of cleanliness. She spent much of the next two months scrubbing walls and floors. She liked the purgative scent of Pine Sol. She vacuumed as if in search of a lost diamond, trying not to miss one square inch. The cleaning process gave her a bracing sense of control over her environment.

She tried to keep furniture to a minimum. Tiffany preferred people to tables and chairs. People brought laughter into her life and were glad to move if she asked them. They would also pick up things for her and help her out of bed. Furniture did little for her but get in the way.

The weather in the summer of 1986 was unbearable. Breezes off the bay rarely reached apartment blocks on Eleventh Street. Tiffany saved her most strenuous housework for late at night.

She kept the windows open and enjoyed speculating on the meaning of an occasional loud shout or gruff laugh in the night. Her father hated the neighborhood and urged her to move into the western suburbs, but Tony would not hear of it.

In mid-July, during a vigorous midnight cleaning of the bathroom floor, Tiffany found she was hungry for scrambled eggs.

Bacon and toast would be nice also, she thought, as she finished inspecting the shower grouting for stains.

What an odd feeling! She had eaten dinner two hours before—chicken, mashed potatoes, and gravy. She rarely became hungry in such heat. Perhaps it was all the hard work on the tiled floor.

She wheeled into the kitchen and scrambled some eggs. She decided against bacon and settled for toast and a generous helping of ketchup. The snack seemed to energize her and she went back to work, this time sorting old papers in the bedroom and filling an old Avon supplies box with trash.

Fifteen minutes later she realized she had made a mistake. Her stomach flipped over and, with no other choice, she vomited into the Avon box.

Tony came in. "Honey? What's wrong?" he said.

"I'm just feeling miserable," she said, making a face. "I've been working on this house all day and it's still not done."

"Maybe we should go to the doctor," he said.

"The doctor can't do anything for the flu," she said.

"Maybe it's not the flu."

"Well, what could it be, then?"

He looked uncertain, unwilling to express a thought. "Well, I don't know," he said.

She did not feel any better the next day, or the next. She couldn't be pregnant, she thought. This wasn't morning sickness. It was morning, afternoon, and night sickness. Maybe it was the flu, maybe the heat, maybe a recurrence of hyperglycemia, her favorite excuse for any ache or pain.

It took two days of Tony's whining and asking questions to convince her to go to Valley Medical for tests. The hospital received her like a favorite stray returned to the pound.

The combination of her cerebral palsy and low income made quick and simple outpatient visits medically risky and administratively ill-advised. The hospital had to comply with Medicaid guidelines if it wanted to be reimbursed. Extensive testing was necessary because doctors refused to trust their instincts with her always complicated set of symptoms. She had to return daily for two weeks of follow-up tests.

They probed her bladder and her kidneys. They took enough blood, she thought, to fill her bathtub. A veteran patient since birth, she was accustomed to being probed and pricked. Doctors marveled at her memory for the dates and results of her various examinations and operations. She did not worry about these latest tests. No one had a miracle cure for her biggest medical problems. Anything else they found would likely seem small by comparison.

When the doctor came into the little examining room with the results, she had her mind in neutral. She would accept all and assert nothing. She still felt ill, but what else was new? Her father's girlfriend, Beth Stuart, was with her. Tony was down the hall looking for cigarettes.

The doctor was short, fat, and courtly, a dark man with a mustache and a trace of an East Indian accent. "Are you her mother?" he said to Beth. His words had an undertone that frightened both women.

"Yes, I am," said Beth, playing the role Tiffany had assigned her. She turned very pale. That shook Tiffany's composure. Did she know something? Were the doctors talking behind her back, as they had when she was a kid? Jesus, what did she have this time?

The doctor turned to Tiffany and smiled. This did not make sense to her at all. She had a tumor or something, and all this guy could come up with was a silly grin.

"Miss Callo," he said, "I hate to tell you, I don't know if it's good news or bad news, but just in case it's good, I'm going to say congratulations. You're having a baby."

Beth looked stunned. Tiffany took in a breath very slowly and held it. She searched her feelings and at first found no definitive response. "Huh?" she said. "Please, tell me I'm dreaming."

"No, I'm serious," the man said. He heard her lighthearted tone, sensing her happiness before she did. "It's for real. You're gonna be a mommy."

Oh, God, she thought. Oh, boy. She let out a war cry: "Aaaaaeeeeeiiiii!"

Beth, still pale, staggered out of the small room. Tony rolled up with a package of cigarettes in his hand. He saw Beth's face and became frantic.

They had forgotten to pack Tiffany's diapers that day. After two hours of waiting for the doctor, she had headed for the restroom too late and wet her pants suit. While Tony was gone, she asked a nurse to get her more adult diapers and a hospital gown. When she emerged from the examining room to greet Tony, she looked as if she had just been readmitted to the hospital.

Tony panicked. He was not accustomed to seeing anyone, except himself, subjected to so many tests. "What did the doctor *say*?" he asked. "What did the doctor *say*?"

She loved having him at a disadvantage. Knowledge was power. "Do you *really* want to know?" she said. "Really, *truly*?"

He nodded in fright and confusion.

She paused for dramatic effect. "I don't think I need to tell you," she said. "I think you can guess."

He looked puzzled, and then a grin began to form and he waved a small fist in the air.

"Come here," she said. "Give me a kiss."

She still hadn't told him. He wondered if he had guessed wrong. "You're not serious," he said, half accusing, half wondering.

"Yes, we're going to have a boy."

He exploded with a sound, a wooooing tone of a train going by. "I knew it!" he said. "I knew it!"

She had no idea if her baby would be a boy or a girl, but she knew what would make him happy. They had talked about children. Early in the romance, during their motel holiday, he had told her, "I can make you happy," and then added, "I can make you a mommy too."

She liked the idea, although she wondered if the time was right. She had just achieved full independence from the courts and her father. There were enormous chunks of the world she had not seen. She wanted much more from her life.

But she knew she could be a good mother. She remembered the missteps in her own upbringing with chilling clarity. She would not be gone twenty hours a day at two jobs like her father. She would not disappear into a void of regret and chemical exhilaration like her mother.

She had time, and knew what to do with it. She appreciated the small moments of a relationship with a child, of what she had had with her grandmother—the looks and the promises and the long, soft conversations. God had denied her many things, but He had given her an appreciation of stability and consistency and the wise use of the 86,400 seconds in every day. She could take life slowly, with none of the guilt of the young executives she saw charging up Santa Clara Street with their dress-for-success suits and thin briefcases. Her baby would get a lot of her time. She was not going anywhere, at least not very quickly.

Tiffany and Tony decided the baby had been inevitable, although they could not point to a moment when they reached any mutual decision about it. She usually wore a diaphragm, but there had been a few days when she was unprotected while her doctors fitted her for a new one. Neither of them had worried about taking other precautions.

Tony, the self-admitted macho Mexican-American, wanted a boy. Tiffany did not mind. She thought she would have some of both before she was through.

Neither of them had more than a moment of doubt that they could raise a child. They had friends and relatives who could help. They thought they could work out an arrangement to live with a relative who would assist during the two or three years when their inability to lift an infant would be a handicap.

They knew little about the law in such matters, although Tiffany had seen firsthand the power of DSS and the juvenile courts. She had recently met a husband and wife not much older than she who had lost a child to the county. That, and her own childhood case, were different—there had been accusations of abuse. That was not going to happen with her baby, and she did not worry about it.

Tiffany called her father that night. Beth had kept Tiffany's secret.

"Yeah, what?" he said in an impatient tone.

"Dad," she said, "you're going to be a grandpa." She heard no reaction. "I'm pregnant," she said.

It took him a few moments to respond, and when he did, the words seemed lifeless to her, nothing close to the excitement she thought her news deserved. "Oh, that's real good, honey, I'm very glad to hear that," he said. "Listen, I got to go. I'm working on a car. We'll talk real soon."

Bob Callo later recalled the conversation differently. He remembered congratulating her, even though the news disturbed him. He had few pleasant memories of parenthood and he did not know if his daughter was ready for the disappointments he had endured. He tried to put the best face on it, but all his daughter heard was his muted distress.

That night the expectant couple ate in the apartment and talked. The conversation turned to the equipment and the money they lacked, and how much more they needed now that a baby was on the way.

Tiffany had bumped against Tony's five-star tastes before. She issued a warning. "I know you're very particular, but we don't have the finances to be all that particular. We can go to, like, secondhand stores and get brand-new clothes, or almost brand-new."

Tony nodded.

"What about a crib?" she said. The thought chilled the conversation. Their child needed a secure, comfortable place to sleep, but to them a crib was no better than a wall safe without the combination. They could not reach up and over to diaper or comfort a baby in a crib, much less pull the child out if he needed exercise or attention.

"The regular ones aren't going to work for us, are they," Tony said. They thought for a while, and came back to the subject several times. The county sent a nurse to the apartment to check on Tiffany once a month. She asked the woman on her next visit if she had heard of cribs for disabled parents. The woman checked, but could find nothing. She had never handled someone with cerebral palsy who was pregnant, and neither had anyone she knew.

The doctors at Valley Medical were not much more helpful, but it was negligence born of ignorance rather than ill will. The idea of someone like Tiffany having a baby was so novel that few people comprehended it. They changed the topic or seemed not to have heard.

Tiffany knew she was breaking fresh ground, which made it all the more interesting. Her father had always insisted she seek out answers for herself—she had mastered the telephone by age nine. She created her own research project, identified each obstacle in her way, and tried to remove them one at a time.

She went first to Valley Medical, rolling down the waxed floors of the maternity ward in search of a doctor willing to answer a few questions. Good fortune led her to a particularly receptive gynecologist, Ray Allen.

She described her situation and asked his reaction.

"Do you have feeling down in the pelvic area?" he asked.

"Sure."

He put her in the stirrups and probed a bit. "Can you feel me touch you there?"

"Yeah," she said, convinced that this particular doctor was not very bright.

"If you're going to have a baby, you're going to have to push. Can you push? Do you think you're strong enough to push?"

Dummy, she thought to herself. "Of course I am," she said.

"Are you sure?" He made her repeat answers to what seemed to her the same questions two or three times. She began to lose patience.

"What makes you want to say that I can't?" she said. "I'm not going to listen to you say I can't. I'm *going to do it*! End of subject."

He smiled. Tiffany realized she had again flown off without clearance from the tower. She had misread him. He was rooting for her. "Oh, I guess I gave you the wrong impression," he said. "I just need to know if you're going to want or need any special equipment, things that will help us help you."

"No, I don't think so," she said, "unless my baby is in some physical distress, but I guess you're ready for that in every birth, right?"

She liked his thoroughness, once it was clear he understood what she planned to do. "Have you ever delivered a disabled person?" she asked.

"No," he said, "but if they can reach me, or if I happen to be here that night, you'll be the first one."

She continued her research. She demanded medical records, called doctors, and consulted with friends and relatives. She liked bearing the weight of responsibility. She would find a way to have the baby and bring it up safely. She had her brain and her power chair and a telephone. Hers was an independent life.

Then, one morning, she found herself sprawled on the floor, gasping for breath and wondering who had moved her wheelchair so far from the bed.

Tiffany's legs could not hold her weight for long, but if she timed it right, they provided sufficient support for her to move from the side of her bed to the seat of the chair, a quick trip of a few inches. Push with her arms, plant her feet, one, two, *three!*— she was in the chair and ready for the day.

She occasionally missed, but this was the second time in a row. Why couldn't she do it? She remained in her small, self-made heap on the floor and considered the problem.

Wake up, Tiffany, she thought, a small light flickering on. Life was changing. It was the weight of the baby. She was no longer the featherweight champion she used to be.

She realized for the first time that pregnancy, birth, and motherhood were going to contract sharply the circle of life in which she moved. The pregnancy was going to make her much less active and restrict her ability to care for herself.

As a severely disabled adult, she was entitled under state law to hire someone up to twenty-five hours a week to do things she could not do for herself. She had considered this an unwanted nuisance and had not hired an attendant because friends or family were always there. Now she began to look for one, a matter of putting her name on a list at DSS and passing the word among her friends.

Her stomach began to bother her. She was allergic to regular milk, but her doctor advised her to drink it during the pregnancy and she developed a craving for it. Her favorite concoction was milk and chocolate ice cream mixed in a blender. She poured it down her throat four or five times a day.

Her bowels rebelled against her increasing appetite and diminished activity. She suffered long periods of constipation, interrupted by stomach cramps and panicky trips to the bathroom that led Tony to fear she was in early labor.

The doctors, curious and concerned about the course of a pregnancy in such a severely disabled woman, did three ultrasound examinations. In each one the infant's growing testicles were a little easier to see. Tony told everyone and seemed to show more concern for her than usual.

Each Tuesday they went to Valley Medical for childbirth classes and sometimes a visit with the doctor. If they had had a van with a chair lift in back, it would have taken less than fifteen minutes to make the drive from Eleventh Street to the hospital complex on Bascom, a quick trip west on Interstate 280. Because they did not have a van, they relied on the Santa Clara County transit system and encountered the frequent mechanical failure of its bus lifts.

The birthing classes began each Tuesday at 7 P.M. If Tiffany wanted to see a doctor, they had to be there at 12:30 P.M. to join the thick knot of Medicaid patients waiting to see whoever was on call. That meant rolling down to the bus stop at 11 A.M. and hoping the lift would work on at least the second or third bus.

Tiffany detected a few odd looks from other couples the first evening in childbirth class. She had anticipated it. People often treated her like a piece of furniture. If she was with a nondisabled person, curious strangers rarely put a question directly to her. Instead, they would say, "Is she all right?" "What is her name?" "How did she get like that?" It was the pet dog syndrome, a universal lament of the disabled. Although she had grown accustomed to it, she still did not like it.

Now it was worse. The baby was showing. One woman she had never seen before walked up to her at the grocery store and asked if the bulge was pregnancy or a sign of her disability. "Yes," Tiffany said, biting her tongue. "I'm a mommy." When she saw the woman frown, she unleashed her tongue. "Listen, what's it to you? How would you like it if somebody looked at you like you were something from outer space? What's your problem?"

Another woman was honest. "I don't think it's right," she said, "a person like you having a baby." Tiffany found she had no words to respond.

The night of the birthing class, the conference room on the second floor of the hospital was full of couples uncertain how to behave in what was a mass baptism of embarrassing self-exposure. When Tiffany and Tony rolled in, the crowd at least had something to do. They stared. Some, Tiffany learned later, did not even believe wheelchair users were capable of conceiving a child.

Tiffany took the stares as a rebuke. Toward the end of the session, she rolled over to one young mother and whispered piercingly, "If you don't stop looking at us like that, I'll blow you into outer space right now."

The young woman looked hurt and distressed. Tiffany realized she had miscalculated. These people did not feel any better than she did about having a very private part of their lives exposed to total strangers. Few people liked to huff and puff and expose their middles in Grand Central Station.

"Okay, I'm sorry," Tiffany said. "I'm sorry for sounding so blunt about it, but you're not the first person who has stared at us. I'm not upset with you, but I'm just tired of so many people being afraid of opening their mouths and asking. We don't mind answering questions, but we are getting irritated at people's reactions."

"Gosh," the woman said, "I didn't mean nothing by it."

"Yeah, I know," Tiffany said. "We think we have as much fun as you do. We may not be able to use our legs, but we can use our brains."

At home they practiced. Tiffany mastered the breathing exercises quickly, although they seemed silly to her. Tony, in his offhand way, tried to help, but the whole idea of a partner at birth warred with his view of a traditional, distant male association with the process. They had begun to have arguments. Tiffany wondered if she could count on him.

Her due date was March 14, 1987. On March 3 she arrived at Valley Medical for what she expected would be one of the last of her prenatal checkups and birthing classes. She felt as if she was sloshing about in her own body. She wanted to expel fluids from every orifice.

The doctor found nothing unusual. "You're fine," he said. "You can go home. I don't see anything to worry about."

She and Tony rolled to the elevator and up to the second-floor cafeteria. Tiffany's appetite had faded as the growing fetus put more pressure on her internal organs, but she picked up a plate of fruit from the counter and found a table.

She played with the food and talked to Tony about the baby equipment they still needed. Her SSI check was late. The five dollars for the meal was probably the last cash they had. She felt a stirring, a bit of a cramp, in her abdomen. She ignored it.

A few minutes later she felt it again. She checked the time. It was 5:40 P.M. The cafeteria walls were full of clocks, a medical fixation on time she didn't share but found comforting at that moment.

She said nothing. Eating always took a lot of her concentration, and she was having trouble focusing on the plate. There was that twinge again. The clocks said 5:50.

Tony peered at her. "Honey, what's wrong? You're so quiet."

"Oh, nothing," she said. She continued to spear at her food. She felt the next contraction, a little stronger, at 5:59.

She looked at him. "Honey," she said, "I don't think we're going to class today. I don't think we're going home today. I think we're going upstairs."

"Shit," he said, his voice rising. "Let's get you *up* there."

She liked his discomfort and decided to let him suffer awhile. "Wait a minute," she said. "You finish feeding your stomach and let me feed your kid and then we'll go. No massive emergency. It isn't like it's going to happen this minute."

He looked astonished. "I don't *care* if I eat. You're *hungry*?"

"Of course. You think I'm going to waste our last five bucks for this meal, buying all of it and not eating anything?"

She chewed thoughtfully and watched him squirm for a few minutes. She had heard all the lectures about false alarms, but she was sure this time. The certainty improved her appetite. When they rolled out of the elevator onto the maternity floor, she felt confident, ready to give orders.

She raised the pitch of her voice even higher than usual to catch the attention of a nurse behind the tall counter of the maternity check-in station. "You guys," she said. "The doctor said I was fine, but I've been having the pains every ten minutes. I know this baby is coming tonight. You better get me in there."

They found a room and lifted her into bed. A nurse peered between her legs. "Looks like you're two centimeters dilated," she said. A few minutes later Tiffany was at four centimeters, but no one seemed in much of a hurry.

Beth Stuart appeared, dragging Bob Callo with her. She had had a hunch—she prided herself on her mystic sensibility—that this was the night. She had insisted they walk over to the hospital and check the maternity ward. The future grandfather retreated to a waiting area, but Beth made some telephone calls. Nancy Naval promised to be right over.

Nurses occasionally strolled in, examined the patient quickly, and walked out. They gave no advice or comfort.

An orderly named Scott whom Tiffany knew walked by. She hailed him with a screech.

"Hi, hon, what's up?" he said. Tiffany was more a fixture than a patient and her presence in the hospital did not seem unusual to him.

"Listen, go get the doctor. The nurse who has this room has her head up her behind. This baby's *coming*. If they keep fooling around, this baby's gonna be *born* before they can get in here, and God knows what's going to happen."

Another nurse arrived and made a quick measurement. "Oh, boy," she said, "she's up to nine." She told Scott and another orderly to push the hospital bed into the delivery room, while the patient continued to give orders and predict catastrophe.

Tiffany had to be moved from the hospital bed to the delivery table, a troublesome maneuver even with nondisabled mothers. They moved her legs over to the edge of the bed to execute the two-man lift, one orderly on either side, but Scott's grip slipped and Tiffany felt herself sliding toward the linoleum floor.

"Excuse me!" she said loudly, with a smile of exhilaration. "If you don't watch what you're doing, if you crack my son's skull, I will have your medical *career*! I'll wrap it around your noses."

"Ooops," the orderly said.

"You're really dumb, Scott," she said.

Tony had donned operating room garments and wheeled himself to a position near the head of the operating table. Nancy was also allowed in. She stood near a wall, reliving a moment she had tried not to think about for nearly twenty years.

The obstetrician on call, Deirdre Lash, looked Tiffany over and seemed satisfied. Tiffany had never seen her before. She was young and self-assured, with a slim figure and long black hair. When Tiffany wasn't too distracted by the pain or the need to push, she watched her work in the mirror attached to the ceiling.

Tiffany thought it was going very fast. By 10 P.M. they seemed to be near the finish line. The doctor, temporarily distracted, had to turn quickly to catch the emerging child. The next thing Tiffany heard was a piercing, gurgling cry, her baby gulping his first air.

"It's a boy," the doctor announced evenly. Tiffany smiled, unsurprised, but happy for Tony.

The child had reddish skin and a small shock of very fine black hair. He weighed seven pounds, one ounce, and was nineteen and a half inches long. He seemed to have all the necessary parts. "You look just like your daddy, boy," Tiffany said, and called Tony over.

The new father peered over the edge of the high delivery table. "Hot damn," he said. "He does look like me. There's going to be another one of us running out in the streets."

She inspected the infant carefully before they took him away. Then she watched in mounting frustration as the doctor tried to stitch her up. The sutures would not stay in place. Tiffany impatiently suffered the repeated needle pricks, with Nancy watching in fear, before they wheeled her away to enjoy a longer conversation with her son.

Tiffany's maternity room was relatively large, with five beds and high curtained windows opening to the west. The orderlies lifted her into the bed, then stepped back as she issued a set of orders to the nurses: Could she have ten or twelve pillows please? Did they have some news on her baby's condition? When would she get to see him again? Were the pillows ready?

She had thought for weeks about how to feed a baby. She had the nurses stack pillows about her until she looked like a harem queen. Six pillows blocked the gaps in the bedside restraining bars so the child could not roll onto the floor. One pillow was propped carefully beside her so the infant could recline and take her breast.

It was midnight. Tony and her family had gone home to bed, but she waited. There was nothing on television, and she did not want to wake the other women in the room. She found a small mirror on the night table and examined her reflection. Geez, she thought, my hair looks awful. She fiddled with the tangled brown strands, trying to frame her face in a symmetrical fashion. She reflected on the child's name, Antonio David, the first name for his father and the second for an uncle she liked, Bob's younger brother, Leonard David Callo. The boy would eventually be known as David, one of many emerging points of friction between mother and father.

She dozed awhile, but woke often to buzz a nurse and ask about the baby. As morning light began to leak through the curtains, Tiffany wearily concluded that something was wrong, and no one had bothered to tell her about it. The nurse who brought her breakfast, a friendly young woman named Kathy, expressed surprise that David had not appeared with the other women's babies. She promised to find out what was happening, but by noon she had not returned.

Tony arrived, eager to see his son again. "Something's wrong," she told him. "They won't let me see him."

Tony snarled and wheeled out the door. Within minutes he returned triumphant with a nurse carrying David, soft and quiet and very hungry.

The nurse held a bottle, which annoyed Tiffany. Against her specific instructions, they had already given David several feedings of bottled formula. They wanted her to do the same. The replies to her questions were vague, but the nurses did not appear confident that she could hold the child or brace herself for a successful feeding.

She felt her breast milk boiling, but they continued to insist on using the bottle. She sighed and agreed to try. The nurses were generally kind and had helped her with the pillows.

The infant took a few ounces of formula but did not seem very happy with it. Tiffany shifted her weight in the bed and asked a nurse to take away the bottle and prop his head on a pillow near her breast. He made the connection almost immediately. His mouth felt warm and wet and somewhat clumsy, but he began to taste something and applied himself more vigorously.

It seemed as if she had stepped up to some higher plane of existence where someone, another human being, was totally dependent on her, a remarkable feeling as new to her as the sticky grip of her son's tiny fingers.

She cooed at him. She admired his hair and his strong hands. She smiled at the nurse who had helped her adjust the pillows. "See," Tiffany said. "He can tell the difference between what's Mommy and what's not Mommy." David fell asleep after a few minutes, his mouth still open but unmoving. She nestled close to him, trying to make the moment last as long as possible.

An orderly brought her lunch. Tony and the baby left. About 2 P.M. a woman Tiffany had never seen before, tall and gray-haired with glasses and a severe manner, walked in. Tiffany smelled trouble.

"I'm a social worker here at the hospital," the woman said. "A man is going to visit you tomorrow to talk about your baby."

"Oh? What's he want to know?"

"He'll have some questions about how you're going to take care of it, about your health and all."

Tiffany sensed what was coming, and tasted bile rising in her throat. She realized a tantrum would not help her cause. The woman was peering at her as if she were a white mouse being tested for reaction to painful stimuli.

"You do this for everybody?" Tiffany said, trying to load every word with sarcasm. "Is this some kind of special service?"

The woman seemed ready for this. She spoke very carefully. "If you don't cooperate with us, you may never see your son again."

The next day the man arrived. His name was Daryl E. Auten. He was casually dressed in short-sleeved shirt and slacks, with a neatly trimmed Afro haircut and a pleasant expression. He seemed eager to deflect the razor-edged looks he was receiving from the tired young woman surrounded by pillows in the bed.

"Ms. Callo, this is my card. I'm an officer with the juvenile court," he said. His voice was even and polite. "The hospital is raising some questions about your ability to take care of your son."

Tiffany broke in. She knew what she wanted to say. "Excuse me, but I think I can do that by myself. I can deal with it with the people I need to. I don't want to deal with you or anybody else."

Her long history with the county gave an edge to her words that she had not consciously intended. She sounded defensive and bitter, even to herself.

"Well," Auten said, "that's just what I'm here to find out. I don't want to take any more of your time than is necessary, but there are some questions I have to ask."

"Your timing is great, you know?" she said, still unable to control her anger. "I've only been allowed to see my son twice in the last two days. I ordered extra pillows. I have the side rails on the bed all fixed. Why don't you just let me see my kid? Just *chill out*. Nobody's asked me what I have planned or what I'm going to do or what I can do or what I can't do. Everybody's just saying I can't do it. I think you're all full of it. They didn't even let me hold my kid for a damn day and you're already accusing me of being abusive."

The man remained calm. "It's not that," he said. "I'm not saying anything like that. It's just that we have to do everything by the law. It all needs to be checked out, what you can and cannot do."

A thought struck her as she glared at him from her mounds of cushions and linen. She thumbed her call button. A nurse appeared.

Tiffany flashed her best social smile and beat her resentment back into a small corner of her consciousness. "Darling, would you please do me a favor? Would you call the nursery and have them bring my son right away? There is somebody here who wants to see me with my son."

The nurse smiled. "I'll be right back. I'll see what I can do," she said.

Tiffany fiddled with the pillows and lectured Auten on the proper handling of a hungry and curious newborn. "You can't lay a baby on their back if they're eating because they'll choke," she said. "You've got to lay them on their side or on their stomach, and then you lay beside them, and when they're done, they lay beside Mommy and go to sleep."

Auten absorbed this with apparent interest, jotting down a few notes. At that moment Tony rolled in.

"Oh, how cute," he said, playing the proud husband. "There's my little mom."

Tiffany greeted him as if he were a Doberman summoned to repulse a burglar. "Yeah," she said, "but this guy's in my face and being a real jerk."

Tony inspected the juvenile officer for a moment. "Uh-huh, how are you sir?" he said. "May I ask who you are?" His antennae were quivering. The smallest suggestion, particularly from any kind of authority, that he could not live a normal life sent him into a fury.

"You're Mr. Rios, aren't you?" Auten said. "I'm Daryl Auten. I'm from the juvenile court, and I'm here just to ask a few questions about your ability to take care of your child."

"What the hell for?" Tony said. "I think you ought to get out of here. Tiffany's got to rest. She's got to take care of my son when she gets home. We'll have somebody that's going to live there with us and take care of the baby. I don't think we need to talk to you."

Auten looked hurt. "I think you misunderstand why I'm here. I don't want to take your baby. It's just that we have a responsibility under the law to make sure children are safe and well cared for. None of these questions are very hard. I'll ask them, fill out the form, and that's it."

Tony growled at him, but Tiffany saw this was a losing battle. Her father had pounded his head against the county's brick wall enough times. Frontal assaults were doomed.

After a few more minutes of aimless invective, she let Auten persuade her to get in her chair and go into the hall, away from the other patients, so he could complete his questionnaire. Tony would later do the same, swearing under his breath about civil rights and improbable operations he wished the county would perform on itself.

"Okay," Auten said. "Let me have your full name."

"Tiffany Ann Callo."

"Your date of birth?"

"April 21, 1967."

The form demanded endless bits and pieces of her autobiography. She told him she had never been arrested and did not use drugs. She described their apartment and the preliminary plans they had for caring for David.

"Do you think you are capable of lifting and carrying your baby?"

"I can probably carry him," Tiffany said. "I can't initially pick him up, but once he's put in my arms, I can do it. I'm trying to get some help from the county and some people I know about getting special harnesses that would help me carry him. I can do it"—she gave him a long, hard look—"but nobody seems to be interested in getting off their behind and helping me."

Auten stiffened, and spoke in a tone that again belied the ogre she wanted him to be. "Calm down, calm down," he said. "That's what I'm trying to do."

"Yeah, right," she said, letting the sarcasm camouflage her need to believe him.

He completed the interview and told her that the next step would be an inspection of the apartment. The county was obliged by law to ensure a clean, comfortable residence free of hazards and controlled substances.

"You guys really have my best interests at heart," Tiffany said, making no effort to hide her disbelief. "All you want to do is come and tear my place up. What do you think I'm going to do? This is a precious, adorable little kid. You think I'm going to hang him upside down and beat him or something?"

"It's not going to be that bad, Tiffany."

She rolled back into her room, refusing to entertain any great hopes. David was back in the nursery, but the room was crowded with friends and relatives—her father, his girlfriend, her mother, her stepsister, her grandfather and his new wife. Tiffany had called everyone she could. She needed more than a stack of pillows to keep David with her. She wanted ideas on creating a home so well lined with legal and financial buffers that even the cleverest social worker could never pry her baby away.

7

Auten visited their new apartment on Ninth Street a week after David's birth. Tony had moved their few belongings there because the apartment was in a better building. Tiffany ached to have her child at home. Her breasts were straining with milk and her arms were sore from polishing every exposed surface of the one-bedroom apartment.

She was particularly proud of the look of the tiny kitchen. With just enough maneuvering room, it was an empire she could rule, a small world she could leave better than she found it.

But Auten, after knocking politely and greeting her with a smile, did not hesitate to invade her cupboards and begin tearing the contents apart. He pulled out pans, sniffed packages, and peered into dark corners. He stuck a finger into the sugar and flour canisters and sampled the white powder. It unnerved her more than she expected it would.

Tiffany clamped her teeth on her tongue. She hated what he was doing to her nest, but the visit had to go well or she might not get David back at all.

He moved from the kitchen to the living room, what Tiffany had taken to calling the nursery. There was not a speck of dust anywhere, but that did not seem to impress Auten.

In the bedroom he looked under the blankets. He turned over the mattress. He pulled clothing and papers out of every drawer.

She had kept the apartment free of extraneous furniture—her old nemesis—so that she could maneuver her chair without incident from the kitchen through the living room to the bedroom. She had spent most of the day working every crease out of the bedspread and arranging the clothes in the drawers as neat as columns on Auten's checklist.

Now he was destroying all the order she had created. She had a dream, one of the few allotted her, and he was reducing it to grimy, picked-over chaos.

Careful, she said to herself, he's got all the power. All it takes is one thing and—*boom!*—David can't come. Careful.

She thought she knew what Auten was doing. He was looking for drugs. The same old stuff. She had spent her life without strong legs or much money, and if a genie suddenly said she could have one or the other, she might choose the money. The assumptions that went with living in this part of town wrapped her as tightly as her old pre-pregnancy jeans and sweatshirts. She did not like it. She gave in to the urge to let her tormentor know.

"What *damn right* do you have, coming in here, turning my baby's nursery upside down?" she said. "I'd have been a fool to use drugs, and if you don't believe me, you can test me. I ain't ashamed to test for nobody.

"I'll go to classes. I'll take counseling. You tell me whatever is necessary. But I want my kid here. I want my kid at home."

Auten ignored the outburst. She was used to that too. Perhaps people did not hear her because her chair was so low. Perhaps it was just another example of how all minorities were treated. Poor or disabled, you were invisible.

Four years before, she had had a glimpse of what it could be like. Beth Stuart, her father's girlfriend, had let her help care for Beth's granddaughter Kimberly, blond and light as a cornflake.

Tiffany had sat in her wheelchair with the brakes locked and faced Beth sitting on the couch. Beth placed the baby in Tiffany's lap and put the bottle in her left hand, the stronger one, to guide into the waiting, questing mouth, like a crumb floating toward a waiting goldfish.

When Kimberly grew bigger, a pillow placed on Tiffany's lap absorbed the added strain. Tiffany experimented. She discovered, by accident, a soothing trick. She could not burp a baby in the usual way. Her brain's confused messages to her muscles would not allow her to grip the small back and rump and hold the infant against her shoulder. But she could place Kimberly stomach down on her lap and apply pressure to the child's back. She didn't pat, she massaged, slowly and lovingly. Small bubbles of swallowed air came gently to the infant's lips and dribbled on a carefully placed towel.

There was a closed, cozy feel to life with Kimberly. Tiffany sat on the couch thigh-to-thigh with Beth as the woman demonstrated the intricacies of diapering. Tiffany wore diapers herself. With practice she could clean, replace, unfold, and fasten almost unconsciously, if slowly.

But why hurry? She and Kimberly had all the time they needed.

Tiffany sought the proper rhythm. Beth watched in surprise as the girl applied her talent for conversation to the small, uncomprehending infant. With coos, trills, and small shrieks of delight, Tiffany turned the process into a game, a lesson in intonation and rhythm by visiting Professor Callo.

Despite her disability, Tiffany had always been a physical child. The chair and her clumsiness had not diminished her delight in wrestling with her father or pounding the floor with her plastic hammer or cheering the thud of bodies in a televised football game. Regular physical contact with other human beings replenished her hope that she had a part in God's plan. The small smiles she received from Kimberly were beacons guiding her somewhere.

Auten found no drugs. He apologized for the mess and left Tiffany to clean up. She didn't care. She had passed.

The next day her father's ex-wife, Lucy, brought David over

from her home. Long before, Tiffany and Lucy had made peace with each other, and that was where the county had temporarily consigned the baby.

Tony had arranged for his sister Irene and her two children to live with them to meet the county's demand for a nondisabled assistant. Tiffany's plan was simple. She would tend to the rhythm of David's life, his feeding and sleeping. Irene would help her do the things she could not, such as put David on her lap or give him a bath in the sink.

The county insisted that Tiffany sign a statement authorizing Irene to take David with her whenever the nondisabled woman left the apartment. It was a backhanded, bureaucratic way of saying the county did not want the mother to be alone with her child. Tiffany scrawled her small, shaky "T. CALLO" in capital letters at the bottom of the paper and tried not to think too much about it.

Tiffany and Tony slept in the ten-by-ten-foot bedroom, which had no room for the crib. Irene slept on the couch in the living room. Her two children, eight-year-old Juan and five-year-old Jenny, shared a mattress on the floor. David and his crib were in the corner of the living room nearest the bedroom so all three adults could hear him easily if he cried.

Each morning Tony left for job interviews or other unexplained appointments and often returned late. The days and most of the evenings were left to Tiffany, Irene, and the three children. The two women enjoyed acquainting themselves with a new baby in the warm spring.

Tiffany found Irene to be very sweet and full of quiet, helpful instincts, a sharp contrast to Tony. The two young women handled the fat, dark-haired David as if they were sharing a favorite toy.

Few American mothers had as much time for their babies as Tiffany. She and David had no motive or means to move very far or very fast. They wallowed in sedentary pleasures. Irene placed the infant on a pillow on Tiffany's lap and left him to be stroked and massaged and entertained with a stream of high-pitched chatter.

"What a *great* kid! What *great blue* eyes!" she said. "Ooooh, what a great blue *smile!*" She giggled and tickled him. The child was unusually alert and listened attentively to his mother's endless comments on the state of the world and his own many fine qualities.

Tiffany diapered and fed and rocked the child, setting her own pace. She breast-fed the baby with ease and pleasure.

She loved to watch David's face move as he tried out expressions and sounds and methods of breathing. She did her best to make her face and voice familiar. A child, she told herself, had to know who his mother was, and that she cared about his life. He had to know that she knew he was his own person, small but vital in the scheme of things.

She loved David's crib, the work of her friend Paul Darius, owner of ABBA Medical Services, where she had her E & J power chair serviced and repaired. Darius was a former Navy nuclear engineer who had become interested in the disability equipment business while investigating the devices he would need for a foster son who had cerebral palsy.

Visiting Tiffany for a chair repair one day, he listened to her describe her frustration at being unable to reach David over the high sides of the crib. It seemed like a simple engineering problem to him. He rigged a hinge that allowed her to pull back one side of the crib and reach the baby easily.

Changing a diaper that way was a leisurely, pleasant game. She pried off the wet disposable diaper with slow care, then placed the fresh diaper on the mattress. She maneuvered the baby to the right spot, molded the paper and plastic to his wiggling bottom, and fastened the adhesive strips.

The process took twenty, sometimes thirty, minutes. Irene was uncomfortable with the delay, but after watching a few times, she decided it worked. Tiffany cooed and stroked and discussed the weather and the state of mankind to keep David distracted. She was a shop clerk jollying her favorite customer. "Hello, little person, and what can I do for you? I'm right here for you, right here, yes, I am. We can worry about this old diaper in a few minutes. You just relax and tell me whatever comes into your head."

If the baby began to fuss at the indignity of remaining on his back with his genitals exposed, Tiffany stopped and tossed a blanket over him. She saw nothing wrong with declaring a break so she could give David a kiss or a toy or a pacifier or a bottle. She massaged him gently and told him he was a good boy.

Sometimes, if she didn't place the blanket over him fast enough, a spurt of urine would fill the air, wetting her hands and her cheeks. "Oooh!" she squealed. "Mommy's not afraid of a little shower. So *what*? Mommy can go in and take a bath. Who *cares*?"

She was fastidious about the cleanup. She used wet towelettes and a warm washcloth, then finished with lotion or powder. Satisfied that her client was dry and clean, she folded the dirty diaper and dropped it into a nearby wastebasket.

Where did all the time go? A day full of ordinary chores sped by quickly.

Tiffany only worried about handling David during baths. Irene would place his slippery form in a sinkful of tepid water, and Tiffany would pull her chair up to help sponge off the soap. While Irene toweled the infant off and dressed him, Tiffany made the bed, nibbled on a piece of toast, and tried to clear the floor of toys that blocked her path around the apartment.

She watched other mothers tend their babies and thought, without saying so, that their mobility made them careless and disorganized. They sometimes forgot that a helpless baby should not be left alone on a changing table, even for a second. They occasionally neglected to set the baby powder, diapers, towelettes, and toys within easy reach.

If they forgot something and dashed across the room to get it, the baby on the table was no safer than if Tiffany tried to sling him under one shaky arm. Under the crib Tiffany stocked everything—diapers, powder, baby oil, rattles, bottles, toys, pacifiers, blankets, and sheets. It was the center of her nest. All might have been perfect if Tony—for reasons she could not understand—had not had so much trouble adjusting to fatherhood.

Before David was born, Tony had anticipated the event with pride bordering on arrogance. He was going to have a son, he assured everyone, and no one would stand in the way of his right to bring up a child like any other person.

He had always been more outspoken on disability rights than Tiffany. She felt strongly about expanding her range of choices and could be a biting satirist of the way people treated her. But she had never been as impulsive as Tony, or as insistent on being treated as if her wheelchair did not exist. She was more than willing to ignore slights and suffer bureaucratic annoyances if that would help her child.

When David was born, Tony glowed in the hubbub of congratulatory relatives and admiring friends. He spoke in awe of his son's size and physical prowess, and the dark, masculine looks that so matched his own.

But he rarely touched the child. He did not volunteer to change diapers or wield a bottle or rise at night to comfort him. It might have been an extreme case of the unease many new fathers feel when adjusting to a child. It might have been Tony's traditional Mexican-American upbringing. It might have been fear of dropping or harming the infant. It might have been a reaction to David as a symbol of a closed, stable family life that he was beginning to realize did not suit him.

Later he would complain that his sister did not let him help. He also denied that his behavior differed in any way from that of other fathers, and to a certain extent it didn't. But it bothered the women he was living with all the same.

"Goddammit, Tony," Irene told him one day after he brusquely rejected a request to watch the baby. "Who the hell is the father around here? It sure as hell doesn't look like it's you. I'm acting more like a father than you are. You haven't even gotten near him."

Tony in turn complained about Irene's boyfriend, a quiet, friendly Mexican immigrant. The man spoke only Spanish, but he was kind to Irene and her children and provided transportation for Tiffany and the baby. He had an ancient Honda, a rattling amalgam of scratched yellow paint and paper-thin gears that somehow got them safely to doctor appointments.

The women thought Tony's ego suffered from the presence of

another man. But the boyfriend became a practical problem as well when the landlord, who had understood the need for Irene to share the apartment, objected to a fourth unrelated adult in a one-bedroom unit.

Tiffany asked Tony to mollify the landlord. The Rios charm had worked on her and innumerable relatives, creditors, and employers. She feared Irene would not stay if the boyfriend was barred.

"Look, I know you don't want this guy around," she said to Tony. "This guy drives me bananas every once in a while 'cause he can't speak any English. But he really is a cool guy. He gives Irene money. He makes sure her kids are fed. He makes sure they have new clothes. He's willing to take Irene everywhere that she has to go. If David has to go see the doctor, he told Irene he'd take him and stay there as long as David needed to be there."

"Sure, I know," Tony said. "I just don't like the guy."

"I know, but you gotta chill out." Tiffany saved her strongest argument for last. "Chill out or you're going to lose your son."

The night it happened Tony had gone to bed early, leaving Tiffany and Irene to care for David, who was fussy because of a cold. Five minutes after lapsing into unconsciousness, Tiffany heard a sorrowful wail from the crib. It would take her a few minutes to transfer over to her wheelchair and reach the child. She knew Irene would be exhausted and did not want to wake her. Tony, on the other hand, could walk short distances without his chair.

"Honey," she said, grasping Tony's arm. "Can you go see if David's wet? Go see if he needs something, go do something. We're tired."

"That's your job," he said, his voice both groggy and icy. "You do it."

She sighed and worked her body over to the edge of the bed, emitting a small squeal of exasperation as she moved. At the edge she felt Tony's foot strike the small of her back very hard. She toppled to the floor and lay there, stunned.

David was still crying. It was dark and there was no convenient handhold for her to pull herself up to her chair. "Irene! Irene!" she shouted.

She hated Tony for making her wake the other woman. She heard him struggling to get out of bed, not a good sign in his mood. She crawled across the floor and under David's crib, whispering encouragement to the baby while making sure she was safely out of Tony's grasp.

She was tired and angry but she felt relatively secure. Tony might hit her, but he would never hit his son. He didn't seem able to find any reason to touch him at all.

"Shhh, David," Tiffany said. "Mommy's right underneath. Mommy's okay, Mommy's right here." The infant was intrigued by the sound of his mother's voice directly beneath him and began to quiet down.

Tiffany heard a hum as Tony, having commandeered her power chair, rolled toward the crib. A wheel hit her outstretched foot and she jerked upward in pain, frightening the baby.

"Irene! Come help me! I'm underneath and I think David needs to be changed."

Irene stood, pried open her eyes, and saw her brother sitting in the power chair in the hallway. He said nothing. She could not see Tiffany at all. David whimpered and she automatically approached the crib. She reached underneath for a diaper and found Tiffany, sniffling and red-faced, wedged among the toiletries.

"What in hell are you doing under there?" she asked, not certain she wanted to know. Tiffany looked so impossibly contorted, Irene could not hold back a laugh. Tiffany joined her, glad for the diversion. "Your brother's trying to attack me!" Tiffany said, unable to stop laughing. David quieted again in response to what sounded like nothing more than a loud party.

Irene addressed Tony as if he were one of her own children. "Listen, you go back to bed. Get your ass out of here and go back to bed," she said. "Don't you fight no more."

Tony twisted angrily in the seat of Tiffany's power chair and railed at his sister and her boyfriend, who sat on the couch unable to understand the torrent of abuse.

It was too much for Tony. There were too many people in his

apartment and too many irritants for what had always been his sensitive ego. If he had been able to find a good job, if Tiffany's attention to David had not caught him so unprepared, they might have worked it out. But he could not get himself back under control.

Tiffany remained under the crib, comfortable for the moment and unwilling to move while Tony roamed the apartment. Irene had given the baby a bottle and a fresh diaper. David slept while the argument, in venomous spurts, filled the early-morning hours. "Why don't you just get the hell out," Tony said to his sister. "Get out and take that jerk with you."

By dawn, Irene had had enough. Tiffany had lost count of the times she had warned Tony: "If you're kicking her out, you're also kicking your son out and you're kicking me out. If my son has to go, I'm going with my son, thank you."

"Tiffy," Irene said, "I really can't take this. This is really too hard."

Tiffany closed her eyes. She could not lose David. "Listen," she said, "we can get an apartment together. I know a lawyer, I can get a restraining order against Tony. I can keep him out of our face. I know who I can talk to about it."

Tony, finally exhausted, had gone back to bed. Tiffany pulled herself out from underneath the crib and looked around the apartment. She had to let Irene go. She could not in good conscience force her to put up with Tony's abuse. That meant David had to go also. Tiffany did not want to risk some makeshift arrangement that might put Irene in legal jeopardy. They had to retreat a step while she found some other way for mother and child to be together.

Irene decided she would stay with one of her sisters until she found a place of her own. Quietly, disguising her feelings as well as she could, Tiffany packed a suitcase for David and arranged for Irene to call her once she reached her sister's apartment. Tiffany watched with resignation, and some anger, as her baby was loaded into the battered Honda and driven away.

Tiffany rode her chair to San Jose State, two blocks from the apartment, where she knew a faculty member who might help.

She had met Gordon Burton, an assistant professor of occupa-
tional therapy, two years before. He was one of the few people she
knew who understood both the difficulties and possibilities of
raising a child from a wheelchair. She had become an occasional
aide in his classes, a cheerful and tolerant guinea pig for student
therapists who sometimes grabbed the wrong parts of her body
or turned joints in directions they were not meant to go.

Together, prospective mother and college professor had
worked out several strategies for raising David. Burton was one
of the few professionals willing to listen patiently to her endless
plans for the future, so it was natural that she come to him to
discuss this crisis. They sat together in his office, exchanging stray
thoughts between long, sad silences. He told her he would do
what he could to find her a place to stay. She would need legal
advice. She would have to talk to the social workers again, as
much as she loathed them.

At one point in the afternoon Tony arrived, spitting fire and
demanding the return of Tiffany and his son. He often carried a
short stick with a plastic hook at one end to snag telephones,
clothing, or other items just out of reach. He used it to rap sharply
on the outside of Burton's office door. "I'm coming in!" he said.
"Goddammit, let me in."

Burton told him to leave. Tony refused. "You know," he
said, "I know a few people who could do you some serious
harm, Doc."

Burton said he would call security. Tony refused to back off.
The two campus guards looked mildly embarrassed as they
wheeled Tony back to the sidewalk and told him to go home.

Stephanie Sandborn, a student of Burton's, invited Tiffany to
spend the night at her home. At first Tiffany declined, then recon-
sidered. She had no base from which to launch a campaign to get
David back, and it would be difficult for Irene to reach her if she
did not have a place. She accepted Stephanie's offer and sat quietly
thinking during the hour's drive to the woman's home in Hollister.

At the house, Stephanie grabbed Tiffany under her arms and
pulled her up the house's front steps on her rump, step by step.

Tiffany's head throbbed. She lay flat on her back on the living room floor, trying to think. Stephanie's dog licked her face, making her laugh and cry. She felt she could sleep for hours. But her dreams were violent, full of faceless men trying to take David. She scratched and punched and kicked each kidnapper, never quite beating them all off.

At nine the next morning, the call from Irene came with the message she feared.

The woman sounded exhausted, whipped. "Tiffy, I really can't take this. This is really too hard. The kids and I don't have a place. I have no choice but to call the agency and let them put David in a foster home." She paused for breath. There did not seem to be any way to soften this blow.

"Listen, Tiffy," she said, her voice breaking. "If you get it worked out with my brother, I'll go to court and help you fight. I know you guys can do it with my help. I just can't help you with my brother's interference in that way. I *can't do it,* Tiffy."

Tiffany tried to tighten her grip on the telephone, so as not to drop it and cut off her last link to David. She had to think of something. She had to stall.

"Irene, don't cry. Let's talk about it," she said. "Before you have to turn him in, can you at least let me meet you somewhere, so that you and I can have just an hour or two with David?" She held her breath.

The older woman considered this. "Okay, Tiffy, fine. Where can we do it?"

They decided on the parking lot of the Sears Savings Bank at First and Market, a downtown location not far from the county office where Irene would have to take David. Stephanie helped Tiffany slide into her gray Nissan pickup. They drove back to San Jose as evening came.

When they arrived, Tiffany asked Stephanie to go inside the Citibank branch on a nearby corner and take a hundred dollars out of Tiffany's account for Irene. She probably had to buy some formula and diapers for David.

Then they waited. Two hours passed. Tiffany envisioned her baby kidnapped, or lost, or worse. At 8 P.M., long after the county agency had closed for the day, Tiffany asked Stephanie to take her back to Hollister. She would call Irene's sister to determine what happened, but she assumed that David was gone, in the county's hands, and she did not want to think too much about that for a while.

Irene called that night. She sounded tired and sad. Her boyfriend's car had broken down and she had had to carry the child to the county office. She did not have the time or strength to bring him to see Tiffany. She wished Tiffany luck, but she had her own problems.

David was at the Santa Clara County Children's Shelter, a place Tiffany knew well. She telephoned DSS the next morning. She had to make sure they had her name in David's file, that the bureaucratic synapses connected.

"Okay," she said after she explained the case to the man who answered the telephone. "I'm living temporarily in Hollister. My friend here has a car, so I can get down there pretty quickly, and during the day you can find me at the university. These are the numbers you can use to get ahold of me.

"Now I want David back. I know I can make it work, if you work with me. I'm getting a new place so I can get under way with getting my son.

"I used to live over there. Please understand, I have nothing against you, but *I want my son out of that godforsaken hellhole.*"

The man sounded bored. She wondered: How many times had he heard this? His words meandered over the telephone line with the urgency of a store clerk inquiring about her shoe size. "Well, good luck," he said. "I hope that you get yourself established first. I hope that you can. You're going to be dealing with a different social worker now. Her name is Shirley Silvani. And I'm sure Shirley will do everything she can to help you. Have a nice day."

Tiffany remembered what it was like to be taken to the shelter when she was eleven. She had not cried the first night, or the second, but by the third she was so homesick, and so confused by the twisted feelings inside her, that she had let it out, slowly, softly, trying not to wake anyone. Where was Daddy? Who would rescue her?

What, she wondered, could David be feeling now, so small and pink and full of her milk and love? She still had scars from the separation from her family, little bits of doubt about her place in the world. Had they just cut David off from his future?

No, that was stupid. They grabbed kids from mothers all the time. She had seen adopted kids. Some of them seemed fine. That was where David was headed unless she did something.

She felt dead. Stephanie's house was a welcome refuge, but it was cut off from David and from her life. She was beginning to realize how much Tony's temper was going to cost her.

No one had warned her about what would happen if she suddenly stopped breast-feeding after four weeks. She woke the next morning with a dull pain in her chest and the sheets soaked with a thin white liquid. In the afternoon at the university, she excused herself to the ladies' room several times and tried to dab away the flowing milk with toilet paper.

That night she retreated to Stephanie's shower. She tried to drown the hate and pain with hot, steaming water. It didn't work. Over the thin whine of the spray, she could hear herself sobbing and feel the salty tears run down her face to mix with soapy water and milk.

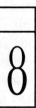

Tiffany waited two days, but no one called. She telephoned the social worker she had spoken to originally, but he was out. She called Auten, who had no information.

After Tiffany tried a dozen more times, a woman returned her call. She identified herself as Shirley Silvani, the caseworker on the DSS petition to remove David from Tiffany's home. Her tone did not rise above cocktail party pleasantry. Tiffany was told she could visit David on April 21, her twentieth birthday, nearly three weeks after he had been taken. By then, their days apart would almost outnumber their days together.

The meeting place was the Santa Clara County Children's Shelter at 1440 Roberts Street. The shelter was, to a first-time visitor, a pleasant, brightly decorated collection of offices, dormitories, and mobile trailers tucked into the middle of a residential neighborhood just south of Interstate 280. Standing in the small parking lot, a visitor had the sense of being transported to a small rural town. Across the street were the grassy fields and occasional oaks of Kelley Park, one of San Jose's few surviving green spots along meandering Coyote Creek.

To Tiffany the shelter was not much better than a prison. She thought the offices were too small and cramped, the barracks and meeting rooms too large and impersonal. It seemed less frightening, but more depressing, than when she first saw it nine years before.

A lot of faces she remembered, some with distaste, some with indifference, a few with warmth. They all seemed happy to see her. "Hey, Tiffy!" "How *are* you, Tiffany?" "Gosh, we heard your baby was here. We'd *love* to see him." Her past overwhelmed her. What was she passing on to her son? Where was he?

Before seeing David, she had to face Tony, who was also in touch with the social workers. He sat in his chair in the waiting area. He wore a clean sweatshirt and the usual blanket over his legs. He seemed calm and confident.

She had refused to take his calls. "How have you been, Tiffany?" he said. "Listen, I called you several times. We gotta talk. Maybe I've been a jerk. We got to work on this together."

She stared at him. "Come on," he said. "We can at least talk, can't we?"

She spit out a reply. "I really loved you, you know. I put in my all. That's a beautiful son that we have, and you're still doing nothing to help out. Maybe we can get him back, but how? You're still not doing nothing about it. I asked you simple things, just to buy *diapers* for him. I asked you to buy formula. I asked you to buy one lousy set of bottles, and you couldn't even do that, and you expect me to tell people that you're a great and groovy daddy?"

Her anger and passion accelerated her usually slow, singsong speech. Tony seemed to shrink, like a witch doused with water. The sight of him visibly softening and cringing moved her. She knew she was sliding into dangerous territory. He looked so sad.

"I know, Tiffy. I know and I'm sorry. Let me do something. Let's see what I can do. What does David need? Please tell me. Can I get him new clothes? What does David need? I got everything for David at the house."

"He needs everything, goddammit, everything," she said, as angry about the love welling up in her as the ease of his reply.

They buzzed their chairs into the central visiting area, full of warm light and soft seating pads. Auten brought in David. This was the final bizarre touch, Tiffany thought, this cop keeping my kid prisoner. Auten set David in his car-seat carrier in the middle of a table and backed off to let the parents wheel in close.

Tony interpreted this as typical able-bodied callousness. "God-dammit," he said, "you'd think they would do more than serve him like a piece of meat." He pulled his chair up to the rim of the table and reached over to undo David's straps. He lifted the baby out of the plastic carrier and cradled him. He called him Antonio, the name he preferred, one of the issues he and Tiffany had never resolved.

Tiffany could not deny that Tony was making an effort. There seemed no other way to recover David than to charge ahead with a united front.

In a way, the birth of David seemed even more important to Tony than it did to her. He had been thinking about having a child for years. She had come upon this miracle almost by accident and considered it a natural part of her entrance into adulthood, while Tony, on his good days, treated the event as some rare, inexplicable wonder.

After a few days, she agreed to move back with him into another apartment, this one with two bedrooms on Tenth Street, a block from their smaller place on Ninth. It was on the ground floor with a ramp up one short step for their wheelchairs. Their living room looked out on a small, dusty courtyard with a dirt rectangle where a tree had once stood. The tenants assumed the tree had succumbed to cooking fumes and rock music, died and been sold for firewood.

Tony seemed to be in a good mood. She found it hard to resist him at such times. As the relationship progressed, she learned that his charming highs were invariably followed by distressing lows. He would tell her one month that she was a priceless jewel, and the next month lock her out of the apartment. In the frustrating weeks immediately following the loss of David, Tony was at his best, making it difficult for her to think clearly about their future together.

His high spirits made it easier for Tiffany to face the prospect of another long summer of weak bladders and enforced immobility, for in May she discovered that she was pregnant again. She doggedly pursued the campaign to recover David, subjecting herself to parent training sessions full of information she already knew. Each Saturday she appeared at the DSS auditorium for her allotted hour with her son, except when she or David was sick or her chair was being repaired.

She and Tony began to talk seriously about marriage. She had not seen many successful ones in her life and still wondered about Tony's ability to sustain a relationship. But it seemed the right thing for David. She had seen what DSS could do to a family. She needed all the help she could get.

In her May 27, 1987, report to the juvenile court on Dependency Petition No. 94106, in the matter of Antonio David Rios, Jr., Shirley Silvani mentioned the Department of Social Services auditorium, known to many of its unhappy inhabitants as the Zoo.

On page two of her report, Silvani indicated that the DSS auditorium would be the site of Tiffany's and Tony's weekly visits with David, brought there by the baby's foster mother. "The agency seems to be the most convenient place for visiting since the parents can get here on their motorized wheelchairs and it is accessible."

Tiffany had heard this rationale. It represented to her DSS's distressing talent for presenting the worst of its services as triumphs of modernity and convenience. Most of the social workers knew the Zoo was bad. Their best psychological consultants, their clients and foster children, and nearly everyone else had been telling them so for years. Eventually they would move out of 55 Younger Street, in part to spare future families the torture of visiting hour in the auditorium.

But in the case of Petition No. 94106, the Zoo was "convenient" and "accessible."

Tiffany approached the DSS building each Saturday with both excitement and dread. The windows on the four-story structure were protected by rows of vertical metal slats that gave the outside the look of an ultramodern cell block. Tiffany looked forward to seeing David, but she knew a headache would always follow the hour spent in that cauldron of noise and emotion.

She rolled through the double glass doors of the building's main entrance and took a sharp left turn to enter the auditorium. The room was roughly half the size of a high-school gymnasium, with one wall of windows looking out on the concrete building entrance and the other walls dotted with indirect lighting fixtures. A large door opposite the windows opened to the parking lot, and a few offices lined the room's north side.

What Tiffany noticed was the furniture, a jumble of couches and heavy chairs and tables that always presented unexpected obstacles in her search for David and Judy, the foster mother. If only, she prayed, some burly bodyguard would clear a path for her through this wood and plastic forest. Tony was sometimes so put off by the Saturday morning chaos he would refuse to enter the room altogether. He would post himself out on the sidewalk and look angry, earning another unfavorable mention in Silvani's services activity log.

The number of people visiting the Zoo on Saturday depended on the level of misery and marital discord in the county the previous week. If there had been a large intake of children, sometimes as many as one hundred people were there, clumped forlornly in family/foster family groups scattered about the room. Some mornings Tiffany rolled from group to group for ten minutes before she realized that David was not there. Judy was occasionally delayed because of traffic. Other times David was ill and the message did not reach Tiffany in time.

Tiffany grieved when she did not see David and rejoiced when she did. But she wondered how much either of them were profiting from the experience. The noise and the distractions of other children kept the infant from focusing well on anything. The beige, speckled linoleum was too cold, hard, and dirty to put him down to play. The boy had begun to establish a bond with Judy, making it that much more difficult for Tiffany to reestablish her relationship with him while the foster mother was there.

Yet Silvani gave little indication in her services activity log that she appreciated Tiffany's disadvantage. She carefully recorded several incidents that indicated that the child did not recognize Tiffany as his mother. Silvani never noted the disruptive, distracting atmosphere of the only place where Tiffany was allowed regular contact with her son.

Shirley Silvani was an experienced, highly regarded social worker in her fifties with a bachelor's degree from the College of Holy Names in Oakland, California, and a master's degree in social work from the University of California at Berkeley.

Her height commanded immediate attention. She was six feet, one inch tall. But what impressed her coworkers most was her energy, resourcefulness, and writing skills. She had begun her career as a probation officer in Stockton, California, and then moved to Catholic Social Services and a succession of higher-level jobs in various California counties after she received her master's degree.

She had worked nearly three years as chief counselor at the San Andreas Regional Center, which provided services to developmentally disabled people in Santa Clara County. When assigned the Callo case, she was a permanency planning coordinator with the highest rating of Social Worker III.

Silvani said in a brief interview that she, like other social workers, always did her best to find ways to reunite families. But copies of her handwritten services activity log entries dating from April 7, 1987, indicate that she doubted from the start Tiffany's ability to care for a child. The log entries also show she considered Tiffany's sons to be healthy, active, intelligent children who would be easy to place in adoptive homes.

Her first entry, apparently based on secondhand information, said Tiffany "cannot provide any care" for David. "She cannot even hold the baby," Silvani said, a statement contradicted by all eyewitnesses and by photographs taken at the hospital.

Silvani seemed to jump to the conclusion that one-month-old David had already rejected his parents—"The baby gets very frightened when they visit because they cannot support his body"—while quoting skeptically the parents' view that David could "sense and compensate for their disability" if they were allowed to care for him.

The negative and often false impressions of Tiffany piled up in Silvani's clear, careful handwriting: "Tiffany is . . . not very realistic about expectations." (June 23, 1987) "Tiff may be using drugs." (October 23, 1987) "If held even with her where her movements are minimal he [David] is okay, but he really is not attached to her." (December 31, 1987) "He does not have any meaningful interaction with Tiffany." (May 24, 1988)

But she missed few opportunities to admire the baby: "He is a beautiful normal one month old infant—fair complected light brown hair." (April 21, 1987) "He is a large, healthy, active youngster who is a happy, outgoing youngster." (October 14, 1987)

Tiffany tried to be honest and candid with her social workers, discussing her difficulties in hopes that they would help her, but often they used the information as a wedge between her and her child. On June 3, 1987, when Tiffany reported that Tony had locked her out of their apartment, Silvani broached the subject of putting David up for adoption. Her report used several abbreviations common to log entries: "I talked about the ct ordering 232 action for David, relinquishment for adoption, open adoption. She could give David the home and permancy she cannot provide herself. She doesn't want him to grow up like herself in placement. She is able to have some openness to adoption, wants to be able to visit and have progress repts. Wants to give him something. Explained that as biological mo she had given him many things he will always have."

When Tiffany complained to Silvani's supervisor, Randall Parker, about Silvani pressing her to give up David, Parker declined to put another social worker on the case. In his own services activity log entry, Parker said he told Tiffany "that Shirley does acknowledge our concern that David have permanent stability, but that she has no bias I can detect about disabled people, nor does she have a bias towards adoption vs. reunif."

The log entries also offer hints of racial bias among social workers handling the case. On two occasions Silvani referred to a friend of Tiffany's as "a black man" and "the Black fellow," without identifying any of Tiffany's other acquaintances by race.

None of the county officials handling Tiffany's case seemed to have been exposed to the latest research on disabled parenting. During a September 8, 1987, visit with Tiffany and David, one unidentified social worker blithely contradicted one of the central findings of research on infant relationships with disabled parents. The social worker said Tiffany "made the statement 'baby knows it's hard for Mommy to change him so he is still to help Mommy.' When I told Tiffany [young babies] are developmentally incapable of purposeful actions she refused to accept this fact and said 'only the baby knows what he does on purpose.' I gave Tiffany written material on child (infant) development to read."

Silvani seemed similarly skeptical. She said Tiffany and Tony "think the baby will immediately sense and compensate for their disability. They are sure they can provide care for him. Unwilling to ackn[owledge] openly any limitations."

Beyond the lack of familiarity with research, official reports filed with the juvenile court reveal confusion, misinformation, and personnel shifts that made Tiffany's effort to regain her children more difficult. Nurses familiar with Tiffany's needs and talents changed jobs. Therapists dropped out for lack of funds or because of reassignment. Some relatives were criticized for visiting David when they had not been told they could not do so, and other relatives were turned away even though they had written authorization from Silvani. David was hospitalized with bronchitis in May, but it took four days before Tiffany was notified.

Perhaps the most distorted report was submitted on May 9, 1987, by the San Andreas Regional Center, a state-supported agency specializing in the treatment of the developmentally disabled, what were sometimes called the mentally retarded. Under state and federal law, anyone with cerebral palsy was by definition developmentally disabled. Yet research showed only a third of persons with cerebral palsy had a significant intellectual deficiency.

The mental institutions established in Europe and the United States in the nineteenth and early twentieth centuries routinely accepted persons with cerebral palsy as patients, even though most of them were as sane and as intelligent as their keepers. Locked up in at worst horrifying and at best dull environments, these people had no opportunity to develop their intellectual gifts. Some deteriorated into a state of senselessness that allowed doctors to justify their original diagnoses.

When legal action opened the doors of large institutions like Pennhurst State School and Hospital in Pennsylvania, many people with cerebral palsy were discovered to have suffered from years of neglect. The San Andreas Regional Center's difficulty in developing programs to help intellectually able people with cerebral palsy was only a faint, almost innocuous echo of the horrors of those old institutions, but it did slow Tiffany's progress.

Most people involved in the regional centers' work endorsed the legal fiction that all people with cerebral palsy were mentally retarded because it allowed some cerebral palsy clients with only physical disabilities to seek services they could not otherwise afford. But regional centers like San Andreas often remained too understaffed, and too focused on the problems of the mentally retarded, to provide useful service to people of average intelligence.

As Tiffany's case unfolded, doctors, lawyers, social workers, and disability rights activists were engaged in a lively debate over the meaning and importance of the "developmentally disabled" label. New research showed human intelligence taking many shapes and dimensions—all mixed differently in each individual. Some critics wondered how useful it was to call people mentally retarded because they failed a test that measured only one or two of intelligence's many forms.

Historian Paul Longmore pointed to World War II employment records indicating that many industries short of manpower had waived requirements that employees pass intelligence tests and therefore had found good workers among the developmentally disabled—almost all of whom were fired once the war ended.

All sides acknowledged that training people with developmental disabilities required different methods than training people with physical disabilities. The San Andreas Center, like other agencies, had difficulty finding the proper mix.

Some cerebral palsy clients, including Tiffany, complained that they spent too much time trying to convince regional center staff members they were not mentally retarded. Tiffany found that the classes she took were often demeaning and irrelevant. Clients of other centers complained that the instruction was often in language appropriate for first-grade children.

The San Andreas Regional Center report submitted to the court buttressed Tiffany's bad impression. Anyone who had spent more than an hour in conversation with her, tested her phenomenal memory, or seen what she could do in her kitchen would not have recognized Tiffany from the description of her by Nancy Cohen, a center counselor with a master's degree in social work.

Tiffany had "very limited use of her arms and fingers," Cohen said. "Tiffany cannot maintain any of her self-help skills" and appeared skilled only in "money management." She said, "Tiffany is unstable emotionally in that she cannot maintain friends or successful interpersonal relationships."

The paragraph on Tiffany's "cognitive domain" sounded like an elementary-school teacher evaluating a kindergartner: "Tiffany recognizes words that sound the same and can respond to familiar objects based on color, size and shape. She associates events and specific times and is able to count utilizing multi-digit numbers with quantities." The vocational paragraph said she "is not working at this time and does not have any desire to work."

The report stated baldly that Tiffany "is diagnosed mentally retarded." This was patently false, and contradicted in other reports submitted to the court. But it remained, uncorrected, in the regional center report made accessible to all other professionals who evaluated her.

Central to the case against—and later for—Tiffany was a videotape of her diapering David in the Tenth Street apartment on September 22, 1987.

The tape itself remains under court seal, but a services activity log entry by an unidentified DSS employee said, "We videotaped both parents doing basic care skills tasks" on that date. Court testimony and an eyewitness report by San Andreas Regional Center skills assessor Mary Bemis indicate what the camera recorded.

"Tiffany can not safely diaper David without assistance," Bemis said, even though her account indicates that the skills assessor herself may have been at fault. Bemis said, "I placed David on the kitchen table" for the diapering demonstration, ignoring several other places in the apartment that would have been less dangerous. When allowed to choose her own diapering spot, Tiffany invariably went to the open-sided crib, which gave her much more control over the baby's movements.

Bemis said that Tiffany "removed his wet diaper, wiped him off, powdered him and replaced a clean diaper. This procedure takes Tiffany twenty to thirty minutes. David is squirmy and bored before she has finished and turns over, making it necessary for someone to be available to catch him as he moves toward the table edge."

Later observers of the same videotape noted what Bemis did not—Tiffany's trills and coos and constant conversation with the child, entertaining him and easing his fears. "Tiffany says David knows she is handicapped and will lay still for her," Bemis said. This, she indicated, was a sign of the mother's "unrealistic views and expectations of the baby," the unshakable position of DSS from the first day it filed Petition 94106. Tiffany, with nothing but a mother's touch to guide her, tried to teach them something about babies, but they weren't listening yet.

The photo editor at the *San Jose Mercury News* asked Eugene Louie to look for an enterprise shot, the sort of aimless exercise Louie did not usually enjoy. The newspaper needed a few individual photographs to lighten pages heavy with type. Finding good ones required an open mind, a good eye, and luck.

The short, black-haired, thirty-four-year-old photographer was dressed that day in jeans, polo shirt, and running shoes. He drove downtown in the brown Chrysler reserved for such assignments, trying to stay below the speed limit so he could scan the sidewalks without risking a rear-end collision.

Louie had a talent for provocative photographs of people in difficulty. He knew the importance of happenstance. He had been visiting the *Longview* (Wash.) *Daily News* for a job interview in 1980 when the top blew off of nearby Mount Saint Helens. Within hours he was taking pictures that would become part of a package that won the *Daily News* a Pulitzer Prize for local reporting.

His eye caught something at the bus stop at San Carlos and Market streets: two people in wheelchairs staring at the passing traffic. The woman was young, with delicate features, brown hair, and wide-spaced eyes. The man was older, gnarled, and seemingly gloomy, wearing a hooded sweatshirt that gave him the look of a dwarf in a story by Grimm.

Louie did not often see wheelchair riders in pairs. Were they related? Married, perhaps? He had nursed for some time the thought of a photo essay on handicapped people in love. He turned the corner, parked, and walked back toward the couple. He shot a few pictures with a telephoto lens before he came close enough to introduce himself.

"Hi," he said. "I don't mean to bother you. My name's Eugene Louie. I'm a photographer for the *San Jose Mercury*. I wonder if I could take some pictures of you. I thought they might make interesting photographs for my newspaper."

Tiffany loved encounters with adventuresome strangers. The idea of having her picture taken was intriguing, although she did not think she looked her best on that dry, windy, hot day. Tony had a more mercantile reaction. "Sure," he said. "Maybe you can help us. We're having trouble with these damn buses. You think the *Mercury* would buy a van for us?"

They were on their way to Valley Medical Center for a physical examination and prescription for Tony's arthritis. The bus was coming, so they had time to tell only a piece of the story—their romance, Tiffany's pregnancy, their jousts with social workers and lawyers. The needle on Louie's human-interest meter swerved to the top of the scale. He would have to tell the desk about this.

He asked for their names and telephone number. Before the bus arrived, he shot off a roll of film of the two waiting at the small, plastic-roofed shelter. Tony assumed a benign expression. Tiffany grinned and leaned seductively in Tony's direction. Neither knew what would come of it, but it was heartening to have a stranger take an interest in their troubles.

Back at the *Mercury News* building, a stucco and stone structure in an isolated industrial park east of the Nimitz Freeway, Louie told the photo editor what he had found. The *Mercury News* was an expanding, colorfully designed newspaper with a circulation of 240,000. It published one of the most interesting front pages in the state—a mix of local investigative pieces, foreign news features, Hollywood gossip, and cuddly animal stories. The paper had just won a Pulitzer Prize for several articles on Philippine President Ferdinand Marcos's financial dealings in the United States and abroad.

Mercury News editors embraced an ancient rule of successful journalism: Write about people, not press conferences. Louie's story about two disabled people trying to raise a child seemed irresistible. The editors looked for a reporter who might do it justice.

Gary Richards, a thirty-six-year-old Iowa native, had been with the newspaper since 1984. He had his own disability, an artificial leg; his own leg had been amputated when he was twelve in an operation that successfully prevented the spread of bone cancer. His sister-in-law had cerebral palsy. But his editors were less interested in his personal history than in his good sources in the county social services agencies and his talent for writing about family issues.

Richards called Tiffany and Tony and went to see them in the Tenth Street apartment. Their full story proved even more interesting than Louie's sketchy account. David was in a foster home, and there was doubt that they would be able to keep the second child. Richards liked Tiffany, once he grew accustomed to her high soprano and unpredictable patterns of speech.

Tony was another matter. He sometimes suggested that Richards pay them for their story and grew testy and short-tempered if a question carried even the slightest hint of doubt regarding his ability to raise a child. Richards's police sources had heard rumors about Tony's career as a minor celebrity of San Jose street life. He had allegedly taken messages for prostitutes, a charge he would later confirm, and had allegedly served as a lookout for burglars, which he later heatedly denied.

Tony's unsavory reputation may have stemmed from the cultural preference for physical beauty, which, in some ways, made his disability perhaps worse than Tiffany's. She was pretty. He was not. People were biased because of his appearance, and might have been more tolerant if he were tall and blond.

Historian Paul Longmore has cataloged many examples in literature and film of repulsive appearance and physical handicaps being attached to electrifying villains, from Rumpelstiltskin to Dr.

Strangelove. "The deformity of the body symbolizes deformity of the soul," he said. "Physical handicaps are made the emblems of evil."

Another problem for Richards as a journalist was DSS. Even if Silvani and the other social workers involved had wanted to comment on the case, they were prohibited by law from doing so. A Santa Clara County counsel's summary of laws and regulations barring release of information on child welfare cases totaled eighty pages. There was no way for Richards to check some of Tiffany's and Tony's statements, short of persuading someone to violate the law. A reporter always feared that such stories might disintegrate the minute they appeared in print.

Richards put his notes aside for several weeks. His regular job was general assignment reporting, and there were more than enough murders and chemical spills and political speeches to keep him busy. But he could not shed the feeling that the couple's story illustrated something important.

In early October 1987 he visited the Tenth Street apartment again and found Tiffany alone. She was candid and much clearer than he had found her when Tony was there. She said she knew her disability made it difficult to raise a child, but she thought she deserved a chance to show what she could do. She had the specially designed crib. She had been practicing diapering and dressing David during her visits with him at the Zoo and during his rare visits to her apartment.

She did not qualify for Aid to Families with Dependent Children because she received SSI. She thought her lawyer was right to ask that money going to foster care be instead given to her to hire an attendant who could help her with the baby. If that was impossible, she wondered if she might find a foster family that would take her and the baby, a package deal. She dismissed Tony's demands and pipe dreams, and presented the picture of a bright young woman who knew the odds but wanted a chance to roll the dice.

Richards thought about his sister-in-law while talking to Tiffany. Barbara's physical limitations were not as great as Tiffany's. She did volunteer work at a hospital and rode the buses of Ames, Iowa, with ease. But Richards was not sure whether Barbara could manage a family or raise a child. If you gave Barbara five dollars, the family saying went, she would go out and spend six.

Tiffany was different. She was quicker, brighter, much more in tune with what was going on around her. She had a keen sense of the worth of a dollar, one reason why she and Tony argued so often about the anemic family budget.

Richards's editor had thought from the start that the story was a natural, but he told the reporter not to write it until he felt comfortable with it. Richards decided that the moment had come. He went back to the office, placed a few more calls, and by Thursday had nearly two thousand words stored in the computer.

Richards had done very few enterprise stories of this length before. He thought it had a chance to be on the front page if he wrote it well. He resisted the urge to manipulate the reader with loaded adjectives and emotional quotes. He had learned in his early days as a sportswriter that the best stories, those with their own emotional resonance, deserved the simplest language. This story would reach out and grab the reader without any unwanted assistance from him.

He wrote:

Tiffany Callo and Tony Rios are fighting to regain custody of their 7-month-old son.

Their fight is that of two wheelchair-bound parents with a healthy child—a fight, specialists in the field say, that has the couple trapped in a society unprepared for the disabled to have children or get help raising them.

And it's a fight they are losing.

Clay Bedford, Tiffany's attorney, provided the most provocative quotes: "The only thing Tiffany has done is to be born with horrendous defects. To think of stripping her of her parental rights is outrageous." The lawyer noted that state law gave Tiffany only eighteen months to persuade the court to return David, or he would be adopted. "What's eighteen months going to do for Tiffany?" he said. "Cure her of cerebral palsy? No."

The story warned that this unusual dilemma might become far more commonplace. "The couple's situation illustrates the kind of problems that may become more frequent as an increasing number of handicapped people learn to live independently and decide to have children, experts said."

Richards presented his subjects' weak and strong points in quick succession:

> Rios' and Callo's case is not simple. They may not be model parents. He is combative and argumentative, according to social worker reports. They aren't married and they have little money.
>
> But able-bodied parents don't normally lose children for such offenses. Callo's and Rios' only crime, say their attorneys, is their inability to care for [David] or pay for someone who can.

Richards saved for last a moment from his decisive interview with Tiffany:

> When she talks about her son, she pulls out a single black-and-white ultrasound picture taken before the baby was born—a memory that reflects the happiness she held before the baby's birth as well as the emptiness with which she now must cope.
>
> "We were so excited about having the baby," she said. "That was the happiest time. Since he's been born, it's been real sad."

Richards's editors loved the story. They placed it on the front page of the Friday, October 16, edition, with one of the photographs Louie took at the bus stop and another showing Tiffany having an ultrasound examination at Valley Medical. The headline read: "Fighting to Keep Their Son, Wheelchair-bound Couple Struggle for Parental Rights."

Tiffany had told Bedford that a reporter was interested in the case. The attorney had no objection. It could not hurt to have some publicity, but he did not think it would help either. He had little experience with the media and no sense of the power of a story that strikes a public nerve.

When Richards called to tell him that the story would be on the front page the next day, he thanked the reporter for the courtesy but felt no particular urgency. He slept late that morning and strolled into his office about ten. His doctor had been screaming about his weight and blood pressure and he was trying to slow down. He had no court appearance planned. He was wearing blue jeans and a polo shirt for a quiet day of office work and thought he might start the weekend a little early.

His secretary greeted him as if he had abandoned her at the bottom of a rattlesnake pit. "There are *forty messages* here for you from *fifteen different media outlets*," she said. She rolled her eyes in frustration. "UPI called, the AP, every one of the TV stations. They want to talk to *you*."

This was not what he had expected. Even Richards and his editors at the *Mercury News* were surprised. They had anticipated some interest from television and other newspapers in northern California, but the national wire services had leapt on the story, and calls were coming to Bedford from Miami, Philadelphia, and even the *Washington Post*.

Bedford drove quickly back to his apartment, put on a suit, and rushed to meet the television crews converging outside the criminal courthouse where he had agreed to meet them. At the Tenth Street apartment, Tiffany and Tony began to entertain a stream of visitors. Tony was friendly and helpful, on his best behavior. But Tiffany was the star, a telegenic, witty interview subject that television producers could not get enough of.

For two weeks Bedford did almost nothing but answer questions in front of television cameras and return telephone calls from the media. He threatened to bill the juvenile court for the hours, but the billing clerk knew he was joking. The psychic rewards were enough, Bedford thought, and it occurred to him that the publicity might create a better atmosphere for the arguments he would make in court, and at the same time might convince DSS that they had to take David's parents, particularly Tiffany, more seriously.

He marveled at her television performances. She was so breathtakingly different from the portrait of a slow-witted cripple in the regional center files that he even enjoyed the moments when she upstaged him.

At the beginning he worried that her speech impediment, the screeching high tones and oddly timed pauses, would make her hard to understand. On the contrary, her slow pace and careful selection of words were perfect for television. Producers and reporters began to remark on her unusual presence on the air, what they called her "charisma." Bedford dubbed her the year's poster child for disabled parents' rights.

Bedford sensed the DSS staff unhappiness at the way they were being portrayed—cold, implacable bureaucrats giving an already unfortunate young woman one more lesson in life's cruelty. The law prevented them from talking about Tony's temperament and the lack of available funding to provide full-time help for the couple. All Shirley Silvani could do was ride out the storm and make sure no cameras got near David or the foster parents. Judy, the foster mother, was aghast to see on television part of her head in a snapshot of David taken from Tiffany's photo album without her permission. Tiffany apologized for not keeping a closer eye on the television crews and promised it would not happen again. She began to tire of the endless series of interviews, and put some reporters off for a while, but eventually decided she needed every bit of publicity if she was ever to turn the county around.

Bedford encouraged DSS and the deputy county counsel Michael Clark to give their side to the press. "My client has waived her privilege," he said. "Tony has waived his privilege." That produced a weary smile. "The baby hasn't waived his privilege," the county attorney replied, nor would the court ever allow him to do so.

The one-sided nature of the media coverage gave Tiffany an advantage, Bedford acknowledged. But with the law and the habits of child-protection agencies stacked against her, he thought it was fair she won at least one round.

Letters and telephone calls began to flow into the offices of the *Mercury News*. Walter Miller of San Jose asked, "Is this Nazism closing in on us—with social workers leading the charge 'for the good of society'?" Shannon Hines Recchio of San Jose said, "By taking away her baby, society is saying Tiffany Callo's physical handicaps make her a less suitable parent than if she were abusive, a drug addict, or even a child herself. How ironic that our child-protection agencies are so overburdened that they are often forced to return kids to dangerous, even deadly homes, yet Tiffany is granted a mere one hour a week with her son."

Tiffany and Bedford began to do a round of talk shows and television appearances, some quite emotional. Joel E. Spivak, the usually sarcastic host of a talk show on WRC-AM Radio in Washington, D.C., had to pause during an interview with Tiffany and Tony to collect himself. "You'll pardon me if I'm just a little bit overcome," he said. "Can you imagine what those people have been through? . . . It's so mind-boggling. It would be different if anyone had seriously intimated that they had done something terrible to the baby or something like that, but there's nothing like that. They just can't pay for full-time help."

Tiffany treasured a letter from Lori Wirthlin, a San Carlos, California, woman raised by parents who had cerebral palsy. "I grew up in a loving, caring atmosphere," she said, "and I feel this child deserves the same opportunity."

Not all responses were positive. One WRC listener told Spivak that "bringing a child into the world carries an enormous responsibility, not only a financial responsibility but the willingness for the husband or the mother to spend time with the child. . . . Can they really fulfill that role as parents? Can they really do the things that a son would want to do? I think not. It's a sad thing that nature is sometimes cruel."

Sharon Dannemiller of Newark, California, told the *Mercury News* that the letters they printed about Tiffany "were completely indifferent to the rights and needs of her baby. It may sound humanitarian to write about the needs of the handicapped adult who is working harder than most of us to be an independent, contributing member of society, but unfortunately Tiffany and the baby's father are permanently and severely handicapped and never will be independent or contributing."

Cheryl A. Davis of Palo Alto responded a week later: "If alternative approaches have not been tried, then the evidence for discrimination on the basis of handicap must be presumed. I believe that both Tiffany Callo and her child have been abused by institutionalized bias against the handicapped. I am not ignoring the child's needs; I say that Tiffany deserves assistance to meet those needs."

Tiffany listened carefully to the arguments erupting around her. She enjoyed her celebrity status. But what mattered most to her was that she no longer felt so alone. The outpouring of concern for her and outrage against DSS had surprised even Bedford. Perhaps his pessimistic assessment of her chances in court would also prove untrue.

In November, feeling huge and lumpy again with a seven-month-old fetus, Tiffany caught the front wheel of her power chair in a small hole while crossing San Carlos Street. The two-hundred-pound chair flipped over and slammed Tiffany, still strapped in, into the asphalt.

She was unconscious for fifteen seconds, an inert mass of mother and baby trapped beneath a metal cage attached to an electrical motor. When she could focus her eyes again, she saw four men in business suits, fuzzy and indistinct, leaning over her. "You okay? You okay?" one said. "Can we move you?"

The baby was pounding frantically. He had not enjoyed the trip.

"Is anything broken? Are you all right?"

She wiggled her fingers for a moment. "I don't think anything's broken."

The men seemed more frightened than she was. "Do you think we can at least get the chair in an upright position?" one asked.

"Yeah," she said, "although you got to be real careful. You got a bouncing baby boy here."

One of the men looked closer, seeing for the first time her swelling midsection. "Oh, God," he said.

Slowly and carefully, they pushed the chair upright, expecting Tiffany at any minute to slide off like a stray tile on a church roof. A bright red line of blood ran down the back of her neck. One of the men ran to call an ambulance while the others inspected Tiffany for more damage.

"This kid's having a great time," she said. "He thinks he's playing football." The men laughed nervously.

"You ought to go in and get the baby checked at least," one said, "and that head needs looking at."

The ambulance pulled up and the paramedics eased Tiffany, and then her chair, into the back. At Valley Medical she lay for four hours in the emergency room, her skull in a special brace. She had split open the flesh at the top of her head. After the usual long wait—she felt as if she had spent half of her life staring at hospital ceilings—the cut was cleaned and patched and her baby pronounced healthy and stable, if a little agitated.

Tiffany began to wonder if the incident was a sign. She had been skating through the events in her life, never quite rooting herself to one spot. She and Tony were fighting hard for David, yet they did not seem to be doing much for their own relationship. They had yet to marry.

She continued to have doubts about Tony's emotional stability, but he was the father of her children. If they were to succeed, she thought, both as partners and parents, they had to keep moving forward. She mentioned the subject of marriage again to Tony and, somewhat to her surprise, he nodded his head. "I don't have any objection to that," he said.

It fell far short of a romantic proposal, but she decided to make the best of it. She ordered a fancy two-layer cake decorated with blue flowers and a bride and groom under a heart-shaped arch. She found an off-white, sleeveless wedding dress, full of fluff and lace but not quite long enough to catch in her chair wheels. Two hours before the ceremony, disturbed that Tony had not bought himself a suit, Tiffany gave him three hundred dollars and sent him to a store that did instant alterations. He returned with only a new white shirt, having spent the rest on liquor for the reception.

The judge who performed the brief courthouse ceremony turned out to be the same man who had married Tiffany's parents, not exactly a favorable omen. The only other people at the ceremony were Tiffany's mother, Tony's godmother, and the god-mother's son.

At the reception afterward in the Tenth Street apartment, Tiffany tried to keep the atmosphere light. Patty Smith, Tiffany's attendant, had cooked fried chicken, steaks, and hamburgers and made potato salad for the guests. Tiffany hugged friends and clinked her champagne glass.

She had put down a root, Tiffany thought. She had made a commitment. But at any moment, Tony could retreat into his own little world. She felt lonely at her wedding banquet, and ter-rified at the thought of separation from the new life kicking within her, demanding more room to grow.

10

Tony found a job at United Handicapped Workers selling light bulbs and cleaning materials by telephone. Money was still short, however, and the long days without David depressed Tiffany and Tony and made their weekly hour in the Zoo that much more of a strain.

With David, Tony was again cold and aloof, rarely touching the boy. He confined his conversations with his son to orders and warnings. When Tiffany and Tony were by themselves, much of the talk was about money—how to get more of it, what they could buy with it, whose fault it was that they didn't have it. Though they had married, it seemed to Tiffany that Tony's feelings for her had again cooled, and she could not decide how to react.

Occasionally he hit her. He used the thin, two-foot wooden rod with a plastic hook, sometimes called a "reacher," that he often carried to snag things too high or too far away. If he came close enough, he could make the stick hurt. She felt humiliated, and wondered if he could endanger their unborn baby.

On December 15, five weeks after the wedding, Tiffany felt unusually ill at ease. The holidays had interrupted the visiting schedule with David. The county had given no sign that it would even consider letting her try to raise the unborn second child. Tony was more distant than ever. He stayed out several nights and ignored her requests for an explanation.

The more she saw David and the more she felt the new baby kick inside her, the happier she was that Tony had given her two small lives to entwine with her own. But it began to occur to her that she had been wrong to insist on marriage. Tony had lived by himself so long, and was so emotionally dependent on his friends on the streets, that he seemed incapable of changing his nocturnal rhythms.

He had little time for sweet talk and caresses. He spent every waking moment in his chair. It gave him mobility, power, and even notoriety among his peers. He had none of Tiffany's love for long hours in bed, talking and loving and dreaming. He did not like being stationary, and helpless, for any reason.

What could she do? A divorce would tarnish her memory of Elnora and the woman's firm Catholicism. It might not help her chances of keeping the children either, although Silvani had once hinted that she had no chance at all if she stayed with Tony.

Tony came in at nine that night. It was early for him, but he was in a foul mood.

The refrigerator was empty. Tiffany was hungry. She thought the child inside her was too. "Honey," she said. "Do you have some money for groceries?"

"What business is that of yours?" he said, thumping his stick absentmindedly on the table. "My money is my money."

"It's just that the baby's hungry, and it's hard to satisfy him if I haven't eaten."

Tony looked at her as if she were a cockroach crawling from under the stove. "I left fifty bucks on the table," he said, "Where is it?"

"I haven't got it," she said. Tiffany called Patty Smith over from the kitchenette. Patty said that neither she nor Tiffany had seen any money on the table.

"You're lying," Tony said. He raised his stick and struck Tiffany on the forehead. There was no blood, but the sharp pain stunned her. She sat immobile for a second, too surprised to say anything, then cried out in pain and tried to reach over and grab him.

He hit her again. "I ought to kill you, bitch," he said.

Tiffany felt the baby jump. Her anger began to wash away much of the pain. "Why don't you get the hell out of here?" she said. "Go cool off or something. You want to hurt your kid? Are you crazy?"

Her vision blurred and she felt dizzy. She could not remember ever being so angry, or so frightened. "You're completely crazy," she said. "Don't you ever do that again." She moved her chair as close to his as she could and pushed herself over on top of him. She reached out with her hand and grabbed a tender spot.

He screeched in pain and struck back, but Patty had already moved in to separate them. She pushed Tiffany back into her chair and yelled for them to stop.

"Come on back!" Tony shouted at Tiffany. "I'll give you something. Come and get it."

Tiffany felt very tired. "Tony, why don't you just get the hell out of here? Go cool off someplace."

Her husband made no move to turn his chair toward the door. He planted himself in the middle of the living room, sputtering a torrent of acidic curses in her direction.

Tiffany lacked the strength to argue much longer. He had her trapped, a moth fluttering in a jar. She did not have the power to relieve Tony of the pain of a lifetime searching for something he could not find. It had done something to his character, and his feelings for her, but she had to protect her children.

"I really don't want to do this," she said to him. "I don't want to send you away from your kid. I'll let you come back and we'll talk about it and all this other stuff. Just give me an hour to think. Leave me alone and stay out of my face for at least an hour."

"Try to make me, bitch," he said.

Tiffany sighed, turned the chair around, and rolled out the door. It was chilly, but she had her coat and she could buy things at the store. Maybe a short break would change the mood.

When she returned a half hour later, Tony had placed his chair against the door and locked the wheels so she could not push it open. Patty had gone. Tiffany yelled at Tony, then sat shivering in the chill air, trying to think.

Her mother walked into the apartment courtyard. Nancy had planned just a quick visit to say hello, but when she hugged her daughter, Tiffany grimaced, as if in pain. "It hurts, Mom," she said. "He hit me."

Nancy inspected the bruises on her daughter's head. She became very angry. The years of earning an occasional living with heavy housework had given her more than enough muscle to force open the door and push Tony and his chair out of the way.

"What did you hit her with?" Nancy asked. Tiffany indicated the stick. Nancy tore it out of Tony's hand and gave him one sharp blow on the head. "How the hell do you like it?" she said.

Tony unleashed a string of sidewalk adjectives and wheeled himself out the door. "I'll get my brother to come over and take care of you, bitch," he said. Nancy jeered at him. "Go ahead and do it," she said. "I'm sure your brother is a lot more rational than you."

Tony went to a corner pay phone and called 911. Several minutes passed. Officer Cindy Bueno, small and unerringly polite, pulled her squad car up to the curb and followed Tony back to the apartment. The officer rapped on the door and identified herself. Nancy let her in and she looked around the living room. She saw Tiffany and noticed marks on her forehead.

"He claims you hit him first," Bueno said. Tiffany laughed, happy to be diverted by such sheer nonsense. "Take a look, Officer," she said. "I think it's clear who is lying."

Bueno went to her squad car and returned with a thirty-five-millimeter camera. She took pictures of Tiffany's bruises and what Tony said were his injuries. The only solution, she said, was for each to leave the other alone for a while. She suggested that Tony go away for a few hours, maybe take a long stroll.

Like most modern urban police, she was accustomed to acting as a family counselor to the poor. She had no office or upholstered couch, but she could arrange truces and separate the combatants, at least temporarily.

For an hour they argued about who had done what to whom, with Bueno as mediator. Tony, seeing he was outnumbered, promised to behave, but he refused to leave the apartment as Tiffany had requested.

Bueno announced that she was ready to jail Tony if Tiffany wished to press charges. "Maybe we can make a deal with him, huh?" Tiffany said. "What I want you to tell him is that I want him to either go down to his dad's and spend the night and give me some time alone or just go out and sit in the damn restaurant for two hours and have a damn cup of coffee like he always does when his wife is sitting at home waiting for him or lying in bed waiting for him to come home." She realized she was not being very coherent, but it was late and this was the first chance in some time to spill out her frustrations to a sympathetic listener. "Why can't he do that tonight?" she said. "Why can't he just give me an hour alone?"

Bueno approached Tony and outlined the bargain. She underlined the consequences if he refused. "Yeah," he said finally. "Okay. I got things to do anyway."

Bueno told him he was not to return without telephoning the apartment and seeking Tiffany's permission. The telephone calls had to be polite, no harassment. Both of them had to behave themselves, but Bueno directed her remarks to Tony. Your wife is in a delicate condition, she told him. It was wrong for you to try to upset her, much less hit her and threaten her.

Tony rolled out the door a few minutes after midnight. Nancy went home. Bueno left too, giving Tiffany a final, encouraging word and one of her cards. Bueno had seen enough of these cases to know that there was a good chance she would see the Rioses again.

Patty returned and she and Tiffany talked for a while. Tiffany was too upset and full of adrenaline to go to bed.

Two hours passed before Tony called. He asked if he could come back. Tiffany said no. An hour later the telephone rang again. The caller was someone else. Tony had enlisted a friend to plead his case, but Tiffany declined to talk to him.

Someone knocked on the door. It was a woman Tiffany knew

slightly, a friend of Tony's offering to help. Tiffany let her in, but before the door shut, Tony rolled in right behind her.

He seemed comfortable and casual, as if his return were part of the bargain. Tiffany could see that this would never end. She still loved Tony. He could be funny and warm, and there was no question he knew how to bring excitement to her life. But, she concluded, she would be crazy or dead if she stayed with him, and he had proven himself an indifferent father.

Tiffany punched in the number on Bueno's card, while Tony sat in his chair, daring her and the rest of the world to tell him what to do.

Bueno arrested Tony, but, perplexed at how to transport him, called a medical van. Seeing what was coming, Tony began to plead with Tiffany. "Come on, sweetheart," he said. "Call this whole thing off and we'll go in the bedroom. I'll give you what you like."

"Oh, that's lovely," Tiffany said. "I'm not stupid. You just want to get me into bed where you can beat me up more."

On the way to jail, Tony convinced Bueno that he needed access to complete medical care. She arranged for him to go to a room at Valley Medical Center reserved for city prisoners, almost directly above the spot where his new son would be sleeping in less than a month.

Tiffany went to bed. She slept until early evening the next day, trying to avoid thinking about what she was going to have to do next.

She dragged herself out of bed and rolled into the kitchenette for something to eat. She did not say much. "Mommy?" Patty asked. "Mommy, are you okay?"

"Ohhh, no," Tiffany said. She tasted a sick emptiness at the bottom of her stomach. "I'm going to my room for a while. I just want to chill."

She rolled over to her bedside table and turned on the radio. Marilyn McCoo was trilling "One Less Bell to Answer," perfect for her mood. The wedding photos had been picked up that day.

She had planned to show them to Tony. She had hoped the memories would break through the barriers he had been putting up. With frustration and fatigue, she inspected the pictures of bright-colored dresses and silly smiles.

The small plastic bride and groom from the wedding cake still sat on her dresser. Her eyes turned to the wall calendar. She calculated that she had a week before the baby was due. She had to tighten her emotional seat belt for another battle with DSS.

She flipped through the wedding pictures one by one. She tossed all the photos of Tony into a pile of their own. She felt herself becoming angry with him all over again. What godawful timing he had. What a mess.

She found a pair of scissors on the dresser and thought about cutting Tony out of every photograph, but discarded the idea. She was too tired to do anything. Why the hell did you do this to me? she thought.

All she wanted, she thought, was the standard dream: a husband and two children and perhaps some way to help other people.

The baby kicked inside her and Tiffany held her breath. David was fading from her life like her old, cherished memories of her grandmother. Her marriage was over. She did not think she had the strength to hold on to this new child, given the number and power of the people who wanted to yank him away.

She had moved into adulthood without having much chance to enjoy the aimlessness of a California urban adolescence, the dances and the music and the sense of moving fast. She could live with that. But she could not bear being denied the bits of life that seemed made for her, the parts that matched her slow pace, like love and faith and hope and trust. She felt as if she had been pushed down a very deep hole, and her arms were too weak to pull herself back up.

PART TWO

Crip Time

11

In the midst of the media blitz over Tiffany's case, Shirley Silvani called Megan Kirshbaum in October 1987 and asked her to do a psychological evaluation of DSS's troublesome client. Her report would help the court decide whether Tiffany could safely raise her children.

Kirshbaum was a short, soft-voiced woman with thick brown hair. She probably had more experience with disabled parents than any psychologist in the country, but San Jose was at least an hour's drive down Interstate 880 from her home and office in Berkeley. Her research and work with local families was demanding and she did not know if she could spare the time.

And yet there was something about the way Silvani described the case that intrigued and concerned her. She sensed that DSS knew very little about how disabled parents could be trained to care for their children. After some hesitation, Kirshbaum agreed to take the case and made arrangements for her first visit with Tiffany at the Tenth Street apartment.

Red tape, Kirshbaum's schedule, the holidays, and Jesse's birth intruded, so that Tiffany did not meet Kirshbaum until three weeks after Jesse was born.

Tiffany greeted the psychologist with weary patience. Silvani had told her that Kirshbaum was a specialist in the field, and would show her how to handle her baby—dress him, wash him, feed him, change him.

Tiffany had heard that before. Kirshbaum was the third or fourth expert she had seen since David was born. Each visit by one of these professionals fit a pattern—a quick, often critical glance around Tiffany's apartment, an hour of detailed instructions on how to do what she had been doing before David was taken, and a great deal of scribbling in notebooks that, as far as Tiffany could tell, said little more than that she was a hopeless case.

Tiffany did not think Kirshbaum looked like someone who could do any better. Silvani had apparently been confused by a conversation with someone who knew Kirshbaum's husband, Hal, who had multiple sclerosis. Silvani told Tiffany that Kirshbaum herself was disabled, but the woman who walked in the door of the Tenth Street apartment did not look disabled to Tiffany.

She assumed that this was another county spy who had little familiarity with disabilities. She braced herself to be treated once again like a three-year-old learning to play with dolls.

Kirshbaum could sense the younger woman's prickly attitude. She ignored it and got to work. Silvani had brought Jesse, a blue-eyed guinea pig in a fresh diaper. Kirshbaum thought Tiffany could manage the infant more easily if there was a safe and efficient way to carry him. With other disabled mothers, she had had some luck with front packs or wheelchair trays. Each mother's physical limits were unique, so she had to see what Tiffany could do.

The wheelchair tray was awkward for Tiffany. The clear plastic device fastened to the side of her chair and swiveled in front of her when she wanted to rest a book, a cup, or a plate. She rarely used it, preferring to push herself up against a nearby table, but Kirshbaum thought it had possibilities.

The psychologist had learned that the best solutions were often the simplest and closest at hand. Her profession was thick with correlation studies and weighted experiments and other academic debris. She preferred to look for something lying in a backyard or gathering dust on a side table that might help perform some small chore. She would grab it and play with it and try to incorporate it immediately into therapy.

Kirshbaum asked Tiffany to snap in the tray and see whether Jesse could ride on it comfortably. Tiffany did not like it. The tray jutted out in front of her in a way that made it difficult to balance the chair and move about the apartment, particularly when she had to make the tight turn in the hall.

"You know," Tiffany said, an edge in her voice, "if you have an idea like this, I would rather you tell me about it ahead of time so I can try to work with it on my own."

"You're not comfortable?" Kirshbaum asked.

"Not very," she said. "I might be able to make it work, but it will take some time. It feels funny to have him out so far in front of me, and I don't like those turns."

Tiffany shifted Jesse over to the bed and began methodically to change his diaper. Kirshbaum watched her for a moment. She liked the way the younger woman handled frustration. Some of the evaluations had said that Tiffany resisted change and lost her temper when stymied. But just now she had expressed herself and moved on to another productive activity without any further sign of agitation.

"You know, I'm glad to try these new ideas of yours," Tiffany said, "but I don't think it's fair to judge me on my first try."

"What do you mean?" Kirshbaum said.

"Well, other people who come in here will try one thing for one time, and then they leave. I sort of feel that what everybody is doing is taking their shot at me and then writing these nasty one-page reports to make me look like some bitch, and I don't appreciate that."

Kirshbaum laughed. "Tiffany," she said, "my report is definitely going to be more than one page long. I'll have to be honest about what I see as your strengths and your difficulties. But first we need to brainstorm together, and figure out how to do things with your babies. I need to hear *your* ideas about how to take care of them, and hear what you think you'd like help with."

That sounded good to Tiffany. She began to relax, without daring to entertain any strong hope that this little woman with the nice smile could do much about her earnest adversaries at DSS.

Megan Light met Hal Kirshbaum in 1960, their freshman year at Antioch College in Yellow Springs, Ohio. They shared an interest in books, people, and the civil rights movement that had become the rallying cry of much of their college generation. They were faced with Hal's initial diagnosis of multiple sclerosis before the end of their first semester, but twenty-five years would pass before the virus progressed to the point where he would have to use a cane and an electric cart to move around.

In her sophomore year Megan transferred from Antioch to New York University and graduated with a degree in English and psychology. She saw Hal often when he came to New York under Antioch's work-study program.

She worked in day-care centers and taught in the pilot project for Operation Head Start. Hal graduated and joined her in New York, working for the unemployment office, before leaving for Berkeley, California, to study philosophy at the University of California. She followed him to U.C. Berkeley, enrolling in a master's degree program where she focused on cross-cultural language development.

They were married in the chambers of an Oakland judge in 1968. In 1971 they moved to Cedar Rapids, Iowa, where Hal taught philosophy at Coe College. Megan had their first child, Anya, and enrolled at Union Institute in a doctoral program in psychology, with a focus on family therapy and infant mental health. She began working on her thesis, a study of hypnotherapist Milton Erickson, who had survived two cases of polio and several other illnesses.

Erickson was considered a therapeutic wizard by young psychologists. He had mastered many techniques for approaching difficult patients in difficult situations, and demonstrated to Megan how the very texture of the words she used could change the atmosphere of an interview.

Small-town academic life in the Midwest did not suit the Kirshbaums. In 1974 they moved back to Berkeley, not sure what they were going to do. Hal's MS was still little more than an annoyance—blurred vision and short episodes of numbness in his legs—but they both had become interested in the growing numbers of East Bay people with disabilities who were talking about launching another civil rights movement.

For more than two centuries, European and American physicians, therapists, and others involved in treating disabilities had argued vehemently over two general approaches. In modern terms, the two alternatives might be described as independence or mainstream.

The independence group was represented by educators like Edward Gallaudet, who advocated sign language for the deaf. They said that disabled people could become most active and creative if they augmented their abilities with helpful methods and machines like signing and wheelchairs, even if this might aggravate popular prejudice against them and isolate them in some ways from nondisabled society.

The mainstream group included inventor Alexander Graham Bell and other oralists who wanted the deaf to learn to speak and read lips. They said disabled people had to try to walk, no matter what the cost in time and energy, and behave as much like nondisabled people as possible or be denied social status and productive employment.

By 1900 the oralist, mainstream faction appeared to have won the argument about deaf people. Psycholinguist Harlan Lane noted that schools for the deaf fired deaf teachers and punished students for using sign language. An Italian oralist told complainers: "Since when do we consult the patient on the nature of his treatment?"

Most models of disabled behavior in the twentieth century were people like Franklin Roosevelt, who tried to act as if their handicap did not exist. But when discrimination against those with disabilities persisted despite such shining examples, activists in the 1960s retrieved the old tattered flag of the independence faction and mounted a new charge.

It began, like the movement for civil rights for blacks, with a focus on education. National organizations led by the parents of disabled children lobbied for more public-school spending and more access to higher education. This led to legal attacks on job discrimination and, like all movements against prejudice, eventually inspired demands for full rights and privileges for disabled people in private matters like sex and family.

In 1973 Congress passed the Rehabilitation Act. It prohibited discrimination against the disabled in any institution receiving federal funds. Many more wheelchair users began to appear on the Berkeley campus of the University of California. The Kirshbaums found themselves drawn into the work of the Center for Independent Living (CIL), the precursor of a national movement to find ways for disabled young people—including many students—to leave their parents and live on their own, often with other disabled people.

The Kirshbaums began to work as counselors at CIL's temporary headquarters on the second floor of an old Berkeley office building. They were good at it, but uncertain at first. Megan had a gentle, almost diffident manner. She felt clumsy with the unfamiliar culture of the disabled community, and was absorbed with confronting her fears about the progression of Hal's MS.

Hal, on the other hand, was relieved to learn at CIL how one could survive with a severe disability—it made him more hopeful about his own future. Tall, bald, and bearded, he had a wry sense of humor and shared Megan's talent for honesty and clarity. His first CIL client, a man in his fifties with cerebral palsy, gave him some sense of where the disability rights movement was going with a befuddling initial question: "How do you meet girls?"

Megan, as a family therapist, tried to salve the wounds of parents who did not want their children to pack their books and wheelchairs and move out. Many young disabled people had discovered sex, something neither their families nor the surrounding community were prepared for. That sometimes required psychological counseling and couple therapy, as well as information about birth control and parenting.

When Megan counseled families, she noticed one common pattern. One parent, usually the mother, would develop an intense relationship with the disabled child—what psychologists called overcompensation. The rest of the family, the other parent and the siblings, would be cut off and the family's emotional health would suffer. The intensity of the bond between mother and disabled child would stifle the child's urge to seek independence in adulthood, and the mother's ability to let go.

In counseling families, Megan sought to restore a balance. The father was encouraged to spend more time with the disabled child. An attempt was made to revitalize the relationship of the marital couple. Ways to include siblings in family routines were suggested. There was pain, she acknowledged, but it could strengthen rather than weaken the bonds of family life if spread around.

Then, unexpectedly, the Kirshbaums received a taste of that suffering and dislocation themselves. In 1978, their son Noah was born with a structural defect in his heart. He spent several weeks among the tubes and beeping monitors of the neonatal intensive-care unit at Children's Hospital in Oakland. When he was nine months old, doctors at the University of California at San Francisco performed open-heart surgery. Another operation would be performed when he was three.

Early in the ordeal, the Kirshbaums were told that Noah's medical recovery might be delayed if they let him cry. They spent long nights trying to comfort the child and saw signs of the same family strain Megan had noticed in her clients.

Megan Kirshbaum began to attend seminars and conferences on the care of disabled infants. She noticed a curious gap. There were no people there with disabilities or knowledge about how disabled adults could function independently. There was remarkably little communication between the disability rights movement, those who were lobbying for jobs and independent living, and the health professionals serving disabled babies. The infant and adult realms did not connect, as if disabled babies had no future.

When it came to questions about parenting—how to prevent overfeeding a baby with spina bifida, how to ease the diapering process for a mother with cerebral palsy—both movements were picking over barren ground. Almost no research had been done on successful techniques for disabled parents. Few therapists even knew if standard psychological tests applied or how to distinguish harmful behavior caused by a disability from mistakes made by any human being under stress. The parents of disabled children were rarely interested in such issues. Some young disabled women complained that as children their mothers had even discouraged them from playing with dolls, for the mothers could not imagine their children becoming parents in the future.

In 1982 Kirshbaum received a five-thousand-dollar grant from the March of Dimes for her work on parenting issues. She founded a nonprofit agency called Through the Looking Glass, a playful tribute to Lewis Carroll and the notion that disabilities might not seem so grim if examined from a new angle.

It was a brave act for a forty-year-old therapist with no equipment and almost no contact with important foundations. She had never before written a grant proposal. She did, however, have the advantage of novelty, which foundations liked. No one else seemed to be exploring the family lives of the disabled in any systematic, nonpathological way. Once she began to complete the grant proposals—a tortuous process that seemed to her akin to writing novels—approval came with surprising speed.

She received twenty-five thousand dollars in 1984 from the National Easter Seal Research Foundation to buy a video camera, recorder, and other equipment to monitor disabled parents working with their babies. Between 1985 and 1987 she received three separate grants of fifty thousand dollars each from the National Institute of Disability and Rehabilitation Research, part of the U.S. Department of Education, to do research and demonstrations and train professionals in infancy and parenting issues from the perspective of the disabled.

The grants were relatively small but impressive for such a tiny operation. For an office, Kirshbaum remodeled a garage behind the family's brown wood-frame house on a leafy street in north Berkeley. She began to hire other therapists. Some social workers sent her cases they could not handle. Juvenile court judges, perplexed at how to evaluate disabled parents, read some of her studies and were impressed. Word of mouth in the disabled community brought many more cases to her door.

Still, many psychologists discounted the work of Through the Looking Glass, for Kirshbaum hired only therapists who were disabled or the parents of disabled. She shrugged off the widespread notion that this would weaken the objectivity of their analyses.

Kirshbaum found to her surprise that many health professionals—doctors, nurses, social workers, therapists—were blithely ignorant of what disabled parents could do. Hospital staffs often sent insensitive or discouraging signals. Her clients told of being peppered with questions and intrusions from the minute they became parents: "How in God's name are you going to take care of your baby?" "Do you really think it is safe for you to do that?" "No, no, that's not right—let me do it for you."

The prevailing assumption was that disabled parents could never do very much for themselves, or for others, and ought not to try. Kirshbaum, watching this theme replayed often in her taped interviews, decided that the only solution was to intervene at the earliest possible moment, perhaps even before the child was born. She wanted to convince parents with disabilities that they could fully participate in the lives of their children. She had to demonstrate to professionals how disabled parents actually managed their children. She hoped that this window on the disabled world would help professionals deal with disabled babies and convey more hope to parents.

Sex had become a favorite topic of activists in the independent-living movement. Publications like *The Disability Rag* and *Spinal Network* printed cartoons and often hilarious confessional pieces on how to leap the hurdles of physical romance. John Callahan, a paraplegic cartoonist in Oregon, gained a cult following with deceptively simple cartoons that teetered on the edge of bad taste. In one, a bespectacled man in a wheelchair examined with interest a streetwalker with a handicap symbol stitched to the front of her skintight pants.

Kirshbaum welcomed the move toward healthy sexuality but cautioned couples about the unforeseen consequences of parenthood. She underlined its stresses and its tendency to change the

pattern of days and careers. She asked about clients' support sys-
tems—relatives, friends, nondisabled spouses. She encouraged
them to stay involved in decisions about their children and not
allow support people to become de facto parents.

When family courts and social services agencies began to ask
Kirshbaum to do evaluations, the growth in the disabled parenting movement and the bureaucratic resistance to it became more
apparent to her. Many psychologists, lacking daily contact with
the disabled and unaware of new research, gave very poor evaluations of disabled people and provided little helpful information.

Kirshbaum's kindness, one of the first things friends remarked
about her, led her to conclude that her fellow psychologists' mistakes stemmed more from innocence and ignorance than ani-
mosity and prejudice. Otherwise intelligent, sensitive therapists
employed blatant stereotypes—a disabled mother's "natural" inability to maintain eye contact with her child, a disabled father's
"stubborn" insistence on overfeeding—that they would have
instantly challenged if directed toward black clients.

Each case helped Kirshbaum conceive more ideas about adaptive equipment—frames, carriers, poles, levers, clothing, computers, motors—that would give a disabled parent the tools to
clean, feed, play with, and comfort a child. A frame could keep a
baby within reach for diapering. A carrier on a lift could let a
wheelchair user raise a toddler from the floor. A front pack would
allow a mother without full use of her arms to cuddle a sick child.
Farther down the road were potential fruits of the electronics rev-
olution spawned in the Silicon Valley itself—voice-activated computers, robots, laser-guided typewriters.

Kirshbaum dreamed of building a sophisticated nest—she
called it a baby-care center—adapted to the level of a parent sitting
in a wheelchair. It would allow a baby to sleep, play, be fed, and
changed in the same place. For that she needed much more grant
money than Through the Looking Glass had ever seen. In the
meantime, she tried to see what she could do for Tiffany Callo.

Kirshbaum noticed from her first observation of Tiffany with
David that the one-year-old was reluctant to approach his mother.

The psychologist suspected that the problem was the wheelchair. Tiffany remembered her own fears about the control lever. She had warned David, as firmly and gently as she could, not to touch the short vertical rod with the plastic knob that ran the motor.

Kirshbaum thought it was more than that. The metal frame created some sort of emotional barrier around Tiffany that separated her from the child. Kirshbaum looked for ways to break Tiffany out of it.

She noticed that David liked balls. She had seen him tossing them wildly in several directions, a way of connecting himself with other adults. It might work with his mother.

Kirshbaum fashioned a long cardboard box that allowed David to roll a ball to Tiffany as she sat in the chair, and let her roll it back to him. But David remained aloof.

Tiffany tried her own experiments. She tossed the ball from the chair or waved it in David's direction. This pleased the psychologist. Disabled people were instinctual tinkerers and inventors, often finding clever shortcuts to simpler and easier lives. But Kirshbaum noticed that when they became parents, they often failed to realize that the same ingenuity would help them adjust to the shortened perspective of a child.

Tiffany's enthusiasm was such that she made no objection when Kirshbaum decided to put both mother and son on the floor. Kirshbaum helped Tiffany slide down onto the stained, thin brown carpet. She gave Tiffany a ball to entice the child. Kirshbaum took Tiffany's seat in the power chair and watched.

David seemed uncertain. He was suddenly seeing this woman from a very different angle. She looked awkward with her legs splayed out and her left hand waving the ball. But he approached her all the same, grabbed the red rubber sphere, bounced it, and tossed it back toward her.

The hour was nearly up. Silvani had returned to fetch David. As usual, the boy began to fuss when he saw the social worker. Most infant specialists, including Kirshbaum, interpreted this to mean that the child missed Silvani and was discharging pent-up feelings of loss over her hour-long absence. It was a bad sign for Tiffany and would be noted as such in other evaluations.

After Silvani held David for a few minutes, the tall woman's angular frame bending around the small, weeping boy, he calmed down. Kirshbaum tried one last experiment. She asked Silvani to sit with the child in the power chair. She did, and David again began to cry.

So perhaps it *was* the chair, Kirshbaum thought. She asked Silvani to remain in the chair with David and move it around the room to see if that would break down his sensitivity. Kirshbaum then took the child and sat down in the chair herself. Tiffany remained on the floor, saying little and calculating the implications of David's tears whenever the chair was near.

At the next session, Kirshbaum began by having Silvani hold David and sit in the power chair again. The boy had the worried look that always came when the social worker was about to leave him. When forced to sit with her in the chair, he wept. Kirshbaum had Silvani move the chair around, then took the child herself and repeated the exercise.

She moved over to a wooden chair in the kitchen and sat down there with David. He quickly regained his composure. He surveyed the room and sniffed the air. She carried him back to the power chair and sat down. He fidgeted and cried.

Tiffany was already on the floor. Kirshbaum hoped that the chair experiments would change the rhythm of the earlier ballplaying efforts. She placed the child next to his mother. He quickly grabbed the ball and rolled it to Tiffany.

His mood changed so swiftly that Kirshbaum was sure he had been put off by the chair. David had preferred Kirshbaum's company to Tiffany's in the past, but he now seemed delighted with his mother. Kirshbaum watched with a mix of professional curiosity and personal satisfaction.

Woman and boy had thrown themselves into the game. David rolled the ball toward Tiffany and waited, his round features alive with anticipation. She rolled it back. His tosses would always be in her direction. He waited patiently for her to guide her resistant muscles toward the ball and grab it. He treated the delay as a special part of the game, a way of prolonging the fun.

As usual, Tiffany talked to him, hoping to repeat the rhythm of words he may have dimly remembered from the days when he was a tiny infant in the Ninth Street apartment. She adjusted the vocabulary to his new maturity, always seeking some response. "Here you go, Davie. Tiffy's got the ball. Whoops! There it is, get it!" He squealed and pounced on it, a lithe, two-legged kitten with a round red mouse.

Kirshbaum nodded slightly and smiled. It was the first time there had been such sustained play between mother and son. She wondered how far they could go.

12

Margaret Jakobson left home early that Sunday morning to be on time for the ten o'clock Tiffany Callo press conference. Jakobson had had polio as a child and, like Tiffany, used a wheelchair. She was also a parent, one of several in the large Bay Area community of disabled people who found themselves emotionally involved in the story of a young woman deprived of her babies.

Jakobson was an attorney with Protection & Advocacy Inc. (P&A), a federally mandated civil rights organization for the developmentally disabled, which technically included Tiffany because of her cerebral palsy. Jakobson had helped organize the press conference and was now on her way to pick up Deborah Kaplan, another disabled parent and attorney who had volunteered to help. They had written a piece of legislation they hoped would solve Tiffany's problem and widen the very narrow limits of disabled parental rights in the state's legal code.

As a pregnant undergraduate at Southern Illinois University, Jakobson had enjoyed thrusting out her abdomen to force a reaction from people unaccustomed even to thinking of disabled people as parents. Her daughter was now in her teens, but the world had not come very far in accepting the idea of people like her having children.

Kaplan's two-year-old son, Desmond, was coming with them to the press conference as a lively symbol of the topic at hand. Kaplan and her husband, Ralf Hotchkiss, a well-known engineer specializing in wheelchair design, had been enraged by the Callo case. Life with Desmond had given them very strong feelings about parenthood.

When Hotchkiss broke his back in a 1966 motorcycle accident, he found himself worrying about two things: (1) Could he still enjoy making love, and (2) could he be a father? A visit by a female friend shortly after the accident eased his mind on the first count. A year recuperating at home and playing with his baby sister Sara convinced him he could also raise a child from a wheelchair.

Kaplan broke her neck in a 1971 diving accident. She could walk with difficulty with a cane, but found her wheelchair easier and safer. When she and Hotchkiss tried to start a family, nothing happened. A physical examination indicated that he had a low sperm count, probably from sitting for such long periods in his wheelchair. They decided to try to adopt, but social services agencies were reluctant to consider a disabled couple.

Eventually they found a private attorney who knew a young woman who wanted to give up her baby. The biological mother was young enough to have been exposed to the integration of disabled children into regular schools. She knew that the petite, brown-haired Kaplan and the wiry, bearded Hotchkiss used wheelchairs, but she told them she didn't think that was an important consideration in deciding if they were right for her child.

They were awarded custody of Desmond Kaplan Hotchkiss, a curly-haired, snub-nosed baby boy. He hit their rambling, tool-strewn house in Oakland like a cyclone, and stimulated an urge to help other disabled people fighting for their rights to be parents.

Kaplan had served as chair of the State Council on Developmental Disabilities during the administration of Gov. Edmund G. (Jerry) Brown Jr. and worked as a staff attorney with the Disability Rights Education and Legal Defense Fund. She knew many people in state politics, and knew what influenced them when it

came to helping the disabled. Hotchkiss, like Kaplan a former associate of consumer advocate Ralph Nader, was known throughout the third world for designing the "Torbellino" (Whirlwind)
wheelchair, which could be built cheaply from steel tubing, can-
vas, and bicycle tires.

Kaplan and Hotchkiss read about Tiffany's fight for her children when the news broke in October 1987. Their difficulty in
winning approval as adoptive parents had shown them how ignorant social services agencies were about social and technological
advances in the disabled world. They and their disabled parent
friends had enough money to hire help and raise their children
without government support, but they thought it wrong that
low-income disabled people like Tiffany Callo were being told
that they ought to forget parenthood.

As Tiffany's story filled the evening news, Kaplan, Jakobson,
and Lonnie Nolta, the chief lobbyist for the United Cerebral Palsy
Association of California, began a series of conversations with Juli
Winesuff, consultant to the California state senate's subcommittee
on the rights of the disabled. The subcommittee chair was Milton
Marks, a popular and determinedly liberal San Francisco legislator
who had recently switched from the Republican to the Democratic Party. He reacted quickly to Tiffany's plight. Dan Mc-
Corquodale, a Democratic senator from San Jose who chaired the
senate subcommittee on mental health, developmental disabilities,
and genetic diseases, also said he was interested in responding to
the case.

Several ideas about helping low-income parents had been bubbling up through disability rights conventions and university social work conferences. The startling increase in foster care and the
severe strain on county and state budgets had led many experts to
wonder whether local governments could do more to help families
keep their children and save the cost of out-of-home placement.
Santa Clara's failure to find an alternative to foster care in Tiffany's
case was only a part of the issue, but it was the one that had caught
public attention.

Marks and McCorquodale knew the importance of moving
fast when the media discovered an issue on their list. They called
a press conference for January 24, a Sunday when news was slow

and maximum press attention likely. They asked Tiffany, Kaplan, Bedford, Jakobson, and several other interested parties to attend.

Jakobson was driving to San Jose in her Dodge Tradesman van with an old-fashioned lift in back. The weathered, gold-colored van had no seats behind the driver and front passenger; after the lift brought her and her passenger through the rear double doors, they could roll to the front and transfer into the swiveling front seats.

Kaplan wheeled onto the lift easily, but a corner of Desmond's car seat caught between the door and the lift and the lift cable snapped.

Kaplan managed to pull herself, her chair, and her son out of the van and went in search of her own car to make the trip south. Jakobson had learned years before to take such moments in stride. She sat and waited for her husband to come and rescue her.

The press conference was at 10 A.M. in the auditorium of the Alfred E. Alquist State Building, two blocks west of the San Jose State University campus. Tiffany grumbled at Bedford's insistence that she meet him at his office at 9 A.M. It meant she had to rise at 6:30 A.M. To get even, she made him walk with her as she negotiated the several blocks of cracked sidewalks and uneven curb cuts between his office and the state building.

She wore a vest over white blouse and jeans. Despite the recent pregnancy, she looked thin again, although that did not lift her spirits as much as she thought it would.

She introduced herself to Kaplan and watched with envy as Desmond tottered about the microphones and cameras, looking for some of the tools he enjoyed in his father's workshop. The child reminded her of David, curly-headed and handsome and curious.

The two senators greeted her warmly and then, the television cameras ready, read their prepared statements. Tiffany sat at the left side of the front table, watching the senators with her head propped up on her hands. She marveled at the ability of elected politicians to move so fast while the tenured bureaucrats she saw every day crawled at a pace much closer to her own.

Marks, stout and balding, thanked the more than two dozen reporters and camera operators who had shown up. It was a spectacular turnout, even for a Sunday. "As you know," he said, "Tiffany Callo recently had a baby. Unfortunately, what should be one of the happiest moments of her life has become something altogether different."

He briefly sketched the background, erroneously referring to cerebral palsy as a debilitating "disease," instead of a condition, but catching no objections from weekend reporters who, with few exceptions, knew even less about the intricacies of Tiffany's condition than he did.

What was particularly appalling about the county removal of Tiffany's babies, the senator said, was that it was completely legal. "California statutes place mothers suffering physical disabilities in the same category as prostitutes and drug abusers when determining their fitness to be parents," he said.

He described two bills—soon to be merged into a single Senate Bill 2762—that he had submitted in Sacramento. It would bar a county from taking a child from a parent solely on the basis of the parent's disability, an expansion of a state supreme court ruling that put disabled parents on an equal footing with nondisabled parents in divorce custody cases. The bill would also authorize payment for attendants to help disabled parents with nondisabled children if that cost was less than it would be to place the child in a foster home or an institution.

Marks reminded his audience that the United Cerebral Palsy Association was having its national telethon that day. "It seems a fitting time to remind ourselves that disability does not mean inability," he said. "Tiffany will need some help in rearing her children. But do we deny her the joys of parenting simply because she has a greater physical burden to bear than most of us? I can't conceive of a just society condoning such a practice."

McCorquodale, a husky giant with graying blond hair, read his statement: "As a nation we have made strides in rethinking our attitude toward the physically disabled. We have removed some of the barriers that have kept the disabled from joining the mainstream of our society. But a situation such as Tiffany's is a grim reminder that we have a long way to go.

"I know the county officials are not insensitive and hard-hearted, and they undoubtedly believe that what they are doing is the best for all concerned. But equating a physical disability with criminal behavior and denying motherhood to a woman solely on the basis of her disability is a staggering exercise in Big Brotherism."

Bedford was next. Despite his success with the press, he remained frustrated with the hit-and-miss quality of the stories. Reporters rarely wanted more than a few sentences; their questions did not always focus on what he considered to be the main points.

For this meeting he had labored to produce a five-page statement that distilled everything he had learned since he met Tiffany nine months before. It explained, to himself and anyone who cared to listen, his spiritual and legal transformation from doubt that Tiffany could ever be a parent to belief that she would be one of the best.

"The essence of being a parent does not lie in the physical tasks that the parent performs for the child," he said. "The essence of being a good parent lies in the installation of a system of values and ethics that will allow the child to become fully equipped to exist in our society. Parenting should be more concerned with providing intellectual guidance, standards of conduct, and appropriate goals and priorities. In the present case, because Tiffany Callo appears to the Santa Clara County Department of Social Services unable to provide some of the physical support her babies need, she may very well be denied the opportunity to instill a system of values in her children and to educate her children about the meaning of life."

He outlined the case and his client's impossible bind. She could not regain her children until she proved she could love and care for them, but she could not prove she loved and cared for them until she got them back. "She is allowed to visit her children for one hour each week," Bedford said. "The only apparent reason she is not allowed more visitation is that increased visitation would place too heavy a burden on the Department of Social Services and the foster family."

Bedford reviewed the requests he had made to the county, each one a little easier than the last. He hoped there would be one that might serve at least as a basis for compromise:

Could they return the babies and give her training, with help from attendants, until she acquired the necessary skills?

Could they place both her and the children in a foster home, so her daily contact with the boys would not be lost?

Could they place the boys in a foster home where she could visit them more than once a week?

By the time the children were five years old, Bedford said, Tiffany's disability would no longer be an important factor in their upbringing. But if she was cut off from them in the meantime, there was no way she could develop the relationship that would allow her to be an effective mother for the majority of their childhood years.

"This case is really about two issues," Bedford said. First, money, and, second, stereotypes. "Tiffany is physically disabled," he said, "but that does not mean that she is incapable of love."

It was Kaplan's turn. She had put Desmond in his car seat and strapped him in. "I can think of few things more basic than having and raising children," she said, glancing in her son's direction. "For many people, having a family is the most important and meaningful part of their lives. Our children connect us to our past and our future. Ironically, many people assume that people with disabilities cannot bear children or should not, even though disabled parents have been quietly raising their own children for all time."

In her first months with Desmond, even the self-confident Kaplan succumbed at times to the doubts of all disabled parents: Was this hyperactive infant really safe in her hands?

She compared notes with nondisabled parents and discovered that they had the same doubts and mishaps. "Desmond rolled off the bed at five months," Kaplan had told one mother. The woman treated this confession as just another play-group war story. "Oh, yeah," she said, "that happened to me too."

Models of intellectual and logical inquiry themselves, Kaplan and Hotchkiss judged their son between ages one and two to be close to certifiably insane. He took chances that made no sense to them, but they had child-proofed the house, as their nondisabled friends had, and discovered several useful techniques for keeping a small dervish in line.

They dressed Desmond in overalls so that they could grab the straps from their chairs and lift him out of peril. They trained him in simple procedures and chores. By the time he was two, he helped set the table each night. When Hotchkiss drove Desmond to day care, the boy would get out of the car on his own, walk across the lawn, and ring the doorbell.

Quick-witted and unusually active, Desmond discovered ways to evade his parents when he chose. If he wedged himself underneath the workbench of Hotchkiss's hopelessly cluttered workroom off the kitchen, his father could not reach him. Father and son would then negotiate, the former Nader's Raider dealing with a small autocrat not unlike some automobile executives he had known.

Although the couple were quick to discipline Desmond for misbehavior, friends detected what they thought was secret delight in the child's adventuresome instincts. Desmond in turn proved fascinated with and proud of his parents' unusual talents and means of transportation. He wheedled his father into making him his own small wheelchair for occasional play.

Kaplan looked at Desmond again before continuing with her statement: "As a parent, I can't imagine anything more painful than having my child taken from me. As a disabled person, I share in the anger and frustration of all others who have lost or may lose their children, and that is why I am here. We are raising our child with the assistance of other adults, and he has benefited as a result. Desmond has many 'aunts,' 'uncles,' and 'grandparents' who have helped us take care of him. This has not kept him from being an outgoing, happy boy, as you can see.

"It takes more than being able to diaper a kicking baby or pick up a twenty-pound child to be a good parent," she said. "We relied on friends and helpers, adaptive equipment, and our own ingenuity to get through Desmond's first two years in a way that was 'normal' for us. We became parents because of our faith in our values and family integrity. Because of the example of our disabilities, our son is learning to be adaptive and not to give up the first time he tries something new. When he helps me set the table, we both know he's contributing to our household in a truly valuable way. As he grows, I expect he will be more tolerant of differences in others."

Kaplan calculated that it would be a long time before she had another chance to share the pivotal lessons of her life with this many people. She read the final paragraphs as carefully as possible:

"As a society, we have encouraged people with disabilities to live independently by removing architectural barriers, to become self-sufficient by providing job training and rehabilitation programs, and, in general, to accomplish as much as possible. Having our own families and children is a natural result of this public policy. Just as we provide public support to disabled people who need help with housing and medical expenses, for example, we need to provide support for keeping families together.

"As a couple, we have been lucky enough to be able to pay for our helpers and adaptive equipment ourselves; others have not. Our society should be extending a helping hand to disabled parents, not out of pity or condescension, but in order to enable us to be the best parents we can be."

The photograph in the *San Francisco Examiner* the next morning showed Tiffany sitting in her wheelchair, looking fragile and very alone. But Kaplan's words had made her feel more a part of the human race than she had felt in some time. When the reporters turned to her, she said she realized she could not raise her children by herself, "but I do have a lot that I can give them if the county will allow me the chance."

As the camera operators rolled up their cables and the reporters pulled the senators aside for a few last-minute questions, Desmond was released from his car seat and allowed to resume exploring. He examined Tiffany's chair, noting its differences and similarities to those of his parents. He smiled at her and she smiled back.

He and she were both part of something new, she thought, but this child was not hers, and that made her feel empty.

13

After the press conference, Tiffany went back to the apartment to think.

She saw that she had allowed too many people to make decisions for her. Just when other eighteen-year-old women were beginning jobs or college, she had met Tony and become pregnant. Just when other young women were learning to make choices, to say yes and no, she had jumped into a new life with little preparation or thought.

She marked down in her mind where she was, and where she wanted to go.

First of all, she was the mother of David and Jesse. If she never did anything else worthwhile in her life, she wanted to remain faithful to them and to her love for them.

Second, she was a young American woman on welfare who wanted to find a way to support herself and her children. She wanted to carve out, if not a career, at least a niche in the working world, some place where she could use her brains and charm and looks, the qualities people often complimented her on when they were politely ignoring her disability.

She would fight to keep the boys. She would pursue her work

with Kirshbaum. She would divorce Tony. She would get a job to bring in some money and put something on her resumé. She would finish work on her high-school diploma and plan for college.

Tony had left her with a few debts that had to be taken care of if she wanted to avoid eviction. He had failed to pay a hundred dollars on the rent, and the landlord wanted the money. "I'll have it to you Friday," Tiffany said, not really knowing where she would get it.

A few days later Tiffany noticed an advertisement in one of the shoppers' guides that littered the apartment house patio. United Handicapped Workers, the place that once employed Tony, was looking for people in telemarketing. She called. The positions were still open.

She had given birth only a few weeks earlier. She felt tired and drained and was not in the mood for the fruitless pursuit of a job that probably would not pay very much. But she had experience in sales. It was something she enjoyed. When she was about fourteen, her schoolmate Liz Balcom hooked her up with Avon Products. The company sent articulate teenagers out to drop catalogs in mailboxes. Interested customers could call the young salesperson and place an order.

Tiffany loved it. She delivered her sales pitch and exchanged small talk with complete strangers who knew nothing of her or her unusual history. She made a little money, although no more than enough for snacks and movies. She needed more than that now.

She pulled on a maternity dress, all that was left in her closet. She buzzed the chair down Santa Clara Street and then up First Street toward the address they had given on the telephone. She thought it was a good omen that Clay Bedford's office was on the ground floor of the same building, the old Bank of America. Construction workers were still tearing up the sidewalk in front, with nothing but a rickety plywood bridge over the gap, but she had come too far to turn back. She bit her tongue, looked straight ahead, and pushed the control knob forward as she heard the thin wood crackle under the weight.

In the old, marble-covered lobby, she waited for what seemed like twenty minutes until the ancient elevator arrived to take her to the sixth floor. The United Handicapped Workers telemarketing operation was conducted in a large room in which several people sat at tables punching in telephone numbers and cajoling suspicious homeowners annoyed at being called during dinner. A thin man with very long hair, no tie, and no visible disability greeted her.

"I need a job right now because I'm financially hung up," she said. "I'm willing to work for it. I'll do whatever you give me."

The man introduced himself as the manager and reached for a form to fill out. She raised a hand. She wasn't finished. "If my attorney comes up to get me, I need to go down with him immediately because that means something is up with my kids." She wanted the point hard and clear. "My first priority, other than making money and keeping busy so I don't think about it all too much, my first priority is to my kids."

"That's okay," the man said. He conducted a quick orientation. Wall displays pasted on heavy wooden boards showed the main items for sale—long-lasting light bulbs, vitamins, and cleaning products. He showed her a prompt book which said what to say to each client.

"I've got previous sales experience, so I know what I'm doing," she said, still anxious. "I can pick it up real quick."

"Well," he said, "if you need extra help, we have one week of training and then you really start and you're expected to meet your quota."

She nodded. He looked toward the coffee machine and called to a short, slightly stooped young man making himself a cup. "Mr. B?" he said.

"Yeah, Jerry?"

"You got room in the morning for another employee?" the manager asked.

"Yeah, you have somebody new?"

"I want you to meet Tiffany."

Tiffany could tell there was something wrong with his posture. He seemed slightly bent. That quick observation was overwhelmed by a tingling reaction to his touch. They shook hands and exchanged a glance that Tiffany could not calibrate. He seemed shy, yet she could sense promising complexity beneath the surface.

"Hi," he said. "My name is Carmo 'Teddy' Brazil."

She liked unusual names. They were fine conversation pieces. "Excuse me," she said. "Did you say Teddy?"

"I said Teddy."

"Which one do you go by?"

"I go by either one, either Carmo or Teddy."

"Which one do you want me to call you?"

"Whichever one you like," he replied, and gave her a bashful smile that made her slightly dizzy.

"Okay," she said, collecting herself. "Brazil? What is it? Is it Spanish or what?"

"No, I'm Portuguese."

She smiled and went into her small-world act, finding some tenuous part of her own background that put her in the same universe as her listener. "Well, my dad's girlfriend is Portuguese," she said, "and if they were ever to get married, I guess you could say I'm part Portuguese."

He smiled at this. "*Fala Português?*"

She had gone too far. "Oh, no," she said. "I don't think she speaks it."

She felt herself slipping into incoherence. She was not sure why. She felt an urge to tell the man she was married but getting a divorce. She wanted to pull him out the door and ask his likes and dislikes. She wanted to memorize the story of his life.

Instead she sat in her chair as the manager described the work schedule and turned her over to this young assistant manager she chose to call Teddy. She looked at him. His brown eyes had a bit of hazel, she noticed. His brown hair was soft and shiny. He was clean-shaven. He seemed to turn slightly pink when something embarrassed him. There was a wiggle in his walk that she found enchanting.

She had to go home. Kirshbaum would be bringing David and Jesse the next day. She had to make sure the apartment was spotless. She mumbled an apology and promised to begin the morning after next. She rode down the creaky elevator alone and wheeled out onto First Avenue to see a full moon and a sky full of stars.

She had dealt with shy men before, but she could not remember one who had attracted her as strongly as Teddy Brazil. She sometimes overwhelmed strangers with loud talk and effusive gestures. She did not want that to happen in this case. She played it slow and easy.

She spent the weekend working out her feelings by fretting about her clothes. She went through her closet once or twice each hour. All she had were maternity dresses and a few formless slacks and sweaters. She rolled up Tenth Street and down Santa Clara, looking in shop windows. She had no money for clothes. She had a good idea what she was going to do with her first few paychecks, after she settled the unpaid rent.

On her first day at work, she started out early in a white T-shirt and jeans. She did not want to come on too strong, but she would make sure she was the first one there.

She arrived two minutes before Teddy did. He smiled uncertainly and raised an eyebrow. "Well, good morning," he said.

"Hi," she said. "How are you feeling this morning? You look awfully chipper."

"Well, today, you know, is just the beginning of another week, but it doesn't look as if it's going to be as boring as it has been."

"Well," she said, looking around the empty office, "is there anything you normally do first that I can help you with?"

"No," he said.

"If the boss walks in, we don't want to be sitting around like bumps on a log. That's not the way to get a good report with a boss who has a short temper."

He looked surprised. "You pick up things fast about people, don't you."

"I've known a few short-tempered people in my time." She smiled sweetly. "If you cross me the wrong way, I can be one of those people too."

He explained the coffee-making ritual and the record-keeping system. Each worker had a folder with a list of telephone numbers, a ruler, and pen. If there was no answer, or an answering machine, they were to draw a straight line through the number. Leaving messages was forbidden; no one ever called back. But a clever worker, Teddy noted with a conspiratorial smile, could talk as if the recorder was a live customer and still get some credit for making the call.

The rest of the staff began to straggle in. He showed her more of the product lines and how they expected her to sell them. Light bulbs came in packs of four, seven, ten, or twelve. Her quota was four bulbs an hour. If she exceeded her quota in any given hour, she was entitled to grab a slip of paper from the money jar. Each slip announced a small prize, maybe twenty-five cents or even a lottery ticket worth a dollar. If sales lagged, they held a special competition: First one to sell a twelve-pack got two grabs in the money jar.

The company had stretched the definition of handicapped out of necessity. It was difficult to find anyone, disabled or otherwise, willing to suffer the minute-by-minute rejection of telephone sales in return for little more than a hundred dollars a week. Only one other person in the room used a wheelchair, Tiffany noticed. She was told that one woman was anemic. At least two of the employees appeared to have no other handicap but old age.

The work began easily. She followed the prompt book, with a few of her own flourishes, and enjoyed the repartee with customers. The nicer ones were retired people with time on their hands. There were several disagreeable types, but she had been dealing with people like that all her life.

While she worked, Tiffany caught Teddy stealing a few looks in her direction. She asked if he would bring her some coffee.

"How do you like it?" he said.

"You guys use milk around here or nondairy creamer?"

"Nondairy."

"Good, 'cause I'm allergic to milk. I'll take one cream and two sugars." Teddy looked slightly uncomfortable. This was a difficult request to interpret. The usual office sugar and sweetener packs were absent, replaced by an old plastic catsup squeeze bottle full of sugar for the convenience of disabled people who might spend a half hour opening a two-inch square paper container.

"We have this squeeze bottle," he explained. "What do you call two sugars?"

She bent her head and peered at him through her eyelashes. "Well, what would *you* call sugar, Sugar?"

He blushed, then turned to fetch the coffee.

The sometimes shy and correct Tiffany dueled with Tiffany the social butterfly. She wanted to encourage this man without terrifying him.

She noticed the telephone on his desk, a multi-button job, and scolded herself for terminal stupidity. She would offer a little information to keep things moving. She wrote something on a small piece of paper and handed it to him.

"What's this?"

"Silly," she said. "What is seven numbers?"

"Oh," he said, surprised. "Are you sure it's okay?"

"Of course it's okay," she said. "I gave it to you, didn't I? Maybe we can have coffee sometime."

He called that night while she was in her bedroom examining her closet. The telephone was in the kitchen. She gunned the chair out the door and found she had approached from the wrong angle. She could not turn it toward the living room in the narrow hall. She swore loudly and backed up into her room again, fidgeting with the directional control as if it were a stubborn branch she was trying to tear from a tree.

Convinced that it was Teddy, she shouted up the hall, "Patty, go pick up the phone and tell him I'll be right there! Tell him it's going to take me a few minutes." She was so angry and distracted that she hit the side of the doorway, but jerked the lever to the right at the proper angle this time and safely maneuvered her way down the hall.

She grabbed the receiver, counted to two, and said hello.

"Oh, hi, it's Teddy."

She had already mentally composed her first few lines, designed to cover his tracks if he was dialing her from work. United Handicapped Workers had strict rules against personal calls, and those recording machines were always on. "Oh," she said. "Is there a problem? Did somebody not show up or what? I can be at work in ten minutes. That's all it takes me."

He laughed at this outburst. "No, no," he said. "Hey, I'm at home."

This, she thought to herself, was a serious call. She dropped her voice to what she hoped was a soft, purry register. "So, what are you doing?"

"Well, I'm kind of bored. I mean, my mom's here to keep me company, but I think I want to do something."

Telephone conversation was her favorite sport. She turned up her vocal thermostat a few notches. "Oh, hmmm, oh, you called 'cause you wanted some company, huh?"

"Yeah, I guess you could say that. I wonder if . . ."

He faltered. Tiffany silently urged him on, a 30–1 horse three lengths from the finish line. Spit it out, she thought. "If what?" she said sweetly.

"If, uh, if you'd like to, um, well, um, I was wondering if you'd like to go out with me."

"Go out with you? Sure! Where? When?"

"I was thinking about maybe tomorrow, um, after the morning shift, maybe for lunch."

"A date for lunch, huh?" She already had her calendar by her side in anticipation of such a request, but she tried to modulate her eagerness. "Let me see, 'cause I do have some appointments this week. . . . Well, I do have an appointment tomorrow, but there's Wednesday, Thursday, Friday, or Saturday." She decided not to tell him her children were coming to see her Tuesday. She did not accept the folk wisdom of 1980s singles that men did not want to date women with children, but she saw no need to press her luck.

"Why don't we make it Wednesday?" he said. It was a date.

Carmo "Teddy" Brazil was born on São Jorge (St. George) Island in the Azores on August 3, 1964. His mother, Dolores Brazil, was thirty-eight years old, long past the age when anyone thought she would marry. She had an affair with a man from a nearby village and Teddy was the result.

She lived with older brothers who accepted the baby as part of the large household. Teddy was a happy if somewhat quiet child, but the family noticed he had trouble keeping his head up. By the time he could stand on both feet, it was clear there was a problem. He seemed bent over. There was something wrong with his back.

In 1971, when he was seven, his mother's brother Carmo, after whom he had been named, invited the two of them to come live with him in San Jose, California. Uncle Carmo said that American doctors might be able to help little Carmo walk straight again. Teddy and his mother moved into the large wood-frame house where Uncle Carmo, Aunt Natalie, and a pack of cousins, Fatima, Gilda, Marie, Jenny, Anthony, Isabel, and Joe, lived.

His mother found a job in a cannery, the first time she had ever worked regularly outside her home. But she began to experience asthma attacks and was told by her doctor to quit.

The nurse at his elementary school in East San Jose took no more than a minute to diagnose Teddy's medical condition. He had scoliosis, a congenital curvature of the spine which might be eased somewhat but never wholly cured. The first two doctors he saw tried a series of braces that accomplished nothing.

His cousin Fatima, a student at San Jose State who dreamed of becoming a lawyer, appointed herself counsel to her young cousin. She called a widening circle of nurses, doctors, and public-health officials and located Fred B. Orcutt, an orthopedic surgeon who had extensive experience with scoliosis. Orcutt examined the boy and gave his opinion. Teddy had learned English quickly and as usual served as his mother's interpreter.

"Okay," the doctor said, "tell her you've got a choice. There is an operation we can do. We go in and straighten out the spine a bit and then we put this metal rod alongside the spine to keep it straight." Teddy struggled both to translate this and absorb the impact of the news. He had grown to hate hospitals.

"Or," Orcutt continued, "we can do nothing, let the condition progress, and when you get older you'll be slanted over even more."

Teddy Brazil, age eleven, began to cry. He did not want to offend his mother or the doctor, but he felt cut adrift and did not see any good way back to shore. His mother, as she often had in the past, found the right words. "You tell him we'll do it," she said. "Carmo, you tell him let's do it."

The next day he checked into San Jose Hospital for three days of tests. Then the surgeon and the anesthetist arrived and his heart raced. "I know you're scared," Orcutt said. "It's going to be okay."

When he woke up in his hospital room, everyone was there, his mother, his uncle, his aunt, all rejoicing. He felt sick and cold and hungry. For five days in the frigid intensive-care unit he was fed intravenously while he glumly studied the cage Orcutt had welded around him. One metal rod encircled his head and another went around his hips. Vertical rods held them in place with screwed attachments that pushed painfully against his hips and the sides of his head.

They told him not to move his head. If he tried, he felt sharp pain. He had to sleep and shower in the contraption. When he returned to school, he was placed in a class for disabled students because he was not strong enough yet for a regular program. But three months later, when they dismantled the cage and removed the screws, he found himself standing somewhat straighter. The postoperative pain dissipated, except for what he insisted was the cold touch of the metal rod rammed up against his backbone.

Teddy returned happily to the life of a disorganized, undirected California teenager. He read comic books and watched soap operas and did not pay much attention to school. He began to apply himself to his studies only when his eleventh-grade counselor told him he would need two years of solid work, including a summer of classes, if he wished to graduate with his friends.

He knew what his mother would say if he did not get a diploma. He spent his last two high-school years doing his reading and counting the days until he would be free of academic routine. When he graduated, his aunt found him a job—at first only as a volunteer—at the Portuguese Center on Twenty-third Street. He answered the telephone, tended the files, and kept track of accounts. After a year they put him on the payroll, but two years later a nun accused him of taking money from a drawer and he quit in disgust.

The state employment office sent him to United Handicapped Workers, where he began, with some trepidation, long hours on the telephone talking to strangers. After a week he had sold nothing and asked the supervisor if he was going to be fired. "Just take it easy," the man said. "We'll give you a chance."

Toward the end of the second week he sold a twelve-pack of light bulbs and took his reward from the grab jar: a dollar bill. It loosened something within him. He began to look forward to the fifteen-minute bus ride to work. He knew he was never going to be assertive, but the anonymity of the telephone loosened his inhibitions. He found he enjoyed easing other people's apprehensions by telling them what a fine product he was offering at such a good price.

After a while he was selling as many as five hundred items a week. His boss asked him to become an assistant manager and help train and supervise new recruits. It meant more money, but the idea bothered him in a way he could not define. He turned it down. He thought it would put him too far above himself and his small world of coworkers and family. He was earning only a hundred dollars a week, but who cared? He paid no rent and his expenses were minimal.

Another assistant manager's job opened and they asked him again. This time the manager insisted and Teddy finally agreed. He continued to look forward to work, even if there was little joy in the rest of his life.

His leisure time was haunted by the memory of the afternoon he went to a party at school and returned to find his mother lying on the couch in the arms of his aunt. She had had a dizzy spell and fallen. He had not been there to help. He resolved that he would never let that happen again. Parties were out. Dates were out. He would come home each evening, and if he could not find enough entertainment on television or in a comic book, that was too bad.

He found some of the pressures of a week at work dissipated if he stopped at Charlie's Liquors on Fourth and Santa Clara and bought a six-pack of Budweiser each Friday evening on his way home. He would drink three or four cans Friday night and the rest on Saturday. He began to buy beer other nights also. His mother said nothing. She rarely criticized anything he did. His aunt told him she thought he should drink less and go out more, but he did not see any way to do that.

Then he met Tiffany.

When he later became accustomed to her almost mystical belief in her instincts, he saw how natural it was for her to have sensed something about him with one look. The first time he saw her, he had also felt a jolt. He had never seen irises of such frosty blue.

He had trouble finding his balance. Calling her at home, even after she had made a gift of her number, required more courage than he had had to summon in a long time.

During their rambling conversation, he found himself stumbling and losing track of his train of thought. He held tight to his one anchor, his plan to invite her to lunch at Ravioli's, an Italian deli run by a Spanish-speaking couple across from their office. "That sounds fine," she said.

He did not watch television news often and had no idea he was making a date with a media celebrity. She had no idea of his history, but sensed from the beginning that he had a genuine quality—cynics might call it naïveté—that meant she would receive honest answers to all her questions.

On Wednesday morning she surprised him by appearing in a new floral cotton dress and full makeup, her lips glowing and her eyes emphasized. At noon they headed for the elevator and made the short trip across the street to Ravioli's, taking a small table by the window.

While they studied the menus, he placed his hand on the top of the table, a little invitation that Tiffany promptly accepted. She held his hand and listened to him talk about the people at work, his favorite television cartoons, what he liked about the food at the deli.

He was as honest as she had expected, and also very funny. She found his impressions of Warner Brothers characters delightful. With each conversational success, his spirits rose. They both ordered chicken enchiladas, one of the many Mexican specialties on the ostensibly Italian menu. She waited for an opportunity to tell him about her boys.

She broached the subject gently, saying she thought there were a few things about her that he ought to know, things that had nothing to do with her feelings for him but would explain some special responsibilities that she had.

"I don't want you to freak out," she said. "If you think you don't want any part of it or think you can't handle it, we can get up right now and walk out of here and go our separate ways and be colleagues and good friends at work, whatever, however we're going to do it, but I need to explain something to you."

She had slipped into her wordiest syntax again, but that was what happened when she felt something. He would have to get used to it.

"I have two children," she said. "The courts stepped in and took the children and I'm busting my ass over backwards. Now that your boss hired me, I do want to be a responsible mother and I will provide what I can for the children."

Teddy was hoping she would slow down. He was having difficulty absorbing everything at once.

"I'm getting a divorce," she said. "I want you to know that there is nobody else in my life right now, except my kids. I see them once a week. They're doing this evaluation of me, and then I'll probably have to go to court to try to win them back. Maybe you saw some of this on television. It was on most of the stations a couple of months ago, you know, disabled mother fights for kids. My Jesse was born just last month, and I was on the news then too."

Teddy searched his memory and found a few vague shreds of recollection, something he might have seen looking through a newspaper in the library or on a news broadcast as he was switching channels.

She watched for his reaction. She wondered if this was too abrupt a way to gauge the character of a man she might love.

Teddy, unaware that he was being so carefully scrutinized, found himself becoming angry. How could any government treat her that way? She was one of the warmest, funniest, most engaging people he had ever met. Who would dare deprive her own children of the gift of knowing her?

He had to do something, he thought. "You know, Tiffany, I'm your employer, so to speak," he said, squeezing her hand. "Maybe I could say something to them. Maybe I could testify for you, tell them what you're capable of and not capable of. I could help you get the kids back." He did not care that she had been married. He did care that she had children. It made her that much more desirable, someone who had already sunk some roots and could be counted on to commit herself to him, as she had to her boys, if that was the way this was going to go.

Teddy began to walk her home from work, down Santa Clara to Tenth and then south, over bumps and bad curb cuts and past the usual assemblage of street people. He did not mind the circus-like atmosphere of Tiffany's apartment. He knew the bad dreams she had when she felt alone. One night Teddy would find six dental hygiene students, friends of another of Tiffany's friends, going over their homework on incisors. Another night he heard heavy-metal rock blaring from the radio as Patty prepared spaghetti for guests.

Tiffany coaxed him into the Friday and Saturday night club scene along Santa Clara. About 7 P.M. they would arrive at the Cactus Club, or the San Salvador, and order salami sandwiches on French bread. They would let the meal settle and sip Dr Pepper until the band plugged itself in about 9 P.M.

Tiffany adored the crowd noises, the friends dropping by to chat, the rhythm of the music pounding in the dark nightclub through every nerve ending, overwhelming, she thought, even her own jumbled nervous system. Teddy would push her wheelchair onto the dance floor and they would gyrate with the rest of the throng, Teddy sliding and hopping on his two feet while Tiffany bounced in her chair and waved her arms.

She monitored her own reactions to their growing closeness as carefully as she could. She knew she tended to gush and embrace too grandly, and this was a man she felt she could not afford to lose. His love for her was genuine. It was impossible for someone so kind to fake sentiment. For the first time in a long time, she was with someone who seemed more concerned for her feelings than his own.

She had begun divorce proceedings against Tony. He had been charming, and often fun, but there had never been any doubt whose interests came first in that relationship. Teddy, despite his Latin upbringing, asked after her regularly and did not make plans without consulting her first. Teddy loved children and clearly wanted a family of his own, but she had to see how he would react to her own small family circle.

Teddy felt playful that morning. He was supervising the morning shift at United Handicapped, and Tiffany had invited him home after work. She was at her desk, apparently looking over some paperwork. His boss had a trick of tickling employees slightly under the armpits if it seemed like they were nodding off. Teddy decided to try it on Tiffany.

He reached under her arm and lightly touched her skin. She squealed and jumped and then swore. This was not the reaction he had expected. She had been holding a cup of coffee that had splattered all over her white blouse.

His voice shook with apologies and he rushed off for some paper towels, but she did not seem very upset. She smiled enigmatically and said she would use the excuse to leave a little early. "Don't forget," she said. "I'll expect you about one o'clock."

He was there on the dot, still wondering at her reaction. He walked in without knocking, as she had instructed, and found the woman he loved sprawled on the floor with a two-month-old baby with bright blue eyes. A one-year-old boy with similar features and eyes a darker shade of blue played in a corner of the room.

"Teddy, sweetie! Come in!" Tiffany shouted. She glanced at a woman with long, thick brown hair who sat in Tiffany's wheelchair with a large notebook on her lap. Kirshbaum was not happy at this intrusion.

"Excuse me," she said. "I'm Megan Kirshbaum and you're . . . ?"

"Oh," Tiffany said. "This is Teddy, my fiancé." She was quick to give him semiofficial status, knowing the way DSS worked. Before Kirshbaum could raise another objection, Tiffany motioned Teddy over and invited him to pick up the baby.

Jesse squinted and squirmed and tried to focus on the new face. Teddy had done this before with young cousins and took a firm but gentle grip on the child. He studied the blue eyes and the upturned nose. This was a small china replica of Tiffany. The boy seemed to sense his fascination and affection and offered a small grin.

"It looks like Jesse likes his new daddy," Tiffany said, daring to barge into the future.

Kirshbaum watched with professional interest as Teddy cooed and giggled and bounced the baby in his arms. Jesse laughed at the sudden motion, like a carnival ride, and seemed to demand more.

The kid has just had a bottle, Tiffany thought. I wonder if I should warn him? But memories of her coffee-stained blouse intruded, and she simply watched to see what would happen.

Teddy was accustomed to Tiffany rushing things, but he did not mind being called Daddy. This was as close as he had ever come to having his own baby, and he liked it. He smiled at David, engrossed in a toy in the corner, and beamed at Tiffany. He didn't help bring these kids into the world, he thought, but, God, it felt like they were his own.

Jesse chose that warm moment to give Teddy his fatherly baptism. One happy bounce brought a portion of the baby's lunch darting back up his throat and onto Teddy's shirt.

Tiffany shrieked with glee. It served him right, of course, but it also brought him into the circle. Kirshbaum could not begrudge a man a few minutes with the boys after he had sacrificed himself this way. The psychologist made a note and then looked for something to help Teddy clean up. Jesse's victim felt mildly embarrassed, and then, to his surprise, pleased. Tiffany seemed more relaxed than ever, and this beautiful baby was acting as if he were one of the family.

When Jesse was taken after his birth, Tiffany spent two days wondering if she was ever meant to have a family. If God had wanted her to be a mother, why would he put so many obstacles in her path?

But after two months with Teddy, she had a vision of what family life could be like—not the resentments and loneliness with her father, or the coldness and uncertainty with Tony, but a sharing of food and music and insights and ambitions. Teddy and she had enrolled in correspondence courses that would allow them to enter college. They had plans for a business.

As the sessions with Kirshbaum continued and Tiffany considered special trays and carriers and other baby aids, the possibilities of parenthood found their way into her dreams again. She was convinced that she was right to have had the boys. All she needed was help in meeting some rudimentary needs and breaking through the DSS prejudice against any possibility of parenting by her.

She had seen enough of good families and bad families to know what worked and what did not. Silvani was not married. How could she hand out advice about what was right for a family?

In some ways, Tiffany thought, her disability gave her an advantage over a nondisabled parent. A parent with two legs who became angry or frustrated or confused could disappear, and many did. Cars were easy to drive. New apartments and jobs were easy to find. No relationship had to be permanent.

She could not move so quickly. She had to give a relationship time; it was the most precious gift she had. Passing an evening with Teddy baking grossly caloric, inch-thick chocolate-chip brownies, or spending an afternoon on the apartment floor with Jesse, she saw how connections were made and how expensive it would be to break them out of pique or let them wither through willfulness and pride.

She felt older, more mature and more certain of what she had to do. She would not give the boys up without a good fight. David and Jesse would know that she wanted them. She found it hard to accept Bedford's vision of a legal marathon that dragged her eight years hence to Washington for a great moment in constitutional law. That seemed like a fantasy, unrelated to her own life.

But she had no difficulty imagining a home with Teddy and David and Jesse. The little house would have a kitchen with all the knobs down low where she could reach them. The shower would have a seat inside. She and Teddy would share a water bed, warm and cozy, while the boys had their own room down the hall. There would be a little park down the block where they would have picnics and birthday parties and barbecues.

And when she was very old, her sons would roll her down the street to gush over her grandchildren, and she would remind them to chew their food slowly and take their time.

14

The hearing that began June 28, 1988, in Courtroom No. 1 of Santa Clara County Juvenile Court, was open only to the parties involved and their attorneys. Under the law, testimony and argument had to be confined to one narrow issue: Should Tiffany Callo be reunited with her two sons?

But most of the people interested in the case, both inside and outside the courtroom, were engaged in a much larger, and politically explosive, debate. Was it fair and legal for a society to tell some of its members that they could not look forward to raising children because they were disabled?

Tiffany saw that Tony was there, presumably living once more on his wits and his street contacts. Poor Tony. Sometimes she felt sorry for him. He had seen the political and philosophical importance of their babies before she had. He was special, sitting there in his chair, quick and bright and proud.

But he had no chance of succeeding in his own legal challenge to DSS. The minute the judge saw the police report from the night he hit her, the minute anyone probed the sources of his extra income, his prospects for winning custody would fade as quickly as the afternoon sun dipping below the Coast Range.

Teddy was there too, a rock to cling to. If only they would let him in the courtroom so she would not have to endure all this legal mumbo jumbo alone.

Clay Bedford rose and addressed the judge. "Out in the waiting room, your honor, is Ms. Callo's fiancé, and while he does not live with Ms. Callo at this point in time, they do intend to get married as soon as the divorce from Mr. Rios is over. And both Ms. Callo and Mr. Brazil would ask that he be allowed to be present as a support person for Ms. Callo, and also as a person who, if Ms. Callo gets custody of the children, will become a person that will be a care provider."

Judge Leonard P. Edwards surveyed the other lawyers. Tony's attorney had no objection. The judge turned to Michael Clark, the deputy county counsel.

"We would object, Your Honor, for the following reasons," Clark said. "First of all, Mr. Brazil is not a relative as contemplated by the Welfare and Institutions Code. In addition, he may be a witness. I do not intend to call him at this time, but he is a percipient witness to some of the allegations, I believe, which are in issue in this case.. And given those circumstances and given the fact that I believe Ms. Callo is still legally married to Mr. Rios, there is just no appropriate basis for Mr. Brazil being present."

Tiffany seethed in silence. She had been shoved into rhetorical corners by lawyers and judges since she was eleven and had never learned to like it.

Bedford made one last try. "While in general I am in support of a motion to exclude witnesses," he said, "I think that it makes sense to exclude Mr. Brazil from the motion on the basis that this really is going to be a fight between experts, between the various Ph.D.'s coming in.

"We are not arguing at this point in time that either child should be placed immediately with Ms. Callo," he said. "We are arguing that she should be provided some substantial reunification services, and then over the next three to six months she will be in a position to take custody. I think at that point in time Mr. Brazil becomes a very important player in these proceedings."

He looked at Edwards to see if the argument was making any

impression. He continued: "I think at this point in time the dis-advantage to any party of having Mr. Brazil present is more than counterbalanced by just simple humanity of allowing him to stay to support Ms. Callo."

Edwards thought for a moment, then denied the motion. Tif-fany would have to do this one on her own. So much for simple humanity, she thought.

Before the bond between disabled mother and child could be ex-amined closely, Bedford had to dismantle the legal barricade the county had begun to erect shortly after it took David.

If Tiffany had been denied her right to raise David and Jesse because of her disability, then she might have a constitutional ar-gument. To counter that, the government contended that her dis-ability had little if anything to do with the removal of her children. Tiffany could not raise her sons because she was psychologically and emotionally unfit to do so, and thus posed a threat of pos-sible neglect or abuse, DSS said. The argument was: Even if she were suddenly cured of her cerebral palsy and could do cart-wheels in the courthouse lobby, it would still be unsafe to return the boys to her.

To make that point, deputy county counsel Michael Clark put his most personable psychologist expert, Amal Barkouki, on the stand and dared Bedford to find a flaw in her character, her anal-ysis, or her expertise.

There was nothing Tiffany's attorney could do about Barkou-ki's character. Her reputation for honesty and good humor was unassailable. Edwards respected her. But Bedford had discovered over the past fourteen months how misinformed nearly everyone was on the issue of disabled parenting. His own ignorance, he realized, had been appalling, and he had found several reports by first-rate social workers and psychologists whose skepticism about Tiffany's raising her babies had no more foundation than his own.

He had to start slowly with Barkouki. If he nibbled on the edges of her psychological evaluation of Tiffany long enough, Edwards would begin to see the holes. The psychologist's own honesty and integrity could be used to undermine the county's case.

Could you tell me what the most common cause of CP is?" Bedford asked.

"I believe that it may either be something," Barkouki said, with an uncertain look, "it is certainly something intrauterine and maybe something at birth. . . . It is considered a birth defect."

"Can it occur after birth? A year or two of life?"

"I suppose it is possible. I don't know that much about it."

Bedford thought Barkouki had tried to make an honest analysis, but she had had to lean on data from other county officials who had made it clear that they wanted the children removed. Silvani's unhappiness at Kirshbaum's willingness to defend Tiffany had exposed the DSS agenda, as had the ragged corners and sloppy paste jobs in other reports. The county had ignored many errors in its haste to wall Tiffany off from her sons with piles of Freudian terminology.

"Is it considered an acceptable practice in general," Bedford asked, "to take the test results of another professional in Rorschach and to reinterpret them yourself?"

Barkouki looked uncomfortable and glanced at Clark. "Let me tell you the dilemma. . . ."

"Well, first answer the question, please," Bedford said.

Edwards tried to help. "Start with a yes or no, or maybe, then you can explain your answer."

Barkouki collected herself. "Under the circumstances, it is an understandable decision," she said.

"Well," Bedford said, speaking slowly and carefully, trying to enlarge the trap, "are there practitioners that would view that as being an unacceptable practice to reinterpret somebody else's raw data on a Rorschach?"

"Not under the conditions."

"So every person who is an expert in Rorschach would say that using Dr. Johnston's data would be acceptable?"

"I didn't say that."

Satisfied, Bedford changed the subject. "Now, the Rorschach test is obviously a visual test, is that correct?"

"Yes."

"Now, does CP involve any visual disability?"

"It is possible."

"Does Tiffany's form of CP involve any visual disability?"

"I think she says that when she gets tired it affects her eyesight."

"Did you ask her whether her eyesight is good or bad, or whether there is any other visual disability?"

"Just what she volunteered."

"But you didn't physically ask the question?"

"No, I didn't. . . ."

"You never asked Tiffany whether she had any visual difficulties which might interfere with her ability to do a Rorschach? Is that correct?"

Barkouki began to look annoyed. The Rorschach was a test of psychological perception, not visual acuity. "What she said about her visual difficulties didn't sound like it would interfere with a Rorschach. I didn't ask her if it would interfere with the Rorschach. I didn't give her the Rorschach."

"If Tiffany has a visual disability that would interfere with her ability to do the Rorschach, would the fact that somebody else had given her the Rorschach and you just relied on that raw data, would that disability still interfere with the Rorschach results?"

"If it interfered, I am not exactly clear how it would interfere," Barkouki said, visibly unsettled. Tiffany felt her spirits lifting for the first time since the psychologist had taken the stand. "How would it interfere?" Barkouki said, the pitch of her voice rising. "If someone was color blind, for example, I think it would definitely affect the Rorschach."

"What you are saying, you are not aware of any . . ."

"That would actually interfere with a valid protocol."

"And if there is some problem that would interfere with the valid protocol, it would make the test results invalid, correct?"

"That is correct."

Bedford turned to the other tests. "Now, let's talk in particular about people with cerebral palsy. Prior to your administration of the MMPI to Tiffany, did you do a research search?"

"No."

"To find any articles on whether the MMPI is applicable to people with CP?"

"No," she said.

"Have you since that time done such a research search?"

"I have not done a research search. I have talked with my colleague, Dr. Mayclin, who is an expert on testing people with all sorts of disabilities, including cerebral palsy, and uses the MMPI all of the time."

Bedford nodded. He had had his own long talk with Nancy Van Couvering, a Northern California psychologist experienced with disabilities who scoffed at courtroom reliance on such tests. There was no objective scoring system. No one had the time or money to study disabled persons' responses to the MMPI and see if they matched the norms set for general use. A good analyst could look at a test and derive useful conclusions, but who was to say who was a good analyst and who was not in a field where so little work had been done?

"You are not aware of any reason why the MMPI might not be applicable to somebody with CP? Yes or no," Bedford said. His tone had hardened.

Barkouki looked exasperated. Tiffany smiled. She was enjoying this.

"I can't answer it that way," Barkouki said. "There are lots of reasons why it might not be applicable if you don't use your brains and your clinical understanding to adjust for its limitations with someone who has got cerebral palsy."

"In other words," Bedford repeated, underlining Van Couvering's point, "there is a lot of subjective evaluation that goes into an MMPI, is that what you are telling us?"

"There is both objective and subjective. It is a clinical test. It is not a Dow Jones average."

Bedford turned to the diagnosis of Tiffany's paranoid tendencies, buttressed by her metaphoric approach to the questions about being followed and being poisoned. The psychologist began an orderly retreat, explaining that she had discounted the importance of the paranoid score because of what she knew about Tiffany and other women under stress.

"When I do custody evaluations," she said, "you can get somebody with a very high paranoid score." Women in the midst of divorce "answer a lot of questions as though somebody is out to get them," she said. "The system is out to get them. People are out to get them. Their ex-husbands are out to get them, etcetera, etcetera. When I look at them carefully, and I understand the context in which they are answering these questions, I adjust the paranoid level."

Tiffany frowned. She was beginning to like Barkouki. She wondered if that was healthy.

The witness, ignorant of the unspoken blessing, continued. "I say she has some paranoid traits. Otherwise, I would have to call her paranoid when the girl is not paranoid."

"If someone was in fact following her," Bedford asked, "would that mean she is paranoid if she believes someone is following her?"

"No, even paranoids have enemies."

Bedford switched to the issue of stress. At the time of the examinations, he asked, "would you expect her to be low on the stress level or high?"

"High."

"That is because she has been through a divorce?"

"Yeah."

"Or at least started a divorce?"

"You name it," Barkouki said, "she has had a lot of stress."

"The kids taken away from her, change in roommates." Bedford checked off the low points of Tiffany's unhappy year.

"Two or three evaluations," Barkouki said. "She is likely to be under stress a lot. She is stress prone, also."

"Now, the fact that she needs always to be doing things, what is this based on? Your observations of her at the house?"

"Observation at the house, her high mania scale on the MMPI, her description of herself, as I said in my observations."

Tiffany recalled the dreary atmosphere the county evaluators brought with them. It was like living in Russia, someone looking over your shoulder every minute. Activity—was that her mania scale?—was a refuge, a way to keep her mind engaged and her emotions in check until they left. Had they wanted her to sit quietly and contemplate the scratching of their pencils on their forms?

Bedford assumed a skeptical look. "And that trait by itself would be enough to say somebody is not fit to be a parent? Is that correct?

"What?"

"The fact that somebody always needs to be doing something—you are talking hyperactivity, right?"

The psychologist saw this inside pitch and sidestepped. "I didn't say hyperactivity, and I certainly wouldn't consider one thing. People need to be doing something. That doesn't make them bad parents. It may make them good parents, a little obsessive. I don't take it on one trait."

This seemed to Bedford a good time to wrestle with the image of Tiffany as a social mayfly, incapable of sustaining a personal relationship. He thought he knew the root of this, a deep bias against disabled sexuality, but that would be difficult to unearth except in careful stages.

"Okay," he said. "You testified that Tiffany would lack the ability to form stimulating and nurturing relationships with adults. Actually, you testified that she would be able to form them but not sustain them?"

"That is correct."

"Now, how long would you expect the maximum length of time she could sustain such a relationship?"

"Well, that is a hard one to answer. It sort of depends on the circumstances and who she is with, and her fatigue or irritability, and their lack of perfection, interaction with each other. But just a wild ballpark figure? I would suspect that with another adult, maybe it would be characterized by on-again, off-again, on-again, off-again, until someone stayed off-again, so maybe two years. But even within that two years, I am just guessing, it will be off-again, on-again."

"So, therefore, if you knew she had friends who had been her friends more than two years, that would be a surprise to you?"

Barkouki was accustomed to this old snare. An evaluation left many holes. "No, it would mean that they were friends, number one, who were very able to tolerate that; who, number two, did not have to be very close emotionally, were not dependent on her emotional consistency with them; perhaps they were friends and helpers who enjoy Tiffany's really charming company—and she really is charming—who can go home to their own place when the going gets tough."

Bedford nodded. "Now, when you said she is not able to form or maintain a nurturing relationship, you are talking about familial types of relationships, not just friendships?"

"Not just friendships. In fact, as friendships I would imagine that a lot of people find Tiffany a very, very good friend. She is helpful, she is gregarious, she is witty, she is intelligent . . ."

Tiffany had heard this one before. Shrinks combed your hair, brushed your coat, and congratulated you on your posture before calling in the firing squad. She wished Teddy or, rest her soul, Elnora was there to talk about relationships.

". . . she has got a heart of gold with her friends," Barkouki said. "They don't get close enough to provoke the intense transference."

There was a portion of Barkouki's report that had sent steam pouring out of Tiffany's ears. The psychologist said Tiffany had pulled out a tablet during their interview and loudly announced that she was taking a birth-control pill. This went down as "inappropriate" behavior. Tiffany insisted that she had made no such announcement, and had not told Barkouki what the pill was until she was asked.

Bedford took a swipe at it, not wanting to ignite his client or focus more attention than necessary on her sexuality, a topic that struck a deep nerve out of reach of cross-examination. "Don't you think it might be important to her to let you know that she is taking care of this at this point in time to make sure she does not get pregnant?"

"She could easily tell me that," Barkouki said. "She doesn't have to act it out."

"So it is the acting out and taking the birth—"

"That is correct. It is the acting out that is clinically inappropriate."

"And you have no information yourself about, talking now about sexually loose in the physical sense in terms of number of lovers and things like that?"

"Only what she told me, no, and what is in the case records," Barkouki said.

Tiffany, once again, was amazed. Me and my big mouth, she thought. She wondered whether some quarterback bragging in the locker room had ever been fined for acting out. She could see it: "I'm sorry, Joe, but what you're saying is clinically inappropriate."

Bedford sifted Barkouki's evaluation for more concealed doubt. "Now," he said, "you referred to the case record as including examples of Tiffany's infantile rage and anger. Could you pinpoint for me exactly where there are examples of her infantile rage and anger?"

"Well," said Barkouki, wary again, "I don't know if it was in writing in the case record, but one that comes to mind immediately is her rage and anger. I don't know how infantile it was since it took a great deal of potency and strength. She told me of the time when her father was drunk and was being inappropriate with her and she threw him hard enough to break four of his ribs. That was her statement."

Bedford had never believed this story, and wished his client would not tell it so often. He had admired Tiffany's imaginative moments. They helped protect her against a callous world that tried to deny her humanity, but they presented certain difficulties in court.

He decided to encourage, gently, whatever doubts Edwards and Barkouki had about this incident. That would be tricky if he ever had to put Tiffany on the stand, but a light touch might work.

"Did she tell you how old she was at that point in time?" he asked the psychologist.

"Somewhere in her late teens, I believe."

"You have never met Tiffany's father. Is that correct?" Bedford wished he had Bob Callo looming beside him, two hundred fifty pounds and counting.

"That is correct," Barkouki said. "I understand he can be, from reading it, that he could be someone one might want to throw against the wall. Let me assure you, I might have done so myself. I don't know if I had the strength to break four of his ribs."

Bedford thanked her silently. "That was going to be my next question. Do you have any information whether or not Tiffany's physical condition was any different then than it is now?"

"No, I don't."

"Now, is rage inappropriate to show?"

"Rage in and of itself is not inappropriate to show. Rage which could hurt somebody else who cannot take care of themselves, I believe, is inappropriate."

"So in a sense what you are saying is that Tiffany was bullying her father?"

Barkouki objected to Bedford's phrasing, and insisted that Tiffany was capable of harming others, such as Tony. "There is a history of acting out violently under maybe extreme provocation," she said. "I'm not denying that she may have been provoked into those—I do not know enough about the instances, nor can I believe anybody enough to be sure about the instances. But I would assume, given her personality structure, that it has to do with being provoked—okay?—even without my knowing what happened. And my hypothesis is that she can be provoked again easily, and that she might hurt somebody under those circumstances."

Bedford looked pained. "Okay, so, therefore—I am having real difficulty with this. Now, at one point in time you are aware that Tony was arrested for battery on Tiffany?"

"Right. He certainly can take care of himself."

"And what you are saying is, *that* is an example of when Tiffany expressed rage and tried to hurt somebody? . . . Can you point to one episode that is in the record anyplace in which Tiffany was not the victim of an assault?"

Barkouki was somber. "No," she said.

"Is it your assumption, then, that if Tiffany is involved in a physical dispute with somebody, that she must somehow have asked for it?"

"No."

Bedford decided to take Edwards a step or two into Tiffany's world, where everybody and everything seemed set at an uncomfortable scale and speed and altitude, where Tiffany always had to adjust to the world, not the other way around.

Bedford asked Barkouki, "Do you think that therapy should be done by somebody who is trained in dealing with people with disabilities?"

"Not particularly," said the psychologist, apparently prepared for the question. "I think they should be trained and dealt with by somebody who is really good at psychodynamic interpersonal long-term psychotherapy."

Excuse me, Tiffany thought, could I have an interpreter please?

Bedford continued. "You don't think a therapist who understands the mental dynamics in a special situation that are going on in a disabled person would be advantageous in that situation?"

"Not particularly if they were not really good therapists. The important thing is that they be very good therapists and very experienced therapists. The issue with Tiffany from my point of view is not her physical disability, it is her emotional problems. So it needs a specialist."

Tiffany stared at the ceiling. Please God, she prayed, save me from the specialists.

"Isn't it possible," Bedford asked, "that some of those emotional problems are the direct result organically of her disability?"

"Quite possibly some of them," Barkouki said.

"And secondly, isn't it possible that some of what is going on is the result of the way society treats somebody with a disability?"

The psychologist's eyes lifted. This was a question she could embrace, and for a moment she seemed to step away from the trial altogether.

"Sure," she said, "more than that. I can give you a whole other extra argument that people in chairs from birth or people who have not had the ability to develop mentally in the ways that most of us are fortunate to be able to learn to master our environment, to have control over our feet, to be able to get from one place to another, and able to reach an object and bring it closer, to do all of the things that infants learn to do, and grow up getting better and better at doing that, will definitely affect a person's personality development."

Tiffany, Edwards, and the small audience listened carefully to this.

"I think that a person to whom you must, because they are disabled, bring things, help attend to, lift, feed, etcetera, is going to definitely grow up with a different sense of their own special-ness and their own narcissism than somebody who has to go fend for themselves in other areas. So I would be the first—any com-petent psychologist would be the first to tell you that just as how tall you are, how short you are, what color you are, what sex you are, also what your physical endowments are, will definitely strongly affect your personality development. My job is to assess the personality development, not the etiology of it."

Bedford paused. She had given him much to work with. "If, let's say, you were asked to go to a different culture, let's make it Japan—"

Barkouki broke in, still keen on this topic. "I spent a year there," she said.

Bedford pushed on. "Does it take any special training to be a clinical psychologist with someone who grew up in a Japanese culture? Are there techniques that you would use with that person that would be inappropriate for using in our culture?"

"More likely vice versa," she said. "There are techniques in our culture that would not be appropriate for working with a Japa-nese person or an Arab-American. For example, to get an Arab-American to tell you how terrible their parents are, that is craziness. You don't tell them how to criticize the experience of parenting. There are lots of things you have to be sensitive to."

"Let's assume that you are working with an Arab-American," Bedford said, "and it is important for him to tell you how bad his parents were in therapy. Could you live with that?"

Barkouki, born in Egypt and active in Arab-American affairs, was in her element. "No, I can't live with that. You have to change

your whole therapy. You have to understand where they are coming from in order to tailor where you want to get. There are things
that one would have to do with Tiffany to establish the rapport
that would allow you to help her change that you might not have
to do with somebody who was able-bodied."

Bedford could see that she was trying to wrap herself once
more in her expertise. There seemed to be several threads to un-
ravel. "I thought you said working with an Arab-American you
would have to understand where they are coming from and adapt
what you are doing, correct?"

"Right."

"And in order to do that, don't you have to have some understanding of the Arab-American culture and—"

"And that person can teach me about it. I wrote *papers* on this.
All you need is someone who understands that culture difference
is an important thing, not that they say, 'All right, in Arabic culture you can hit your kids, so now it is all right to hit your kids.'
Now, that is crazy. You have to be able to understand, yes, it is
different for them. You have to understand that you don't neces-
sarily assume that somebody who does it has an impulse-control
disorder, as I might with an Anglo in Saratoga."

Having seeded the ground for Kirshbaum, Bedford moved on
to other matters. "Do you have any problem with somebody who
has a special relationship with God?" he asked.

"No," Barkouki said.

"And do you have any problem with somebody who believes
that her destiny is to have children?"

"That by itself, no."

"If we put those two together, does that give you a problem?"

Barkouki thought for a moment. "When you begin to put
those two together and other things together, that is when I begin
to have a problem, yes."

Bedford made a note. That was the answer he expected. "Now,
is it inappropriate for Tiffany to dream of having a three-bedroom
house after she gets married?"

"The dream is not inappropriate," Barkouki said evenly. "The
fact that she is implying that you can do this on four dollars an
hour is."

"Did she ever *say* they are going to be able to move into a three-bedroom house on four dollars an hour?"

"No, she didn't say that."

Heather Hyde, the court-appointed attorney representing David, asked Barkouki about what she called in her report Tiffany's "lack of empathy" with her children. Could Tiffany be expected to develop empathy if she only saw them once a week?

"One can develop and improve their capacity at empathy and understanding," Barkouki said, "but you have to have a significant amount of capacity there for it to start to work. If you have it, you can get more of it, and if you don't have it at all, it is hard to acquire."

"Then would you say that Tiffany, because of who Tiffany is, is lacking in empathy?" Hyde asked.

"At this point in her life, yes."

"And would interactions with her children develop empathy?"

"I think the level to which Tiffany is limited in this area is serious enough and debilitating . . . enough that it would be very hard for it to develop naturally enough or quickly enough."

There was something about this line of argument that seemed to Hyde inconsistent. "So it is possible that if she did learn some interactions with her children, that would tend to bring out the empathy?"

Barkouki peered at the attorney. "That would not be empathy," she said.

"What would it be?"

"That would be going through the motions of looking empathetic."

Tiffany felt a chill. Why try with such people?

Hyde was fascinated. "So the fact that she learned, for instance, to move a child by pulling a blanket, that is an interaction or a way of facilitating?"

"Correct," Barkouki said, "handling a child." She brushed off Tiffany's success at pulling Jesse on his baby blanket as "a useful thing that you can learn," like "a household hint in Heloise," but nothing more.

Everyone in the courtroom had heard that Kirshbaum had made progress with Tiffany and the boys. When Tony's attorney had asked Barkouki earlier if she had alerted Tony to ways he could be a better parent, she curtly dismissed the question. "It was not my job to do that," she said.

Clark appeared to think that this left an unfavorable impression and saw a chance to cut some ground out from under Kirshbaum in advance. "In your opinion," Clark asked, "is it possible for an individual to be both a therapist and a neutral assessor in the same clinical situation with a patient?"

"Absolutely not," Barkouki said. "I refuse to see people in therapy that I have ever evaluated. I have recommended to the county that that be county policy. And when I am called as an expert witness as to somebody that I have been their therapist, I am very clear that I am there usually under duress, not as an expert witness, but as that person's therapist."

"And why can't a person be both a therapist and an assessor?"

"It is just plain, ordinary, you know, experimental bias," she said. "You can't study an experiment if you are mucking around in it, obviously you can't. I mean, you wouldn't put up with that in atomic physics."

Tiffany studied her lap. In a perfect world where therapists all shared an encyclopedic appreciation of the problems of the disabled, the Barkouki Rule might work. In the world she lived in, almost no one understood her situation. The County of Santa Clara, its well-meaning social workers and foster parents and attorneys, had been her guardian and guide for nearly half her life. Yet it was only now, after she had defied them and pushed them to the limit, that she had found one of the few people in the country willing and able to help her.

And Barkouki, for all the right reasons, wanted that door gently shut in her face.

Bedford rose and looked at his notes. He had to turn Barkouki's scientific caution against her.

"If somebody was hired to do a study as to whether or not

somebody was physically capable to taking care of children and formulated a plan for that," he began, "would that come within your rule that the person that formulated that plan should not follow through with the plan?"

"Personally, yes, that is my personal rule."

". . . Now, you said that your test results showed that Tiffany would have a complete lack of empathy with her children, correct?"

"No, I didn't say that. I said that my test results indicate that she is very limited in that area, and limited enough for that to be debilitating."

Bedford shuffled his papers, looking for something. "Okay," he said. "Your written report says, 'Her lack of empathy,' not her limited lack?"

"It doesn't say her total lack of empathy, Mr. Bedford."

"Okay," he said, taking an agreeable tone. "Well, then, your test results say that Tiffany lacks empathy?"

"That is correct."

"Now, if Dr. Kirshbaum did observe this empathy, which would be more reliable, a test result that says Tiffany is not capable of empathy, or an observation that she is displaying these traits?"

Barkouki thought for a moment. "It depends on who is doing the observation, and what kind of position they are coming from, background they are coming from, and I believe the same thing about empathy."

"Let's say you test somebody and the test says that they lack empathy, you then observe them and observe them displaying empathy?"

"It depends on what empathy means to me."

Bedford asked for a definition. "Empathy is the capacity to put oneself in somebody else's shoes," she said, "to feel the world from their point of view. For me to see that, someone would have to be able to articulate it or to demonstrate it."

Bedford was ready with his sharpest needle, looking for the right spot to puncture Barkouki's scientifically neutral balloon.

"Let's assume," he said, not planning to assume anything at all, "that Tiffany is trying to change David's diaper, and let's assume

that David is six months old at the time. And let's assume that due
to the fact that the clothes that David is wearing have snaps
on them—"

"Instead of Velcro," said Barkouki, signaling Bedford that she
was ready for this.

"—and it is inappropriate," Bedford continued, "for Tiffany,
in view of her disability, and let's assume she is being videotaped
and that there are various people who are there—authority type
people, social workers, people from San Andreas Regional Center—and let's assume it takes her approximately twenty minutes
to perform this operation from start to finish.

"Now, would the fact that during that changing of the diaper
she is cooing at the baby, the fact she is talking to the baby and
saying things like, 'I'm sorry, we will get this over soon,' the fact
she is handing the baby toys during the operation, would that in
your mind be a display of empathy?"

Barkouki smiled. "Yeah," she said, "it could be."

"Okay, and once Tiffany has that ability, it is your testimony
she would not lose it?"

Barkouki seemed to sense she was losing ground here. "You
said it was a display of empathy," she said, pausing for a moment.
"I don't know. Someone may have coached her and said, 'Go "coo,
coo, coo."' I don't know. I mean, it is not something that I can
relate to, I wasn't there, and I don't know what the ambiance was."

"And would you expect the baby to regress if minimal advances had been made in eye contact and she hadn't seen him in
six weeks?"

"I think that a child as young as David could, if it was just a
one-time learning, and it hadn't been demonstrated for a long
time, I think he would lose it over a week's time, even."

Bedford could see Barkouki had a human heart. He had to
remind Edwards again of the tenuous connection between that
and her cold, hard, white porcelain treatment of Tiffany.

"Let's say Tiffany was—let's say she was playing ball, trying to
play ball with David in an age-inappropriate way, and let's assume
that you realized, Hey, there is a different approach she could
take—if she tried this, it might work better. As I understand it,

your testimony is that it would be inappropriate in view of your job role to make the suggestion, 'Why don't you try it this way,' is that correct?"

"Mm-hmm," said Barkouki, ready to take this rhetorical journey one more time.

"Now, on the other hand, if you had said, 'Why don't you try doing it this other way,' in that type of situation would that not have helped you understand and see what Tiffany's reaction to criticism or suggestions would be, and whether she could incorporate what you said? Wouldn't that information whether she could take that criticism have been helpful in your diagnosis?"

He described Jesse squirming in his mother's lap. "If Jesse is not able to get comfortable," he asked, "would you expect any increase in bonding on that particular day or from that particular episode?"

"If, in fact, the only experience the child has with a person, whoever that person is, is discomfort, I don't think they will bond," she said.

If mother and child could not bond after fourteen months of weekly visits at the Zoo, he asked, "might that also suggest that there was something wrong with the conditions under which Tiffany was meeting with David? . . . Would that not suggest that something else should be tried, such as having visitation at home or changing, also, who is present, that sort of thing?"

"Sure," Barkouki said. The truth about her was that she preferred counseling to evaluating, even if she refused to mix the two. "I mean, I am not saying that it would work, but I certainly would try all sorts of other things. Obviously, what was happening wasn't working."

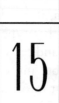

15

Megan Kirshbaum was scheduled to testify on the second day of Tiffany's hearing. She accepted Margaret Jakobson's offer of a ride to San Jose. Jakobson, the disability rights attorney from Protection & Advocacy Inc. in Oakland, had been advising Bedford on California and federal law. He asked her to attend the hearing in case the argument took an unfamiliar turn.

Jakobson had fixed the lift on her old van, and it rattled down Interstate 880 without further mishap. During the ride she talked with Kirshbaum about the psychologist's research and about raising teenage daughters, a challenge they shared.

They arrived in time for a hasty lunch of sandwiches and soft drinks in the narrow library of Bedford's office. He outlined his strategy and tried to familiarize Kirshbaum with his line of questioning.

Kirshbaum had testified in court only three times before. The emphasis seemed backward to her. There was so much concern about legal definitions and protocol and such an adversarial focus that it seemed hard to express views in a complex and balanced way.

One thing at a time, Bedford said. Jakobson told her to relax, listen carefully to each question, and try to respond directly. She should feel free to elaborate if necessary.

They walked into court, and Kirshbaum took her seat in the witness chair to Judge Edwards's right. She smiled at Tiffany. Throughout the afternoon she glanced at the young woman to see how she was reacting to the testimony. Bedford identified Jakobson, who maneuvered her power chair next to Tiffany's on the left side of the court, in front of Tony's chair.

Bedford began his questioning of Kirshbaum with a not-so-subtle reminder of Barkouki's failure to demonstrate much experience with disabled parents.

"Do you think that it takes special training to properly evaluate a parent/infant interaction?" he asked.

"Yes, I think so," Kirshbaum said, "and I think that is generally not available. I think it takes a lot of training, not just of those measures, but the new specialties that are developed."

"Is there a difference between this type of training and the training one would receive in developmental psychology?"

"Very few programs in the country have any specialized training of any depth in infant observation or infant/parent observation."

"And the fact that somebody has had a clinical psychology practice dealing with family issues for twenty years, would that be a substitute for this type of training?"

"Definitely not," Kirshbaum said. "There is almost no infancy work in the family therapy field. Most of the work is focused on age three and up."

Barkouki had had her shot at Kirshbaum, and now the favor was returned—two kind and thoughtful women forced into opposite corners by the adversarial system of American justice.

"And do you believe that the conclusions reached by a clinical psychologist who does not have this specialized training would be valid?"

"I would question them in the area that pertains to observation of infants and their interaction with their parents or their families."

"Now, to change the subject a little bit, first of all, you were contacted by the Department of Social Services to perform certain evaluations of Tiffany Callo, correct?"

"Yes."

"And basically most of your practice is related to disabled people and parenting issues related to disabled people, is that correct?"

"Well, I have worked with families in disabled issues as a family therapist, also, for approximately fifteen years, and with all ages of people in the family with disabilities from infancy to middle age. And since I founded this agency in 1982, I have focused on disabled parents and their babies, both in research and services and training of professionals."

"And based on your experience with people with cerebral palsy, can you tell us whether or not you would expect Tiffany's condition to improve, stay the same, or deteriorate over the years in terms of cerebral palsy?"

Kirshbaum paused. She was having trouble understanding the point of some of Bedford's questions. "Cerebral palsy is not a progressive condition," she said. "The only thing that could possibly change it is if there is a traumatic arthritis from an unusual mode of mobility. But that is usually with ambulatory people. It is usually considered a stable condition that would not change over the years."

"And is there anything that would indicate she would have anything shorter than normal life expectancy?"

"Well, with the current quality of medical care for people with severe CP, I think it would be normal life expectancy pretty much as long as she uses good self-care."

Bedford asked why Kirshbaum had insisted on seeing Tiffany so many times—eight sessions totaling seventeen and a half hours—before finishing her evaluation.

"Our program has developed a period of assessment that seems to work," Kirshbaum said. "We assess a minimum of five to seven weeks usually for a disabled parent and baby. Most infant mental-health programs do assess for that period of time and do consider it important to have a fairly long-term assessment partly because of the variation in states in babies from one time to another."

"Is there any reason why you wanted these observations done in Ms. Callo's home rather than someplace else?"

"We have concluded over years of doing this work that the observations are much more valid in a home setting."

Bedford asked her about the Zoo. "I have been told about the auditorium for visitations and considered it a very inappropriate place to meet for many reasons," she said.

"What are those reasons?"

Kirshbaum hesitated for a moment, wondering how explicit she should be. DSS was already unhappy with her. The department had assumed she would take their side, and appeared stunned by her report. But she had not acted out of any desire to provoke them.

She told Bedford that a foster mother had complained to her about the DSS auditorium. "She said it was very distracting and hard to focus in that setting. I wanted to work with Ms. Callo in as optimal a situation as I could without [the presence of] other people who had charged relationships, either to Ms. Callo or the babies. I wanted to be alone with her in our work, also."

Tiffany gave Kirshbaum a reassuring smile. The younger woman wondered what her life would be like if she could speak as subtly as the psychologist and tell people what she thought without hurting their feelings.

"Let's deal with the social worker," Bedford said to Kirshbaum. "Why would you not want a social worker present for these sessions?"

"It is like it is—it is very difficult to have a, first of all . . ." Kirshbaum said, and paused. She did not want unnecessarily to alienate DSS any further, and sought a way to avoid this and still address the important issues.

"It is like having a third party during a therapy session," she said, finding the thread. "It is not conducive to work, to any aspect of the work, and tends to be a distraction from it. The other point would be that by having a foster mother or Ms. Silvani, the relationships were complicating what I would have been observing, so in my opinion it would have obfuscated my observations. I could explain why, if you want."

"Yes, please."

"Well, because, particularly with David, he had quite an attachment to Ms. Silvani. He had a lot of contact with her, so he had a very strong preference for her as opposed to any able-bodied or disabled person that was present.

"And, also, there seemed to be sort of a charged relationship between Ms. Callo and Ms. Silvani. The kind of work I was doing, it was very difficult to do in that situation. And there have got to be charged emotional issues between a foster mother and birth mother, so that complicates what you would see in observations."

Bedford thought he had established Kirshbaum's unique experience in such matters. He began to tread softly into the heart of his case—how his client's natural touch with her children had fared during a year of anxiety, separation, mishap, and abuse.

He would take Kirshbaum out of her office, free her from the technical language needed to establish her credentials, and let her describe what she discovered on the stained carpets of the Tenth Street apartment.

"In your experience," he asked, "do very young babies adapt their behavior to a disabled parent?"

Kirshbaum took a breath. This was something she knew as much about as anyone in the country, but she did not want to be too clinical. "We have observed and documented that in videotape in our research study as young as one month of age," she said. "It doesn't always occur, and we are trying to understand why.

"But we have videotapes of a baby as young as one month of age. When the mother lifts the baby with one hand, the baby becomes still and tenses its body for the lift, so it is cooperating apparently with the mother during the lift so she can do it more easily."

Bedford smiled. "And one of these adaptive behaviors," he said, "does that include a baby not rolling around as much when a disabled parent is trying to change the baby's diaper?"

"Yes, it is common to see them lie extremely still for a disabled parent, and being incredibly patient during a long process of diapering in which some parents have more skill at facilitating than other parents."

Kirshbaum smiled at Tiffany. "Tiffany, Ms. Callo, has some excellent skills which we call bridging techniques, which apparently no one has taught her, for helping her baby be patient through diapering."

She explained: "There are simple things that help a baby to be patient, like offering a pacifier, bottle, or toy, or talking to them, or breaking up the care into a little relating in the midst of it. That was done with David, also, at six months, although the diapering took a very long time, which is very normal for a parent with CP. Her interaction with the baby during it had many strengths of those sort."

Kirshbaum said the infant's sensitivity toward the disabled parent's slow pace was verified by observations of disabled parents and their nondisabled spouses. "We have seen in our clinical cases babies incredibly still and patient for a disabled parent, and when the able-bodied parent diapers, they are all over the place, the same baby, the same age level," she said. "The same thing happens with sighted and blind parents with babies."

"And just to take that one step further," Bedford said, "once a baby becomes a toddler, have you noticed that toddlers will react differently to voice commands by disabled parents?"

"It is quite common for the babies to come more readily to the request of the disabled parent than the able-bodied parent," she said. "But, again, it depends if they have facilitated that, because a lot of parents work very hard on achieving that."

Jakobson listened intently from her wheelchair in the aisle. Kirshbaum, as she had feared, could not discard her diffidence and soft tone of voice. The attorney would have liked the psychologist to sound more *positive.* But Kirshbaum's exhaustive research and sincerity came through. That, Jakobson hoped, would be enough.

Bedford thought Kirshbaum was doing fine. It was time to show that Tiffany and her sons shared the same bond Kirshbaum had detected in other families.

"Now, in dealing with Ms. Callo," he said, "at some point in time did you become concerned that David was displaying some sort of aversion to contact with Tiffany?"

Kirshbaum welcomed the question. This was why she had come all this way. "Yes," she said. "He was very clearly displaying aversive behavior toward her until, you know . . ." She caught herself losing the point again. "It was a predominant, his predominant reaction until I started working with her in my last three visits."

"Okay, and at some point in time, did you reach a conclusion about what may be causing David to be staying away from Tiffany?"

"Well, I was trying to problem-solve around that all through my work and eliminating one thing after another, and I was basically exploring the hypothesis that he was aversive, that part of his aversion had to do with her being in a motorized wheelchair.

"I tried to get him in contact with her while in the wheelchair by having keys or something attractive in the wheelchair, or by trying play while she was in the wheelchair that was interesting to him, and that sort of thing."

"Were there a lot of moments when Tiffany would be frustrated in dealing with the children?"

Kirshbaum had so much to say on this topic that she had to grope for the proper starting place. "Well, see, there are lots of . . ." She felt frustrated by this legal obsession with questions and answers. "There are really no people who have developed proper adaptive equipment for disabled people. I was working with her and trying to work out baby-care strategies using just what equipment we had available or I could scrounge to bring."

Tiffany smiled. She was proud of the experiments the two of them had done. Bedford coaxed Kirshbaum along, encouraged by Edwards's intense look as the judge chewed on his pen. "I would bring a front pack and it wouldn't be properly adapted because such front packs don't exist at this point," Kirshbaum said, "and it would work in certain respects and be frustrating in other respects.

"There was another point where I experimented with her own wheelchair tray and did baby care on that," she said. Tiffany had struggled with the tray and told Kirshbaum it would have been better to warn her so she could have a chance to practice with the device. The emotional outburst predicted by Barkouki never occurred.

"Once she stated that to me," Kirshbaum told Bedford, "and that was clear to me that that would have been a better thing for me to have done, then we sort of moved on to other things, and there was no explosiveness. It didn't end the work at that point. She moved from that into doing a very appropriate diaper change with Jesse in the bed that was quite sensitive to him. So she didn't remain in sort of any kind of agitated state or anything of that sort."

Bedford led Kirshbaum through a detailed account of their efforts to rid David of his fear of Tiffany's wheelchair, and of Tiffany's increasingly active play with David on the apartment floor.

Describing this now in court, four months after the fact, Kirshbaum shed some of the psychological terminology that had studded the earlier part of her testimony. She relived the moment. Edwards turned his chair to face her. The courtroom was very still.

"He started playing with Tiffany," she said, "and this time there was a lot of parallel play with her, and a lot of interaction with her, and the beginning of vocalizing with her. The baby will say something, the mom imitates, the baby imitates, and the mom imitates. It goes like that, which requires a lot of sensitive reading of baby's signals for the mother.

"You don't see that very often in low-functioning moms and, you know, so there was a lot of imitative play going on. He was much, much, markedly less anxious, markedly more comfortable with the whole situation. He had had some anxiety on the previous visits, but during that visit it was markedly less."

Kirshbaum described how mother and son rolled about the brown carpet as if they were playing handball on a high-gravity planet. David giggled and smiled and shrieked at his mother's teasing. She would fake a throw in one direction and then roll the ball another way to see how fast he could change directions. Her freshly laundered jogging suit had picked up bits of dust but she did not care. She could be as patient as David, perhaps more able than most parents to match the crazed persistence of a child who never wanted a game to end.

When Silvani arrived at the end of the hour, David looked up in surprise. Kirshbaum waited for the usual tears, the sign of relief that his preferred attendant had finally returned. They never came. David smiled at Silvani but play with his mother continued.

The psychologist was surprised, and pleased. The time on the floor had worn away some barrier between the small, sensitive child and her client. Whether it was, as Tiffany thought, old memories of her high-pitched, coaxing voice, or the renewed physical contact, or the absence of the chair, David's mother had again become part of his world. He was no longer interested in leaving her so quickly.

At one point, Kirshbaum noted, Tiffany had reached for the ball but missed and it had rolled away from her. David paused for a moment, then dashed over, picked up the ball, and carefully handed it to his mother before moving back so she could throw it in his direction.

Kirshbaum asked, "So what do you make of that, Tiffany?"

Tiffany, understanding her interest, said, "He knew that was hard for me and tried to help." Kirshbaum smiled and recorded a few more details of the session in her notebook, then prepared to leave.

Tiffany did not need to write anything down. She had recorded every second in her heart. She watched, her usual guardedness softened by fatigue and David's unexpected reaction, as Silvani gathered her son up and carried him out the door.

"Bye-bye, Davie," she said. She felt unexpectedly serene. He would be back.

16

Now, had you noticed that Tiffany had difficulty making eye-to-eye contact with either of her babies?" Bedford asked. One sweet moment on the apartment floor would intrigue Edwards, he knew, but winning back the boys would take evidence that Tiffany had overcome, or at least was gaining on, all the other obstacles left by the long separation and Kirshbaum's late start.

Bedford could see that Kirshbaum's energies were flagging. She had been on the stand for two hours. But he did not want to lose the momentum.

Kirshbaum was prepared for the eye-contact question. "I saw that some difficulties looked like they were developing with Jesse," Kirshbaum said, "and she told me, 'Oh, that happened also with David when he was little.' In the same way I was exploring about the wheelchair, I was exploring about the eye contact and what could be going on with that."

She had several theories. One of Tiffany's eyes wandered slightly, which might bother a baby. In addition, the infrequent visits and the nature of life in the Zoo might have taken their toll.

Tiffany had trouble finding the best distance between her eyes and the babies'. Because of her uncertain muscle control, she felt an urge to move very close to a child to nuzzle. Her eyes were too close then for the baby to return the look comfortably. Often the infant would look away.

Kirshbaum said, "Another theory I was exploring was if I stabilized, if I made the physical care situation better and eliminated what we call adaptive stress or stress pertaining to disability, if I got the mom in a secure, comfortable position and got the baby in a secure, comfortable position, would that facilitate eye contact?"

She and Tiffany resumed work with the wheelchair tray. If Jesse was placed on the tray or a table at about the same height, Tiffany could move her head farther from his without fear that she would drop him. He could see her clearly at the proper distance.

On March 31, when Jesse was ten weeks old, Kirshbaum recorded happily in her notes the official establishment of eye contact. She called it a "mutual gaze," but that did not adequately describe Tiffany's feelings about the moment. Her baby gave her a sudden, sweeping grin, and inspected her face carefully for signs of reciprocal love and approbation.

Knowing Edwards had read several pages of analyses and heard hours of Barkouki testimony about Tiffany's psychological profile, Kirshbaum tried to underscore the principal lesson of her six years of research on disabled parents: Assumptions and unexamined speculation were deadly. The eye contact problem "seemed to get worked out . . . by having the position less stressful for the mother and baby. I often see with disabled parents that their eye contact problems are due to positioning," she said. "And so that always needs to be worked out before you make some kind of esoteric conclusions. Before you conclude that there are emotional reasons for it, I always like to eliminate the physical alternatives."

"Do you have any personal knowledge . . . whether anybody else offered her any help on that issue?" Bedford asked.

"There was no indication that she had had any help," the psychologist said.

Bedford could see that Kirshbaum wanted to escape the court's inquisitional straitjacket, but he insisted on guiding her carefully through the story of Tiffany's growing awareness of her abilities as a parent.

"In other words, she listened to what you said, she changed her behavior, and got a positive result?" Bedford asked.

"Yes," she said, "but it is also a very hard thing to change a habitual thing, which may have to do with her motor control."

He turned to Barkouki's image of Tiffany as a self-absorbed child, killing off friendship whenever someone did not want to do things her way. "When you offered your observations to her, did she get defensive at all, or interested in what you were saying?"

"She seemed to be quite curious about some of the things I said that could have been taken as criticism," Kirshbaum said. "I also taught her to soothe the baby, Jesse, when he was a newborn by holding his arms on his chest, and that could have been taken as a criticism . . . but she seemed quite curious about it and interested in it rather than defensive about it. Then she incorporated that into her subsequent care of him in my presence, also, very nicely."

"In other words, she was trying to improve the way she took care of the babies?"

"Yes, and she did."

He took her through each of the sessions that followed their breakthrough on the apartment floor. At the very next meeting between David and his mother, Kirshbaum said, "there was a wonderful imitative game between them, and I am especially interested in the sequences of imitation because they necessitate a lot of observation and acuity about reading his signals on her part and sensitivity to where he is."

That day David had gotten into some of the plastic kitchenware, residue of Tiffany's attempt to sell Tupperware. Tiffany thought they might serve as interesting toys. One tall container particularly intrigued the boy. He held it and inspected it and chewed it before discovering that, if he tilted it at a certain angle, he could squeal into the mouth of the object and produce an eerie echo.

Tiffany heard this and found an identical container for herself. She blew a note into the mouth of the suddenly magical instrument. Her son laughed in recognition. The toots and squeals, amplified and echoed, went back and forth, a Callo symphony.

They spent most of the session on the floor, tossing the ball again and looking for other games. At one point David was so eager to reach a toy car that he climbed over his mother to get it. She laughed and hugged him. They wrestled.

Kirshbaum, intrigued, made several notes as she watched. The moment pleased the mother in her, but was also significant to her research because David had recovered so quickly from his aversion to bodily contact with Tiffany.

Again, Silvani arrived and David reacted calmly. He had no pent-up feelings to release.

On April 14, the third visit after the initial floor play, David and Tiffany began a tickling game. They touched and laughed and made faces at each other.

Their games became more complicated. He brought her a small pot and indicated that he wanted her to remove the lid. She did, then suggested he try. "*David* fix it," she said. He smiled and made a booing noise, a sound of triumph over a foe, and she repeated it back to him. With her encouragement, he put small blocks and rubber balls in the pot and pulled them out.

Kirshbaum suggested to Tiffany that she feed him some Cheerios. This had not worked before. He had not let his mother give him a bottle or solid food, no matter how gently and carefully she approached him. This time he sat still, accepted several mouthfuls of the oat circles, and crunched them with pleasure. She squealed a compliment to his appetite, and he smiled.

Tiffany felt the relationship with her son sailing ahead. She shuddered at the thought of Silvani coming to take him away. Mother and child had finally tuned themselves back to the same frequency. "Here, honey. Here, David. Sit down here," she said. He did so. "Bring Mommy the balloon," she said. He beamed, grabbed the bouncing red object in both hands, and carried it over to her, while Kirshbaum scribbled in her notebook.

The psychologist had noticed how sensitive the child was to

the slightest sound. David's eyes widened at the click of a refrigerator door or the rattle of a toy. Now he focused that sense on the interesting woman who liked to lie on the floor and play with him. Tiffany, Kirshbaum noted, had a talent for putting words to each of the child's actions. He would wave a hand and she would squeal, "Oooh, that's right, Davie. *Wave* to Mommy." A childish belch would bring laughter and motherly advice. "What a *good burp,* David! Always remember to chew and swallow." That was the way children learned the language, Kirshbaum knew. Tiffany had enough verbal skill and intensity for four or five children to absorb.

The next visit both David and Jesse came. The floor of the apartment became a squirming mass of flesh and toys. Tiffany and David continued to play with words, balls, and plastic containers. Tiffany's contact with Jesse was more subtle, but progressed rapidly.

The two days Tiffany had had with Jesse at Valley Medical were unlikely to have left any trace in the baby's shadowy memory, and their weekly visits at the Zoo had not added much. But on the floor of her own apartment, without the chilly formalities and jarring noise of the DSS auditorium, Tiffany found a way to communicate with her younger son.

He lay small and curly-headed in his carrier, staring at her as if he was trying to divine what game they were playing. Tiffany waved a soft rattle in his face and smiled. She cooed at his yawns and let him suck one of her fingers. If he was tired or hungry, Tiffany seemed to sense it before anyone else.

Tiffany should have a chance, Kirshbaum told the court, to demonstrate continued progress in communication and care of her babies, with the help of better services and more home visits. She would have to make a serious commitment to pursuing psychological therapy to address her own childhood traumas and to developing and practicing with adaptive equipment and child-care strategies. In time she ought to be allowed to show that with a backup attendant, she could handle sustained care of at least one of the children, most likely Jesse since she had more chance of developing a full relationship with the younger child.

Bedford asked the question that depressed Tiffany the most: "As each day goes by, are we losing time with either or both children in terms of providing the type of services that you are talking about?"

Kirshbaum responded emphatically, the kind of answer Jakobson liked. "Yeah, for sure," she said. "It is difficult enough ordinarily separating babies and parents in terms of the ground that they lose in their relationship. That is hard to regain; the impact on babies of removal is very profound. And it is very profound in its impact on the interaction and attachment to the parents."

Kirshbaum glanced at Tiffany, sitting very still and absorbing each word. "But I think where the parents' disability enters into it, things are more complex because of the problems with working out the reciprocal collaboration between parent and baby that can happen around the disability."

Bedford asked a question that intrigued Tiffany: "How would it be helpful to David to have Tiffany as part of his life?"

Kirshbaum was uncomfortable with hypothetical questions, but this was an area where she trusted her instincts. "I think it can be very strengthening to have a disabled parent," she said. "People can develop more tolerance, and facilitation of their patience."

The questions and answers went back and forth, teetering on the edge of possibility, while Tiffany listened and wondered what she should do. She was getting closer to what she wanted, but sitting in the courtroom aisle still made the boys seem very far away.

Bedford had kept Kirshbaum on the stand for more than three hours, but he needed more time to drain the swamp of psychological jargon that had flooded the court record. He would make sure he had the judge's attention by starting with sex.

"In the reports of the other psychologists, Dr. Terry Johnston, Barkouki, and Winter, there are some substantial references to sexual acting out, is that correct?"

"Yes," Kirshbaum said, ready for this one.

Tiffany permitted herself a small smirk.

"And do you have any theories why this didn't occur with you whereas it did with them?"

"I can only speculate," Kirshbaum said. "I know in my experience working with therapists who are inexperienced with disabilities, especially young people, it is very common for people who are inexperienced with disabilities to have difficulties with their sexuality. One of the main stereotypes that is involved with disabilities is that disabled people should be asexual. Parenthood, in fact, from my research, is even more threatening than sexuality."

Kirshbaum recalled her years as a family therapist with the Center for Independent Living, where she counseled bright young people like Tiffany who, if they detected a disapproving look or a dubious tone of voice, reacted strongly. "It wasn't unusual," she said, "to see disabled people picking up the nuances of people not being able to tolerate their sexuality, and putting out a lot of that material, sort of acting out with that when they were young."

Bedford referred Kirshbaum to the report by Terry Johnston, one of the other psychologists, which mentioned Tiffany's "terrible fears of being alone." He asked, "Is that common among people with disabilities?"

"Yes," Kirshbaum said, "I think it is common with a number of people with especially severe disabilities, understandably, you know, if you are needing to depend on outside assistance for your physical care, and also given that in society disabled people are stigmatized socially to such an extent, I think that is common in clinical work with perfectly normal disabled people."

"In that sense, the fact that Ms. Callo has a fear of being alone would not be significant to you?"

"The issue of dependency, and conflicts around independence and dependency, and fears of being alone, are extremely common in a normal population of disabled people in clinical work."

He asked her about Barkouki's description of Tiffany as "extremely vivacious and dramatic."

"In my first session with her there was a slight performing aspect, which I always expect with an intelligent person," Kirshbaum said, "but basically she did not behave in a dramatic or labile way with me."

Johnston, Bedford noted, had complained about Tiffany trying to feed Jesse while he lay on his stomach. "I never saw her feed in that position," Kirshbaum said. "It was a real pattern to the feeding, and always she was very careful about burping him."

She recalled Tiffany's insistence on feeding the baby while he lay on his side to prevent him from choking if he spit up. "A lot of disabled parents do feed their babies on their back because sometimes that is for severely disabled people a more practicable position that is workable. But Tiffany was extremely cautious on that point, and she was always very careful to have him on his side, usually had him propped up with a blanket."

"And I assume that feeding a child on its side is appropriate?"

"There is nothing wrong with that."

Bedford asked about Johnston's contention that Tiffany failed to change Jesse's diaper, even after noting he was wet. "She always changed him when I was there," she said. "That was a large part of our work together, so she was always doing that, she did that each session."

Kirshbaum quickly dismissed Johnston's statement that Tiffany made no attempt to burp Jesse. In her own report Johnston described Tiffany placing the baby on a pillow and rubbing his back. It was "a feasible way of burping him," Kirshbaum said. "In fact, he always burped in that position. It is a contradiction right there."

Johnston had accused Tiffany of "force-feeding" Jesse. Kirshbaum bristled. "I just thought that was a very inaccurate description of what she had previously described, and a very judgmental and exaggerated way of stating it. In all of the feedings that Tiffany did, I had never seen anything of that nature."

Kirshbaum knew enough about the juvenile protection business, the legal reallocation of young lives, to realize what forces were at work. She could not resist delivering a short lecture to a room full of experts on the subject. "Now, overfeeding a baby for comforting when a foster mother has just previously fed a baby is not an unusual thing to do," she said. "I think the natural impulse of a mother is to want to feed her baby. Many, many, many mothers who have custody of their babies overfeed their babies for comforting."

She remembered doing it herself when Noah came back from the hospital and they told her to make sure he didn't cry. What an awful thing to tell a parent! She had asked that the babies not be fed before being brought to Tiffany so that her feeding exercises had some chance of success, but the message did not always reach the foster parents.

Johnston's "force-feeding" comment really bothered her. Her tone of voice sharpened. "I think it is just, the phrase there is just extremely hostile," she said, "and not an accurate representation of what she previously described, so I found it a little bit surprising."

Bedford asked about Barkouki's complaint that Tiffany had not established "a clearly positive relationship with David" despite a year of weekly meetings. Kirshbaum said, "From the beginning I have viewed the visitation pattern that occurred to be extremely inappropriate, inadequate in its frequency and in an inappropriate setting, almost completely in a non-home setting. So I think it was predestined—what is the word?—predetermined how that is going to turn out."

She paused to think of a way she might underline her irritation. "If you wanted to set up a situation where you have a poor outcome between a parent and baby, you would set it up like that with a disabled parent and baby."

What about Tiffany's lack of empathy, as characterized by the psychologists? Bedford asked.

"From the very first visit there were examples of empathic talk to her babies," Kirshbaum said. On February 4, her notes showed, Tiffany was full of encouragement for Jesse during a long diapering change. "I know this is hard," Tiffany had said. "I'm sorry it is taking so long, Jesse."

Kirshbaum gave another short lecture on the hazards of evaluating disabled parents without full awareness of their history and habits. If an evaluator noticed unusual silence from a disabled parent during a diaper change, it might reflect a healthy reaction to their situation that would have no real bearing on the upbringing of the child.

"In our research we note in situations where a parent is what we call 'adaptively stressed,'" she said. When performing a chore like dressing or diapering that takes an unusual amount of time and concentration, "you see less interactive sensitivity, just like when you are preoccupied with anything.

"Sometimes you will notice that parents who usually talk really nicely to their babies and be interactive will be completely silent with their babies during a change," she said. "Completely appropriate, psychologically normal parents can be very silent and insensitive to the cues of the baby, like one of the parents that we videotaped with severe CP. As she changes her baby it is as if she lost all of her interactive skills with her baby."

She glanced over at Clark. "If you assess—or if you take too seriously the assessment during that kind of situation and don't weigh it, balance it, with looking at the situation in less stressed times, then you get a real inaccurate evaluation of the relationship between the parents and baby."

Bedford read another psychological indictment: "an overidealized attachment to the therapist, making childlike demands and becoming angry if these demands are not met, run away from treatment as her basic conflicts were being denied."

"She definitely has not had that pattern with me so far," Kirshbaum said. "She has never been overdemanding with me. All of this stuff, these descriptions of insatiable needs and demanding—in my experience with her, there has been no evidence of that."

Bedford liked the way the afternoon was going. Kirshbaum had blurred, and in many instances erased, the image of his client as a crazed juvenile hopeless in the presence of her children.

But he had not confronted the videotape, the county's trump card. Tiffany's excruciatingly slow pace as she diapered David, painful to an uninitiated observer, required context and an explanation. Edwards had been given the tape that morning, and Bedford could not allow him to watch it without taking him first, with Kirshbaum's help, into the sea-bottom world of the disabled.

Bedford's witness was ready for this. He asked for her observations on the tape, more of a cue than a question.

Kirshbaum thought for a moment, collecting herself. "I think that it is important for people to know about the pacing that happens with disabled parents." Tiffany listened very carefully. This seemed to her the heart of much of her irritation with the outside world, the impatience she sensed in able-bodied people. It was magnified several times, she imagined, in those who wrote the reports for her file and watched that damned tape.

"Their diapering is very slow," Kirshbaum said. "The professionals, nondisabled professionals, can get very judgmental about that, but it focuses on the slowness of the enterprise, and indeed there can be incredible slowness in the care. But the fact is that parents and babies can get through that in a very appropriate way."

She looked at Bedford. "In some ways the slow pacing, which is, in the disabled community, sometimes called 'crip time,' in different families seems to be almost a cultural characteristic of a slower-paced life, slower-paced approach to work, more tolerance of slow pacing.

"In some ways," she said, "I think this is advantageous to babies because it helps to maximize their own functioning, their own mobilizing."

That month Kirshbaum had published a long paper on her experience with Tiffany and other mothers. It had a message for anyone quick to disparage the ability of a parent to care for his or her child. Watch the child, Kirshbaum said, before being moved by old assumptions to snatch the child away.

"It is usual for the children of disabled parents to consider their parents' disability equipment, wheelchairs, reachers, etc., an ordinary part of their environment," Kirshbaum wrote. "A reacher is twirled like a baton, a wheelchair is usually a wonderfully entertaining and useful object.

"I think we have much to learn from the children of disabled parents; from their viewpoint the definition of childhood can often include disability in a matter-of-fact way."

Bedford began to dissect the DSS videotape of September 22, 1987. He asked about the snaps on the pajamas David, then six months old, had worn.

"I would never use the kind of clothing he was wearing," Kirshbaum said. "It was about as bad as you can get in working with parents with her disability. It was amazing that she could do it at all."

"And once you worked with Ms. Callo in terms of diapering Jesse, was she able to do it in a time-appropriate fashion?"

"It is slow," Kirshbaum said. "I am not saying that her pacing and diapering is not slow, but what I am saying is that it is feasible to be a parent with a baby with such slow pacing, and that can be worked out fine in the relationship, and I have seen that many times."

"Did you observe during the slow period that it took Tiffany to change diapers and get the pajamas back on, did you observe any acts she was doing that were beneficial to David?"

Kirshbaum recalled two other mothers she had observed, both with severe cerebral palsy. "Her skills were better than both of those mothers in what we call 'bridging strategies' and eliciting cooperation from her baby to help her baby be patient through the long change."

She had expected the tape to show some of the diminished sensitivity, the preoccupied, spaced-out look, that often came over disabled mothers when carrying out a complicated maneuver. A mother might have so little control and self-confidence that she would fall into a battle with the child, grimly trying to force the baby to hold still.

Instead, the DSS tape showed Tiffany talking to David, praising him for his patience, offering him a toy. If anything, it was not Tiffany's disability that interfered with her progress, but the skills trainer who had been assigned to teach her what to do. The trainer "was doing more than she needed to do, and sometimes in an interfering way, sometimes interfering with things that I thought Tiffany had done that were good."

Tiffany had stopped at one point during the taping to chat with the baby, but the trainer objected and hurried her on.

"Actually," Kirshbaum said, "the breakup of care is something that we facilitate in such situations, that there is a little break of relating to the baby, then the baby can kind of carry on and be more patient, and the whole thing can turn out nicer between them. She was doing techniques without having been taught by anyone that I know."

The trills and coos echoed in Kirshbaum's mind. "It was her vocalizing to the baby that I was really impressed with, and her praise of the baby that showed a lot of strength in her acts with the baby in one of the most stressful situations when parents often look really terrible who look great otherwise.

"It is the kind of thing that I saw her doing with me all of the time, during every single diapering she did things like this, and she was very much in tune and sensitive to her babies at these times, which I have found to be very stressful times."

Whoever had set up the diapering taping seemed determined that Tiffany fail. "It was a horrendous setting for doing it," Kirshbaum said. "A diaper change with a rolling, pivoting baby, and there were three dropoffs on each side, and no one bothered to put the table in the corner.

"I would have at least put the table in the corner and put some things to block off one side of it so she just had one open side in front of her. I would never recommend that position, and it seems a really odd position to assess someone in."

Tiffany had seen the point immediately. During the assessment she had felt herself the captive of the evaluator's impatience and interest in setting up the camera. She rarely changed the baby on the kitchen table, and was only trying to accommodate the camera operator, who wanted the baby in a good light.

Kirshbaum mentioned several other small triumphs in their work with the boys. Tiffany had learned how to pull Jesse around the floor on a blanket, rather than dragging him by an arm or leg. They talked of ordering pajamas with Velcro fastenings and perhaps designing their own supervest, an all-purpose garment with hooks and hand clasps perfect for lifting small babies.

In Kirshbaum's last session with mother and sons, a slight change in Jesse's expression had brought a firm note to Tiffany's voice. "Jesse's getting hungry, Megan," she said. "Can you hand me the bottle?"

Kirshbaum had seen nothing to indicate hunger and thought

the infant had been fed before he arrived. She looked more closely. Jesse was making a small, almost imperceptible inward kissing motion, as if his lips were sore.

"Look," Tiffany said, somewhat impatient, "the kid's starving."

Kirshbaum fetched the bottle and gave it to her. Tiffany shifted her position so she could lightly, if somewhat awkwardly, steer the plastic nipple toward the baby's lips.

He clamped on and sucked greedily, soon emptying the bottle. Kirshbaum made a note. The woman knew her child.

Michael Clark, deputy county counsel, had done little to interrupt Kirshbaum's testimony. He had maintained a lawyerly reserve throughout the case, perhaps because he thought it unlikely he would lose.

Bedford had been able to ruffle him only once, and that was outside the courtroom when a polite discussion of procedure deteriorated into a shouting match over the county's motives. "You know what you guys are doing?" Bedford said. "You're in the baby market business. You've got two cute, adoptable kids here and you don't want to let them go."

Clark looked at Bedford in disbelief, angrily denied the charge, and walked off, ending the conversation.

In court Clark resumed his serene demeanor. But he had to do something about Kirshbaum. If she was to be the key support for Bedford's case, some sharpened cross-examination was necessary in order to whittle her down.

"Now, Dr. Kirshbaum, you hold a Ph.D. in clinical psychology?" Clark asked.

"Mm-hmm," she said, nodding her head.

"Are you licensed by the state of California?"

"Mm-hmm, I have an MFCC license."

"You didn't answer my question."

"No," she said.

"Are you licensed by the state of California to practice clinical psychology?"

"No, I am not a clinical psychologist."

"Are you licensed in the National Registry of Health Care Providers?"

"No."

"Now, in the course of your graduate work at the Union Graduate School, what special training did you receive in parent/child bonding?"

"I did a great deal of work on my graduate degree in that area through my—"

Clark interrupted. "Let me go back and ask the question again. I said in your training at the Union School while you were doing your Ph.D. work in clinical psychology, what training did you receive there in conducting parent/child bonding studies?"

"I did my training, my internship at the Children's Health Council, which was part of my graduate Ph.D. program, and my work with a pediatrician/neurologist named Tom Forrest, who was on my committee at Stanford. All of that was intensive training as a person who specializes in infant/parent bonding and interaction and development, and that was the nature of all the studies during that period of my Ph.D. program."

Clark persisted. "My original question was, what courses you had taken at Union—"

"Well, I don't have—"

"—dealing with parent/child bonding. Do you remember taking any?"

Kirshbaum refused to back down. "It wasn't called that, but that was the content of it, that was working on attachments and interaction as an infant specialist in clinical work with infants in that setting."

Bedford, sitting and watching, guessed that Clark was going to dip into the psychological tests again to see if he could shake Kirshbaum's confidence. Kirshbaum felt as if she had been up all night with a sick child. She had not undergone such an interrogation since she defended her doctoral thesis. She was uncomfortable and tired and hungry, and not terribly happy with the vague and often contradictory nature of the questions she was being asked.

Tiffany rooted quietly for the psychologist and admired her stamina, but she found her mind wandering to the boys. She wondered what they were doing at that moment.

"To what extent would the presence or absence of psychological disorder in the parent bear on child bonding?" Clark asked.

Kirshbaum blinked, thought for a moment, and then allowed herself to be openly irritated. "I think that is an unanswerable question. How could I answer that question?"

"You don't understand the question?"

"I understand it. I just think there is no answer to that. How am I supposed to determine to what extent that could be?"

"Okay," he said. "If you are preparing an evaluation and you are assessing the level of bonding between a parent and child, would it matter to you whether or not the parent suffered from any psychological disorders?"

"Yes."

"And why would that matter to you?"

She decided that it was not entirely Clark's fault that she was so weary. She tried to cooperate, looking for some way to frame the question that might have meaning. "If I had to determine, if I knew that to be true, why would that matter to me?" she suggested.

"Yes," Clark said.

She thought for a moment. There was no hope for it. "There is something strange about that question, too. There is something really fuzzy about that question. Can you try that again?"

Clark persisted: "If a parent has a personality disorder, and, let's say that the parent along with that personality disorder shows evidence of a stress disorder of paranoid traits, of narcissistic personality traits . . ."

My goodness, Tiffany thought, to whom could he be referring?

". . . how would those impact the process of bonding between a parent and a child?"

"That is a completely different question. Is that the question you want answered?"

Clark smiled. "Please," he said.

"Okay," Kirshbaum said, concentrating. "It would, if these

things were true, if those diagnoses were true, affect the bonding with the child. It would affect the interaction with the child, and you should be able to pick that up in sustained observations of the parent and baby's interaction in a really concrete, nitty-gritty way, the way I was observing it."

She recalled how she had detected some psychological problems in parents simply by noting how difficult it was for them to form a working relationship with her. "They frequently are not able to hold the relationship between session to session," she said, "and you have to reestablish the rapport between them every single time you go. That was not true with Tiffany."

Clark seemed ready to quit. Kirshbaum would not waver in her reluctance to focus on psychological disorders. It was too pathological. She preferred to present both strengths and weaknesses.

Clark's questions had triggered more memories, and Kirshbaum rolled on, too tired to stop. She did not want to leave the stand until she had explained to Edwards everything she thought was important about Tiffany's reaction to what was the greatest crisis of her young life.

"She is very, very strong and very capable in responding to her babies when she is given some hope," Kirshbaum said. Tiffany smiled and Kirshbaum felt herself energized by her client's encouragement. She spoke as much to Tiffany as to the court.

"I think she has been without hope in relationship to her babies," Kirshbaum said, "so I think that she is having more difficulty with a baby who is very unhappy and crying, and feeling basically maybe someone else had better take care of this, and maybe could do it better than I can, and handing them over and not retaining a lot of central focus as a parent."

It was true, Kirshbaum said, that Tiffany often magnified in her own mind her four weeks with David after his birth and her brief moments with him since. "I found this very poignant," Kirshbaum said. "I found this very understandable, and maybe functional in the sense that she is trying to maintain that sense of her motherness with him, building it up and exaggerating the tiny fragments of contact with him into something bigger than it was."

She looked at Tiffany again. It was important that this young parent, any parent, recognize that there was nothing wrong with hope, as well as nothing wrong with admitting weaknesses and dealing with them. Both Tiffany and Kirshbaum were thinking about the day on Tenth Street when a mother had come down from her chair and rediscovered her son.

Kirshbaum turned back to the county's attorney. "She was trying to think of parenting him in the future," she said. "You could view that as very functional, even though it does involve denial and distortion, but it may be functional in terms of preserving the relationship, and it was very moving."

17

Tiffany thanked Kirshbaum and Jakobson, checked the hearing schedule with Bedford, and left Courtroom No. 1 as fast as she could. She rolled through the inner and outer lobbies, up the ramp to Guadalupe Road, and turned south toward downtown.

Teddy had gone to work and she wanted to join him. A few hours punching telephone buttons and sweetly singing the praises of long-term light bulbs might cleanse her mind of psychological multisyllables and lawyerly circumlocution.

She was weary of the legal process, but she had been thrilled by Kirshbaum's testimony. The woman had seemed fragile and uncertain at first, opening-night jitters, perhaps. But her answers gradually gained momentum until, by the end, Tiffany felt like waving pom-poms and singing a fight song. She welcomed any evidence that David, Jesse, and she could share some sort of life together, be connected by something more substantial than the blue pigment of their irises.

She hoped work at United Handicapped would quiet the worrisome flurries of doubt, like mosquitoes on a warm night, that distracted her whenever she fantasized about her future with her sons.

It seemed so simple when she reread her news clippings piling up in a shoebox in the apartment. She would get the boys back, and live happily ever after, or she would not get them back, and resign herself to bitterness and regret.

But that was not the way Bedford explained it.

The lawyer was honest about his excitement at the attention the case was receiving. The constitutional issues were unique. The county's defensiveness was encouraging.

Bedford was the one young court-appointed counsel in ten thousand who had a chance to take his case to the U.S. Supreme Court. There would be more articles, news bites, maybe even a movie. Both he and Tiffany liked the idea of traveling and meeting more people.

But Bedford, while enjoying the carnival, had always reminded Tiffany that it would eventually end and she would still have to make a choice.

First, she could fight the case to its legal conclusion. As strong as Kirshbaum had been, and as sympathetic as Edwards seemed, Bedford did not expect to win at this level. At the most, and it was the slimmest chance, Edwards might give Tiffany custody of Jesse, but that could be so delayed by appeals and other red tape that it would be wrong for her to count on it.

He needed to add as much evidence about disabled parenting as possible to the court record. He needed help from senators Marks and McCorquodale, whose bill was still alive in Sacramento. He had to find some way to fortify his argument that the county was overlooking resources it already had for reuniting mothers and children. His principal constitutional issue on appeal would be the violation of due process represented by the county's, and the court's, reliance on psychological tests that had not been designed for disabled people. The legal maneuvers, he told Tiffany, could last as long as seven or eight years.

Even if the courts eventually agreed with him on the constitutional issues, the judges would probably still leave the boys with their foster families on the grounds that, after so much time, it would exact too much emotional cost to uproot them. And if by some chance the boys were returned to her seven years hence, she faced the personal ordeal of reconciling with two bewildered, frightened children who had seen her only periodically for half of their childhoods.

She loved the boys, and she liked Judy and Angelo, the foster parents who had them. Would she be capable of hurting all of them?

If, after a long legal struggle, she lost her case, the county could easily cut her off from any further contact with her sons, particularly if the struggle had turned bitter and the foster parents no longer wished to deal with her.

Her second choice was to make a deal. Her relationship with Judy was excellent. Bedford thought the county would accept an agreement letting Tiffany see her sons twice a year. Judy had promised to explain to them who their natural mother was and why they had been given to another family. Tiffany was intimately familiar with the etiquette and rhythms of life in a foster home. As a child she had been able to balance the emotional demands of having more than two parents, of being part of a family and something more. Perhaps her sons could too. Tiffany realized that she as a parent could adjust to that awkward system much better than her father had.

The endless calculations whirled inside her head. She found it annoying that Bedford balanced so carefully the arguments for every course of action. In conscientiously suppressing his own eagerness to take the case all the way to Washington, he had left her confused about what he wanted. He forced her to solve the equation, to provide the emotional weight that would swing the scale one way or the other.

Sometimes she argued with him. She was so accustomed to receiving discouraging advice from people close to her that she assumed he was urging her to give up. "There is a higher court," she said heatedly. "I'm not stupid, you know."

"Yes," he said, unwilling to back off the point. "But I'm worried that if this goes to the Supreme Court, we're going to lose and then you might never in your life ever again be able to see your children."

Bedford was glad she could not detect his strong interest in going forward. He felt she had to make the decision herself.

After the long day in court and three hours at Handicapped

Workers, she felt as if she had been encased in concrete and dropped into the bay. At home, she could barely lift her head. She asked Teddy to feed her some soup, but she could only take a little of it before feeling ill. Her head hurt and she began to cough.

She played the choice game, her version of Russian roulette. There were four choices, she thought, only one of them very good. She could lose both boys. She could lose just David. She could lose just Jesse. She could win both boys, someday, maybe.

There were moments when she thought that Bedford, like nearly everyone else, treated her like a child. He explained the alternatives to her repeatedly. He seemed to forget that she had had a great deal more firsthand contact with the juvenile court system than he had had.

She was not certain she could recall clearly what had motivated the frightened teenager she once was to bounce around the foster-care system. In hindsight, it might have been better if she had returned to her father. But that system and those years had their own logic, and forced her to reflect on what her father's struggle to win her back had gotten him. Not much, she thought.

Patty helped lift her into bed. She let her unhappy choices dance about in front of her eyes for a few minutes before she tumbled, with a slight headache, into sleep.

She awoke terrified, full of some unmentionable fear. She moaned and began to weep. She felt like screaming but could not summon the energy for it. Patty ran in to comfort her. In a few moments she quieted down. She could remember the dream, and thought she knew what it meant.

She had been a ghostly presence in someone else's house. From the look of the big television set, the clean furniture, and the scattered toys and blankets, it was Judy's house. She could see the foster mother sitting at the kitchen table. Tiffany knew somehow that this was a little window looking five or six years into the future.

As she watched, a boy who was unmistakenly David, if somewhat taller and huskier, ran into the kitchen. He seemed to have just woken up and was upset.

"Mommy," he said to Judy, "where's brother? Where is Jesse? Where he go?"

Tiffany's dreaming subconscious supplied the context. This was a future world in which she had won what Bedford often called her best shot—some temporary custody of Jesse while the courts slowly digested the issue of permanent placement of both boys.

It did not seem to have brought much happiness to her elder son's life. "Mommy got brother back, and Mommy not want me?" the dark-haired child said. "Why was I so bad that Mommy didn't want me?"

Judy, soft and consoling as usual, tried to calm him. Tiffany could not hear her words clearly. Her son's anguish seemed to reverberate in her skull.

She had torn her family apart while trying to save it. She had no good answer to the boy's question, and neither did Judy.

Tiffany took a deep breath and looked bleakly at Patty. "I'm going to lose them either way, aren't I," she said. It was a statement, not a question. Patty, cooking breakfast, looked over at her but did not respond.

Tiffany thought for a few more minutes. She had to have some plan. The hearings would proceed and Edwards would rule and some of her maneuvering room would be taken from her. Bedford had indicated that the earlier she decided, the more negotiating power she might have. She had to make up her mind soon.

She remembered the Bible stories from her childhood. She recalled the faces of the preachers and Sunday-school teachers. The Baptists used to pick her up in a bus. Elnora read to her from Catholic devotional books kept on a living room shelf. The Mormons gathered at the Howell house. They had told their stories with slightly different emphases, but she remembered the one that had occurred to her more than once in the last several months.

Her mind seemed to retain the King James version best:

The one saith, This is my son that liveth, and thy son is the dead, and the other saith, Nay, but thy son is the dead, and my son is the living.

And the king said, Bring me a sword. And they brought a sword before the king.

And the king said, Divide the living child in two, and give half to the one, and half to the other.

Like the mother in the story, she faced the rich king with the long beard. He was wisdom personified, an ancient embodiment of all the lawyers and psychologists and social workers and doctors strung out through her life in courtrooms, hospitals, county offices, and schoolrooms. She could not outwit such people. She had to listen to her heart, with all its moody fluctuations, and find the core of what she held dear.

"That's it," she said. "I'm not going to put my babies through any more of this crap. I'm going to do what they want."

Patty sat down at the kitchen table and examined Tiffany's face for some clue to how she should react to this decision. Tiffany sniffed and wiped her nose. She did not feel like crying anymore. She had to conserve her strength. Maybe there was still some respite. Maybe the county would give up the minute she rolled into the courtroom. Maybe she would sell her chair for scrap and join the Rockettes.

Patty decided what she wanted to say. "I know it's hard, Mommy," she said. "But you know what? You're probably right."

It was not the heartiest endorsement Tiffany had ever heard, but she could see the other woman meant well. "Yeah," she said, "I think so, but that makes it all the harder to do."

Teddy took the early bus from his mother's house and met Tiffany outside the apartment building for the long walk to the courthouse. She told him about the dream and her decision. It still seemed tentative to her. She could not discard her last hope that someone would find a way out.

Teddy was heartbroken at the thought of losing the boys. He knew how much Tiffany disliked the legal proceedings and how much she loathed the idea of subjecting her children to the uncertainties of her own youth. But he loved the boys. They brought a sparkle to his life. Only the thought that she could bargain for regular visits sustained him.

She pushed through the buzzer door into the inner courtroom lobby and looked for Silvani. She saw her in a corner of the room, her lean frame folded into one of the plastic blue chairs as she fiddled with the paperwork she often brought to court.

"Shirley," she said. "Can I talk to you?"

The older woman looked at her expectantly.

"Okay," Tiffany said. "I'm willing to do it your way." She was not enjoying this. The words were not coming easily. "If I can't have both, I don't think I should take either, 'cause it isn't fair. I don't want one aching over losing the other."

Silvani said nothing. She knew Tiffany's rhythms, and waited patiently while the young woman plucked out, bit by bit, everything she wanted to say.

Tiffany raised her voice for emphasis: "But I *want them in the same house,* swear to God."

Silvani waited to see if there was more, then asked a question: "Did you talk about this with your lawyer?"

"No," she said. "But we've talked about this before. He said it was up to me. I just want to cut through all this stuff and decide it, right now."

This was so typical of Tiffany's impatience with DSS that Silvani laughed. She seemed to be feeling a great relief, which amused Tiffany, who rarely saw her so relaxed and happy.

"I think this is a good decision, Tiffany," she said. "I think it will help."

Tiffany did not reply. She felt her mood blackening as the weight of her sacrifice pressed down. Silvani would handle it, as she had been eager to do from the beginning. Tiffany would have to fight a rearguard action to maintain contact with two children Bedford had always said would be prime merchandise on the adoption market.

Bedford arrived late, so she waited until a recess to tell him. She could see, somewhat to her surprise, a touch of disappointment. "That's not what I wanted, but I know it has to be done," he said.

She felt as if she was sleepwalking through the hearing, as if her dream had taken over her life. She was a ghost haunting the courtroom and all that was said there left her without a shred of pain or even curiosity.

Teddy joined her as she rolled out to Guadalupe, turned south on the sidewalk toward downtown. She stopped to pull him down to her for a kiss. "Honey, when we get to a phone, can you call work and tell them I'm not going to be in today?"

Teddy smiled. "Sure, hon," he said. "You ought to take it easy."

She was so numb she wondered if her head was still on her shoulders. Perhaps God was using it for a basketball, or Silvani had saved it to shrink and hang from her office door.

Sooner or later, she knew, it was going to hit her. "You know," she said to Teddy as they resumed their trek south, "I'm glad I don't have money stashed in a savings account or a checking account. I'm so numb right now, so wrung out from all this bull, I don't know what I'm going to do next. If I had some money, I'm almost sure I would have died tonight because I'd probably be at the bottom of a bottle and nobody could have pulled me out of that one."

Teddy felt queasy and frightened. She saw the look on his narrow face, his eyelids fluttering. She smiled, a toothy grin that ended a millimeter short of a grimace. "But I'm not going to do that," she said. "Not ever. Because I've got you here, and you are some hope for me, as well as help. That's the way I need to stay."

He walked her home and helped put her to bed. They kissed good-bye and Teddy walked out toward the bus stop.

He was happy that she had reached a decision, but it was going to cost them a great deal. He was going to miss the boys. They had been a start on the dream of a family. Perhaps that was what this moment was also, a start.

For the next several months Tiffany thought about where her life should turn. She tried to keep her balance, a skater doing figure eights over an icy surface of disappointment and disagreeable detail.

The Social Security Administration informed her that her SSI payments would be reduced by the amount she was earning at United Handicapped Workers. She had enjoyed the work and thought it had demonstrated how serious she was about earning a living for her family, but if there was no financial advantage, she thought she ought to use the time to complete her high-school work.

Her dilemma was one shared by many disabled people seeking self-sufficiency, even those with advanced degrees and offers of good jobs. Paul Longmore, a professor of history and noted author, faced a similar problem. A childhood bout with polio had rendered his arms useless and forced him to sleep with a ventilator. His teaching career had prospered, and he had just published a book on George Washington. But the rules said that if he earned more than twenty-three thousand dollars a year, he lost the benefits that paid for the equipment that kept him alive.

In most cases, private companies would not insure the disabled. Longmore's choices appeared to be either to resign himself to a life of volunteer work or pay for the medical equipment himself and ration carefully the little money left for food and lodging. Deborah McKeithan, founder of Handicapped Organized Women, said, "Let's face it. Self-worth depends on how much you get paid. I'm tired of being a volunteer!"

Bills introduced in Congress would allow disabled people to break out of the trap by working and buying Medicare insurance on a sliding scale. "Defining disability as a total inability to work no longer makes sense," Longmore said.

Bedford, Heather Hyde, the county attorney representing David and Jesse, and Margaret S. Johnson, the attorney for Judy and Angelo, spent several weeks discussing the language of the agreement on custody. On August 25 Johnson sent Bedford a letter attached to a final draft:

This agreement is for visitation by Tiffany Callo with the children and assumes a legal relinquishment of parental rights to the children by Tiffany Callo and a legal adoption of the children by [the foster parents].

Tiffany Callo has the right to two visits with the children each calendar year. These visits are to be of no longer than four hours duration and shall be supervised by an adult to be selected by Angelo and Judy. . . . Tiffany Callo shall initiate the visit by contacting the Adoption Unit of the Department of Social Services no sooner than five months after the last visit.

Tiffany scanned it and felt a bleak sense of completion. They seemed to have thought of everything, in their inhuman little way. The adoption unit or the court would mediate disputes. One paragraph struck her as bizarre:

Birthday or Christmas cards may be sent by Tiffany Callo to the children through the Adoption Unit of the Department of Social Services, and shall be given to the children. Any other correspondence from Tiffany Callo to the children shall be given to the children at the discretion of [the foster parents].

No one who knew Judy and Angelo could conceive of them withholding anything from those boys, particularly a cheerful card from that wheelchair lady they knew. Judy had agreed to tell the boys who Tiffany was when they asked. As long as Tony was out of the picture, which seemed likely considering his own appeals were being rejected, Judy was happy to welcome Tiffany to the periphery of her life. After a decade of watching television dramas about adopted children in anguished searches for their natural mothers, Judy thought this was a way to avoid much unnecessary pain.

The campaign for disabled parents inspired by Tiffany's case continued to grow. There was talk about a broader approach to child placement, perhaps expanding the idea of spending foster-care money on special treatment to handle all families about to lose their children. If a little more help had enabled Tiffany to keep

David and Jesse, who was to say it might not also have helped keep a child like Tiffany with a parent like Bob Callo?

The fears and the arguments and the erratic history of her life seemed to be turning in on themselves. She saw connections to her struggle everywhere she looked. As she and Teddy began to look at business opportunities to support them while they took turns returning to school, she read more about the disability rights movement, alcoholism, and dysfunctional families. She saw ways she might be able to help.

In January 1989, a year after Jesse's birth, Tiffany traveled to New York with Teddy and Bedford to appear on "Donahue" for a discussion of disabled parenting that convinced her that the future was much less predictable and more hopeful than she had imagined.

The two other women guests she met on the show inspired both sad memories and happy thoughts. She was pleased that people still felt that what had happened to her was important. The questions were, with some exceptions, supportive and encouraging, and she had rarely seen so many friendly faces in one place.

By the end of the hour, almost all the questions from audience members and telephone callers had been addressed to Tiffany. She was the liveliest and most attractive of the three guests, a press agent's dream. Phil Donahue, apparently warned to expect fireworks, treated her as gingerly as a letter bomb, but she was light and funny, and inspired laughter with guileless answers to Donahue's sometimes convoluted questions.

Yet she did not have her sons with her, while the two other women on the program, Debra Weston and Patty Cecere, each with some disabilities more severe than her own, had brought with them sons whom they had been allowed to raise.

Weston had the Hallerman-Streiff-Francois syndrome, a type of premature aging which produced dwarfism, small eyes, baldness, prominent nose, receding chin, and cataracts. She had had plastic surgery to reduce the number of sickening stares and, by artificial insemination, conceived and gave birth to her son, Casey, who did not share his mother's condition.

Cecere had Down's syndrome and appeared on the show with her husband, Tony, who had a learning disability. Despite opposition by others, they had married and had their son, Danny, also with Down's syndrome, five years before. Danny had been taken away in the hospital, but the courts and the child welfare authorities in Buffalo, where they lived, had drafted an unusual training and visiting schedule to bring him back.

Bruce Goldstein, Cecere's attorney, said that in the beginning, the couple was able to visit Danny three hours at a time for parenting training. "Then they brought Danny home for three hours at a time, then it was six hours at a time, then overnight," Goldstein said. "And they got all the training so that after a year, finally the judge ordered that Danny could come home with Patty and Tony and that they were able to take care of him, and services were brought in to assist them in the home to take care of him."

To Tiffany, these were tales from a better world, a sign that there were social workers on the planet who might allow her to raise a child. She recognized the crucial differences: Weston had no physical disability, other than poor eyesight, to keep her from parenting. The New York authorities who handled the Cecere case probably recognized that they would have had difficulty permanently placing a Down's syndrome child anywhere other than his parents' home. But they had each found a way.

Tiffany, who was wrestling with a bad cold, gripped a purple handkerchief in her left hand and tried not to sneeze. She was wearing a black suit, with the jacket open, and a silk blouse. She sat in her standard chair, since her power chair had been too wide for the airplane aisle.

"Who should have a baby and who should not?" Donahue said, his arms raised in his favorite interrogative pose. "And if you feel that some people should not have a baby, who should decide, and under what circumstances?"

He moved through Weston's case quickly and then turned to Tiffany. "Have you read about Tiffany Callo? Lots of people have. She's from San Jose, California. You are twenty-one, Tiffany?"

Tiffany smiled and nodded. For about the five hundredth time in two years, she outlined the extent of her disability—spastic cerebral palsy, lower half of the body could feel but could not support her weight, bad hand coordination and vision. Her sons were in a foster home, which, she said, "has been really hard on me. But they're two beautiful kids. They have all my traits, if you see—"

Donahue tried to flirt. "Then they must be very beautiful," he said.

Tiffany grinned and plunged on. "If you see me with—on a visit with the kids, you can tell that they're my kids, you know."

The visits, she said, were "two hours max."

"And then you have to say good-bye," Donahue said.

"Yes," she said. "It's very difficult."

Bedford was introduced and summarized the legal history. There was much interest in disabled parenting now, he said, but for Tiffany and her two sons it had come too late.

"And the really sad part of it is if the children had been disabled," Bedford said, "there would have been state money to help them live with Tiffany. But the fact that they're both able-bodied, there's no money available to help design the equipment that she needed."

While Donahue deftly retrieved Tiffany's handkerchief from the studio floor, she and Bedford described David's bonding with Judy over the fourteen months between his removal and the custody hearing. She skipped lightly over her Solomon's choice and the agreement to have the brothers raised together.

Donahue moved on to the Cecere case, then asked the audience for questions. Joel Steinberg's manslaughter trial in the child-abuse slaying of his adoptive daughter Lisa was under way in New York. The horror of it hung in the air. "If Lisa Steinberg had been given to parents like this," one member of the audience said, "she'd still be alive today."

A woman with polio who raised four children called to express her support. A woman with cerebral palsy called to say that she had lost custody of her three children to her husband and had only been able to regain custody of the eldest, a fourteen-year-old daughter, "because she was supposedly, quote, old enough to take care of me."

At the end of the show, a woman in the audience had one last question: "Tiffany, what are your plans if you do have another child?"

It was a question she had many answers to. She could see herself and Teddy, lounging on a lawn, watching an infant take its first steps. But the woman wanted a more practical perspective, and Donahue, she sensed, would like something light to close an intense hour.

"What are my plans?" she said, grinning. "To have a whole lot of money and a good attorney."

Donahue gave Tiffany a good-bye kiss. The three Californians headed for their limousine. The typed schedule said they were to depart for the airport, but Bedford noticed they had three hours before their flight left. Why not see some of the city?

Tiffany and Teddy quickly agreed. The driver shrugged and took them over to Fifth Avenue, where they disembarked and strolled down the boulevard. In one shop Tiffany found purses for two hundred and fifty dollars each, a comforting sign that in certain parts of the country even her wealthiest relatives would feel poor. Bedford bought her a tiny vial of "Tiffany" perfume as a souvenir. He helped Teddy lift woman and chair up the stone steps of St. Patrick's Cathedral, where the two young Catholics admired the stratospheric ceilings, smoky icons, and candle-lit alcoves.

They stopped for hamburgers, and then, almost by accident, found themselves in Rockefeller Center, looking down into the skating rink that had graced a dozen of the Christmas television specials that Tiffany loved to watch. The weather had turned sunny, and although the breeze was chilly, Tiffany had forgotten her cold. She gazed at the skaters.

This was part of her dream. She would have ankles of supple steel, and twirl about some holiday-festooned rink while musicians played German carols and young men vied to be her partner. She hugged Teddy and whispered, "Don't you wish that could be us?"

Perhaps it was, she thought. She had kept her balance. She had found the measure of trust and compromise that would let her sons grow tall without losing sight of her. That very day she had glided across a slick studio floor and into the homes of hundreds of thousands of people she had never met. She had learned what she might do to have another baby and emerge this time a winner, the gold medalist for parenting on four wheels.

Bedford checked his watch and signaled that it was time to go. Teddy hugged her and turned the chair toward the limousine. She was flying.

18

On June 8, 1988, the California state senate passed the Marks-McCorquodale disabled parenting bill, SB 2762, by a 27–1 vote. On August 24 the state assembly passed the same measure 66–6. Tiffany heard the news from Bedford. It made her happy. Maybe some other mother would profit from her bad luck and slow start.

In order to tempt the fiscally conservative governor, George Deukmejian, to accept the idea, the sponsors had whittled down the initial five-hundred-thousand-dollar proposal to a pilot project in Alameda and Santa Clara counties that would cost no more than twenty-five thousand dollars to start and another hundred thousand to complete a three-year cycle. In the last two months before the bill was passed, nearly every major interest group dealing with disability rights announced support, and some of Tiffany's allies testified at committee hearings.

Deborah Kaplan left Desmond in her husband's care and wheeled into the senate appropriations committee to tell legislators they were wasting taxpayers' dollars fighting cases like Tiffany's. "First there is the cost of an investigation and case development by Children's Protective Services," she said. "Then there are costs in bringing the legal system into the situation: court costs, court-appointed attorney's fees and costs, and the attorneys representing the state. Most difficult to estimate, but perhaps more costly in the long run, are the fiscal and social costs of separating families, placing children into the foster-care system, and then the potential behavioral and delinquency problems of these children later in their lives."

No one ever bothered to estimate the total costs of Tiffany's fourteen-month struggle with DSS, but it was likely to have equaled the projected cost of Marks's modest bill. Kaplan reminded the senators that Tiffany would be only the first of many. As the independent-living movement spread throughout the country, she said, "there are more and more people with significant disabilities leading normal lives. That includes marrying and having children." Without some initial help, Kaplan said, "a rather modest need for intervention, adaptive equipment, or in-home support can become a much more serious problem, possibly endangering the well-being of the children in the family or the ability of the family to stay together."

Lonnie Nolta of the United Cerebral Palsy Association of California said, "Some children have been removed and placed in foster care without a realistic assessment of the family strengths, identification of the types of support services which might assist the parents in retaining the family unit, or options provided to the parents to enhance their parenting ability."

Megan Kirshbaum told the senate committee that her experience with 125 families with disabled parents had revealed "severe problems with professionals' abilities to accurately assess such parents." In the past year she had helped twenty-nine families with at least one disabled parent, including eight cases where children were in danger of being taken by child authorities.

The Marks bill authorized the pilot project counties to enlist the aid of groups like Through the Looking Glass to help disabled parents. This, Kirshbaum said, "could provide the first model of and data on private and public agency collaboration concerning disabled parents—an effort that would be likely to be replicated nationally."

The State Bar Legal Services Section, the Organization of Area Boards on Developmental Disabilities, and the State Council on Developmental Disabilities supported the bill. It sat on the governor's desk for a month. On September 26 Deukmejian issued a statement saying he was returning it unsigned, thus killing the bill.

"There are existing programs to assist individuals in maintaining an independent-living condition and keeping children in the home," Deukmejian said. "The state currently provides funding for such services as attendant care and independent-living skills training. I believe this proposal to establish a new program would duplicate existing services."

That was news to the people who had wrestled so long over David and Jesse. Kaplan, Kirshbaum, and Jakobson shook their heads and went back to work. This was to them just one setback in a very long campaign. Nolta, who thought she had developed a hard shell after a decade as a Sacramento lobbyist, was surprised at how disappointed she felt. She scolded herself for letting the euphoria of the landslide legislative votes convince her that they had a chance.

Tiffany did not hear the news immediately. She had enough problems as it was, for the county had reneged on what she had thought was its agreement to keep her sons together and had not even bothered to inform her. It was Tony, calling shortly after their divorce became final, who gave her the bad news.

She and Teddy had just moved to a tiny studio apartment off Nineteenth Street. The telephone rang with a call from Tony, full of charm and concern. "Honey," he said, "did you know that they moved Jesse?"

Tiffany's response was a hiss. "Get the hell out of my life," she said. "Don't ever call me on my phone."

"I just thought it was something you ought to know," he said.

She listened. The story was too wearingly familiar not to be true. Judy and Angelo had decided they could not keep Jesse and had returned him to DSS. The county had known that Judy would have trouble taking care of both boys and a little girl she already had. Silvani's log entries showed the foster mother had complained of the strain even before the hearing.

But DSS had not revealed these problems when Tiffany agreed to relinquish custody on condition that the boys be kept together. Once the department had her signature, she would have little choice but to accept its decision on placement, whatever its oral promises.

Jesse was soon placed with another couple. Tiffany met them and thought they were kind and considerate people. But communication with them and Jesse was limited by DSS rules.

A few months passed and Tony called again. Jesse's foster parents had decided to move out of the state and take Jesse with them.

Tiffany's agreement with the county still held. She was entitled to a visit every six months, but the distances were going to make this difficult.

Tiffany took the news of Jesse's out-of-state transfer very hard. She did not leave the apartment for three days. The foster parents assured her that Jesse and David would be reminded of each other's existence and allowed to see each other as the parents' schedules and budgets permitted. But this was just one more in a series of assurances that, in the past, had often fallen short.

Tiffany called Silvani and worked out her frustrations with a blistering barrage of accusations. Why did she have to hear this from Tony? Had Silvani decided to cut her off from her children permanently, agreements or not? Where was Jesse going? When could she see the boys? What the hell was going on?

It was the verbal equivalent of going into a gymnasium and doing thirty hard minutes with a punching bag. She felt a little better afterward. Teddy lay in bed with her and held her for hours. They talked about the child they would have someday, a skinny, brown-haired, blue-eyed wonder who would never see a social worker as long as he lived.

One year after David and Jesse were permanently removed from Tiffany's care, the California state legislature acknowledged the impending collapse of the national foster-care system by passing Assembly Bill 558. The legislation attempted to provide, in a broader, vaguer sense, the services that Tiffany had sought for herself in hopes of recovering her sons.

Legislators had been hearing stories like Tiffany's for years, although all of them involved mothers with fewer physical barriers to caring for their children and less desire to fight the system. Drugs, divorce, and a weakening social and religious commitment to the two-parent household had put far more children in government hands than child welfare agencies were equipped to care for.

By 1991 there would be 407,000 American children in foster care on any one day and 240,000 more housed in juvenile detention facilities, mental-health institutions, or other forms of out-of-home care. In 1989, when California passed and George Deukmejian signed AB 558, one of every 100 California children was in out-of-home placement. State child welfare officials calculated that the number of children under four in foster care had increased 165 percent in four years, and out-of-home placement of newborn babies had increased 235 percent.

The cost of out-of-home care in California alone approached $1 billion, and was expected to double by 1994. Yet the average monthly payment to a foster parent was only $540. Nationally, only 125,000 foster homes were available as the number of children thought to need foster care approached the half million mark.

AB 558 was another tentative effort to prove a point through pilot programs. Four counties were asked to experiment with devoting much more than the usual amount of time and money to rescuing a few families in danger of losing their children. About half the states in the country had begun to try forms of what was called the "family preservation" approach, inspired by the Tacoma, Washington, "Homebuilders" program created by psychologists Jill Kinney and David Haapala.

Some counties not included in the original bill, including Santa Clara, decided to go ahead with their own family preservation plans. James L. Fare, director of the Santa Clara Department of Family and Children's Services, and his boss, Richard R. O'Neil, director of the Social Services Agency—the new name for DSS—had been active in the movement to promote family preservation statewide and were impatient to begin in their own county.

They selected a supervisor, five of their best senior social

workers, four beginning social workers, and a teaching home-
maker for what they called an "intensive intervention" program.
The team was assigned ninety-seven families, each to receive an
array of services and advice over a ninety-day period. Each social
worker had a caseload of fewer than eight families, much less than
usual, and had the time for lengthy conversations with troubled
parents and daily checks on their progress.

If a mother felt helpless disciplining a hyperactive child, the
social worker could spend several days demonstrating techniques
and even pay a specialist. If a child needed medical attention, the
social worker would get him to the doctor. If the family had budget problems, the social worker would help the parents find jobs
and learn how to manage money. If the parents were quarreling, a
marital counselor would come to help them talk it out. Each senior social worker was in charge of seeking money or support hidden in odd corners of the welfare system that might help each
family's special problems, just the kind of work Bedford had
asked DSS to do for Tiffany in 1987.

After a year, only 5.2 percent of the families in the Santa Clara
program lost their children, a remarkable rate for people who had
had much previous contact with the child welfare system. Nearly
80 percent of the families completed at least half of their service
plan goals during the ninety days.

The most important political result of the experiment was the
cost. Fare and O'Neil calculated that for every dollar they spent
on the intensive program, they saved $1.72 in federal, state, and
county funds, not even counting court costs.

At the same time, the federal government took a surprisingly
large step to remove barriers to employment and mobility for Tiffany and the other 42 million Americans with significant disabilities. At a huge ceremony attended by two thousand people on the
South Lawn of the White House, on July 26, 1990, President Bush
signed the Americans with Disabilities Act, one of the most com-
prehensive and potentially expensive civil rights laws ever passed.

The law bore the stamp of Iowa Sen. Tom Harkin. His initial
proposal had been so radical, business lobbyists called it the "make
the world flat" bill. He eventually compromised with the Bush
administration on a law that required most businesses to provide

reasonable physical access for people with disabilities and banned job discrimination because of disabilities.

Some of the adjustments required by the bill would be expensive, Harkin said. But others would be quite easy. He told the story of his deaf brother, who complained during a hospital stay that no one responded when he pushed the nurse's call button. Harkin pushed it himself and heard a voice through a loudspeaker: "Hello. May I help you?"

In early 1991 the administration began to propose detailed rules for implementation of the law, including a requirement that five percent of hotel rooms be equipped for disabled guests, restaurants have strategically placed movable tables, and every supermarket checkout counter be wide and low enough for a wheelchair user.

As with other civil rights legislation, the ADA promised more than it had the power to achieve. Some of the administration's rules on employment seemed at odds with the new law's intent. The Equal Employment Opportunity Commission said a company did not have to help a worker if he might be "a danger to himself," a subjective judgment that could bar many productive people. The rules would also free employers from the need to help disabled workers use the restroom or eat lunch.

Mary Johnson, editor of *The Disability Rag,* said the rules turned the new law into "nothing more than an empty promise." That issue and a hundred more associated with the ADA would wind up in court, with lawyers arguing over economic costs and benefits while bright and resourceful people used the new law and whatever other leverage they could find to reveal something about themselves and the future.

The Tiffany Callo case is only one of many signals of a fitful, almost unconscious transformation of human culture to an era when physical strength and agility, even mobility, will be unnecessary for productive life. Tiffany and the many other disabled people are, in a way, rewriting the popular conception of Darwinism, survival of the fittest.

The number and variety of people affected is astonishing. Historian Paul K. Longmore has estimated that 18 million Americans have a physical handicap, including 7.4 million with limited or no use of their legs. The other disabilities include limits on hearing affecting 14.5 million people, limits on speech affecting 2 million, limits on sight affecting 1.7 million, and mental retardation affecting 6 million. He adds 12.5 million with learning disabilities not usually included in the total of 42.2 million. The ideological range of the disability rights movement is quite broad, from "Cure— Not Care" activists pushing for spinal cord research to wheelchair users resolved to a life on wheels who want all architectural barriers removed.

In a world so specialized that an entire field of science and engineering concerns itself with the twisted strands of a single molecule, in a world so automated that robots replace thousands of assembly workers each year, the most useful human talent in the next stage of history is likely to be analysis and decision.

There were many things that Tiffany can do already with just a motorized wheelchair and a telephone, the two principal tools of her existence. The cornucopia of gadgets inspired by the ADA is likely to produce a quantum leap in efficiency and creativity.

Nearly all the mechanical and some of the simpler intellectual functions of the body can be performed by computers. Keyboards can be manipulated by head-mounted spotlights, eye-sensitive cameras, or even by voice. A man in Oakland, California, with severe cerebral palsy produces elaborate digital maps on a computer despite his disability. A blind physicist working for the National Aeronautics and Space Administration designs interstellar communications equipment with a computer that reads and speaks. One of the world's most celebrated theoretical physicists is Stephen Hawking, whose amyotrophic lateral sclerosis forces him to use a machine to speak.

In the future, there will be work for any good brain, whether it walks, rolls, or finds some other way to get itself to a computer console. Some futurists predict that the need for creative thinking is so great that the range of choices for disabled people cannot help but increase, with law and social custom forced to catch up.

The nation's politicians have been moved by stories like Tiffany's and they, like most Americans, have a friend or relative with a disability. They have won applause by passing the ADA and spreading the safety net a little wider. But it is unclear how much this will mean to young people in wheelchairs who dream of raising families.

In 1991 Lonnie Nolta in Sacramento began to talk to the old Tiffany coalition about resurrecting Milton Marks's disabled parenting bill. Deukmejian was gone, replaced by another Republican, Pete Wilson, who was eager to have government intervene to help people avoid being expensive drains on state funds.

Kirshbaum continued to experiment with adaptive equipment, but she needed much more money than she had to make working prototypes of the complicated devices inspired by her videotape research and the frequent exchange of notes and impressions with her staff. The director of the National Institute of Disability and Rehabilitation Research (NIDRR), which had given Through the Looking Glass three small grants, said he liked Kirshbaum's ideas, but was she sure she was playing in the right league? She was told if she affiliated with a large university, like Stanford or the University of California at San Francisco, she might have a chance.

Kirshbaum felt like a minnow being asked to play with whales. She declined, and kept sending in her grant proposals. Then, without warning, NIDRR turned around in 1991 and gave her $125,000 a year for three years, much more money than she ever expected. She hatched plans to hire Ralf Hotchkiss, Kaplan's engineer husband, as the rehabilitation engineer on the project. In 1990 Hotchkiss won a $250,000 MacArthur Foundation award, one of the "genius" grants given without warning to those the foundation thinks are doing interesting work. Television news crews visited the Kaplan-Hotchkiss house and recorded Desmond doing his chores. Hotchkiss demonstrated a pulley which allowed him to climb trees to terrifying heights, a middle-aged substitute for his ill-starred youthful motorcycle riding.

Kirshbaum fretted about finding the right fabricators for her new equipment. She wrestled with liability problems. Her insurance company had rejected coverage for the new adaptive equipment enterprise; it seemed too hazardous and had no precedent.

She sought other options. "I'm really naïve," she said. "I just keep trying to do things."

Tiffany called Kirshbaum to consult about the front carrier design they had worked on. She had a few more ideas, and volunteered as a guinea pig. Someday, she thought, I'll have someone small again to practice with, and this time everything will be ready.

19

Tiffany had a new apartment. The rent was subsidized by a small trust set up by her grandmother. She and Teddy had left it almost bare of furniture—she still hated the stuff—and filled it instead with people, particularly children. Nine-year-olds with grimy noses would stop by to chat with Aunt Tiffy and watch a few cartoons on her tiny black-and-white portable. On several occasions she had kept children overnight for neighbors who had been called away in emergencies. She involved herself in the lives of everyone within a radius of ten units in the beige stucco ground-floor apartment complex in southeastern San Jose.

"Don't go bouncing off the walls when your mommy comes to get you," she warned one young neighbor, "or your mommy's gonna kill me. You've had more sugar than I know she wanted you to have."

When one couple she knew was evicted, the husband partially disabled by a broken back, she volunteered to take care of two of their children for what turned out to be two months. George, ten, and Misty, six, proved to be an interesting challenge. They had not been well disciplined at home, and they resisted many of Tiffany's efforts to set bedtimes and limit sweets. It was a little like dealing with Tony, she thought. She discovered that if she remained firm, they eventually accepted the inevitable.

The ten-year-old made her a keepsake before he left, a ballpoint pen drawing of a heart hovering over a pastoral scene with the words "I Love You, Tiffany" in careful block letters across the top. She put it on the refrigerator and refused to take it down.

She continued to pursue the National Education Corporation high-school diploma correspondence course. Her scores were often in the 90s, and college no longer seemed to be such an impossible goal.

Teddy and she experimented with business ventures. They passed a course in therapeutic massage and tried their hand at mail-order sales. They had become very sure of each other and spoke of marriage. She complained about the long hours he spent caring for his mother. He complained about her fondness for having friends drop by at all hours. They shared jokes and memories and kept David's crib in their second bedroom for the day when they would need it.

David had grown tall and muscular. He loved Judy and Angelo, the foster parents who were close to adopting him. Angelo, a distributor for an ice cream company, had a natural affinity for children. Judy was a well-organized mother who carefully watched each sniffle and seemed to sense the child's every mood. She was warm and honest and committed to raising David with full knowledge of his origins.

When David was three, Judy tried to explain how he had come to live with her and Angelo after being born to Tiffy, the lady in the wheelchair. The story seemed to confuse him and he asked no questions. Judy told Tiffany that the next time she tried to explain the relationship to him she would make the story sound more like a parable or a fairy tale—a simple base upon which to mount the more complex truth when he was older.

Tiffany and Teddy spent a long, easy afternoon with David, Judy, and Angelo a month after the child's third birthday. During the past year Tiffany had bought something for the boy every time she happened to be in a store.

Judy and Angelo pulled into the parking lot in their red van and unbuckled David from his safety seat in back. David had forgotten his old aversion to Tiffany's wheelchair. "Hi, Tiffy!" he said, and leaned close for a kiss.

The boy seemed unusually strong and agile. Judy showed that he was capable of taking Tiffany's door key and putting the key in the lock—just as Tiffany had always told Silvani and Bedford he would be able to do. They strolled over to Round Table Pizza a quarter block from their apartment. They ordered two large pizzas—one pepperoni and one pepperoni and mushroom.

While waiting for the food, David saw the three battered video games near the front door and begged for a chance to run Sprint Rider, the race-car game that allowed him to crash car after car with no discernible injuries. Judy had left her purse in the car and was reluctant to let him ask other adults for money, but Teddy offered to supply some quarters and Judy relented. Not realizing David's appetite for action, Teddy gave him five quarters at once rather than one at a time. He put quarters in every machine he could find, all at once, before Angelo could stop him.

Teddy bought the boy a cola. It was too large for him, Judy thought, and not a flavor he was accustomed to, but he gulped it down in minutes. Tiffany, convinced of the evils of sugar, fretted that he would be up all night, but Judy said that was his habit anyway. He was an active child, with his mother's and father's love of mischief, and there wasn't much she could do about that.

They returned to the apartment to let the food settle while David played with the new yellow Tonka truck Tiffany had bought him. At 6 P.M., when Judy told him it was time to go, he resisted for a while, the sweetest gift he could give his natural mother. The boy then helped pick up his new toys and put them in a bag Tiffany had given him for the occasion.

"Don't worry, Davie," Tiffany said. "You can come back and see me soon."

"I love you, Tiffy," the child said. Tiffany glowed. Whatever preparation had gone into the moment, it did not sound the least bit practiced to her.

They walked out to the apartment complex parking lot and watched David climb into the van and buckle his own seat belt.

He waved as the vehicle pulled out, leaving the emptiness Tiffany and Teddy had anticipated. Teddy stayed in the apartment with her for two straight days, leaving his mother to fend for herself while they thought about their future.

While the wind kicked up the dust under the eucalyptus trees on Monterey Road, Tiffany and Teddy waited on the sidewalk. Jesse was coming. They had planted themselves on the sidewalk for an hour already, imagining the dark brown curls, blue eyes, and widely spaced teeth atop the taller, leaner body they had seen in the pictures.

They went back inside to see if Mel and Lee Anne had called, but the machine had no messages. Tiffany did not know precisely where Jesse and his foster parents lived. The postmarks on the letters and cards forwarded to her by Silvani were stamped in Seattle and other parts of Washington State. She thought she once heard Silvani say Tacoma, but she was not permitted to write to Jesse directly and had no address.

It would be a long, sixteen-hour drive, Lee Anne and Mel had said. Jesse's foster mother, soon to be his adoptive mother, was thirty-nine years old and had been a schoolteacher and an airline reservation agent. Her husband, fifty-two, had been an employment counselor.

The foster parents were well-educated people. Tiffany knew Jesse would have the rigorous schooling that had been denied her, and she liked that. The child would have a much better start than she had had.

Mel and Lee Anne had underestimated the time needed to reach the far southeast corner of San Jose's massive sprawl. They pulled their white sedan into the apartment parking lot an hour late. Just turned three, Jesse resembled his older brother, although his hair was not quite as dark as David's and his eyes a lighter shade of blue. He wore green overalls and a blue T-shirt with a star on the back.

Jesse was shy at first. Tiffany did not demand the kiss that

David would have granted willingly. The boy radiated pink-cheeked health. Mel said he and Jesse jogged at least once each day. The four adults let the boy grow accustomed to the unfamiliar smells and expanses of bare gray-green carpeting. He finally accepted Tiffany's offer of a Teenage Mutant Ninja Turtles ice cream bar, one of her several purchases the day before.

Lee Anne had brought homemade apple sauce and a photo album so that Tiffany could collect the colored snapshots Lee Anne had been sending at irregular intervals. Tiffany liked Lee Anne. She was slim and attractive, in slacks, blouse, and jacket, with close-cut, light hair in tight curls. She had met her husband, long divorced from his first wife, in 1985. They married the next year. When they learned they could not have children of their own, they volunteered as foster-adopt parents. They had thought a great deal about what they were doing and had many questions for Tiffany.

Mel was thin, with a receding hairline and an athletic build. He had a wry sense of humor and bore a physical resemblance to a young Mel Brooks. In the unseasonably warm February weather, he wore jeans and a colored T-shirt. Mel said Jesse had proved to be very strong and a great runner. The boy had a favorite football almost as prized as his large toy Mickey Mouse, whom he called Bo Bo. He loved to play with Mel's carpentry tools.

Although the conversation rarely focused on the foster couple's occupation, Tiffany learned that they ran a small business in a neighborhood where there were no other children Jesse's age. To compensate, they took him to a day-care program one day a week for four hours.

When Lee Anne sought help in recalling the circumstances of Jesse's birth for a family history, Tiffany was delighted to oblige. The foster parents listened, jaws slightly agape, as Tiffany repeated the much-told story of her sudden labor, the panic on Tenth Street, and her furious objections to the paramedics' taking credit for a birth she had orchestrated herself. Lee Anne made no comment when Tiffany described leaving the hospital after a day. Tiffany spared them an account of how it felt to cut short breast-feeding a second time.

Lee Anne marveled at the younger woman. Lee Anne and Mel

had told Jesse that Tiffany was his "birth mother" and Tony, whom they had not met, was his "birth father." In turn, Tiffany often looked for ways to acknowledge Lee Anne as Jesse's mother. At an early meeting, when the boy was only twenty months old, he had asked for a bottle of Sprite that Tiffany was holding. "You'll have to ask your mommy if it is all right for you to have some," Tiffany said. Lee Anne was not sure she would have been as magnanimous in Tiffany's place.

Tiffany had occasionally wondered what all that pain had been for. God, she believed, had a purpose in tragedy, otherwise her own birth might be shrugged off as some cosmic mistake. In the wide-eyed, happy boy in front of her, she could see a bit of the divine plan. Jesse seemed so far away from her, when but for an accident of timing—a few more weeks in her mother's womb—she might have been able to raise him herself.

Lee Anne and Mel had to leave at 4 P.M. Jesse was tired, and they had another appointment before they could put him down for the night. The visit had lasted only two hours, but ever since the day he was taken, Tiffany had become accustomed to treasuring each minute. She did not want to tarnish with complaints her relationship with a couple who seemed to be trying to keep her in touch with her son.

Lee Anne felt badly for Tiffany. She could only imagine the emptiness and loneliness that would intrude when they left.

Toward the end of the second hour, Jesse lost some of his shyness. He moved close enough to the woman in the wheelchair to have his picture taken with her. He cuddled a bit and thanked her for the books and a toy bear she had given him. They went outside and Tiffany asked to see Bo Bo. Jesse proudly pulled the doll out of the car.

"Wait a minute, Jess," Tiffany said. "In the picture Bo Bo has a necklace."

Jesse nodded vigorously. Mother and son shared a keen memory, and to them this was an important detail. Tiffany had studied each of Lee Anne's snapshots for a long time.

The child found the necklace and brought it out for Tiffany's inspection. It was made of colored beads that he had painstakingly strung together.

"Time to go, Jesse," Mel said.

"Good-bye, Tiffy," the boy said. "Good-bye, Teddy."

Tiffany and Teddy watched as the car safely merged with traffic, made a U-turn to return to the highway, and faded from sight.

They stayed rooted in the spot for another twenty minutes. They did not say much. If crip time meant savoring each moment and not rushing after ghosts, then they would make the most of it.

Tiffany would sometimes wonder, as she watched other parents struggle with their children, why the lessons she had learned about disabilities, families, and love were not obvious to everyone.

Parents with disabilities, like all parents, wanted to carve out a place of security and enchantment where a child could grow at a safe, smooth pace. Care and caution were paramount, as they were for anyone moving about in an often dangerous world. Speed could kill.

The effort to show abusive parents how to save their families had the same goals—slow down, peel off nonessentials, focus on health and safety and food on the table and gentle fun.

It was an old-fashioned contradiction of the lifestyle of much of the country, but the focus had to be on the child. The government was unlikely to solve the problems of child poverty and child abuse without a million parental commitments to the well-being of their children.

Tiffany composed a letter on the subject once, a message to her children she hoped would someday make it easier for them to understand why she had tried so hard to keep them, and then saw it was best that she let go.

The important thing, she said, was to live her life as if someone always depended on her, and when a decision arose, decide what was best for that small, vulnerable soul. "If the grieving mother who loves her son wants to see her son again," she said, "she'll fight for her rights to live, eat, breathe, and sleep properly for her son."

Tiffany thought if everyone behaved as if they were someone's mother, and remembered each day the slow, sweet care that required, it would be a better world.

During Tiffany's afternoon at the pizza parlor with David, the child had quickly run out of quarters for the video games and asked Angelo for more. Angelo's pockets were empty, and Judy still did not have her purse. Somewhat reluctantly, Judy suggested that the child ask Tiffany for more.

The boy headed eagerly in that direction. Tiffany was in her wheelchair in the far corner of the room, on the other side of the scattered wooden tables and chairs, waiting for the pizza order to be announced. She smiled at the boy.

"Tiffy? Money?" he said.

"No, baby," she said. "I don't have any money." She spotted Teddy waiting to buy drinks. "See Teddy over there?" She waved in that direction. "Go ask Teddy for the money. Teddy's got *all* the money. See? Tiffy doesn't have anything."

This saddened David. He did not seem as sure of his influence on Teddy. "No," he said. "I don't want to go by myself. Tiffy come with me?"

The boy surveyed the route. Several of the chairs had been pulled from the tables. He saw no clear path for Tiffany. Without another word, he began to pull some chairs out of the way and push others into tables, a small Moses parting a sea of furniture.

Tiffany watched, astonished. She had envisioned a moment like this—his legs and arms and her brain becoming one. She turned her chair toward the road he had opened and began to roll through.

David smiled and then thought of something else. He ran behind her chair, grasped the handles, and began to push. Tiffany and son were on their way.

EPILOGUE

On January 15, 1992, Jesse's fourth birthday, Tiffany and Teddy exchanged wedding vows in the chapel of Bally's Hotel in Reno, Nevada. The bride wore a cream-colored brocaded gown she had snatched from the discarded wardrobe of a neighbor. The groom wore gray slacks, a sweater, and one of his wife's flowery shirts—artfully hidden under the sweater when he discovered his own shirts were missing.

The Rev. Charles Sances, a retired Los Angeles sheriff's deputy, read a service full of promises of commitment the couple before him had honored for some time. He included a modern version of First Corinthians with meaning for Tiffany. "Love does not demand its own way. It is not irritable or touchy," he read. "It is not glad about injustice, but rejoices when truth wins out."

The bride and groom had known each other for more than three years. Teddy's caution and gentleness fit well with Tiffany's ambition and gregariousness. Their love had survived some of the worst days of their lives, as well as a few quiet years without lawyers and reporters and social workers recording their every move. They had had some luck with home sales, such as Teddy's work with Mary Kay cosmetics. They thought they would have enough money eventually for at least one of them to begin college.

But what they wanted most was a child. They lived for their short, irregular visits with David and Jesse, both now legally adopted by their foster parents. They knew their ties to Tiffany's sons would be distant and somewhat ambiguous until the boys grew to understand how Tiffany had fought for them and why she had given them up. They would have a chance to rediscover their mother in adulthood, just as Tiffany had.

The law, she vowed, would never take another one of her children away. While Teddy thought of ways to turn their second bedroom into a comfortable nursery, Tiffany spoke to Clay Bedford and other attorneys about how to prevent further county interference in their lives. She and Megan Kirshbaum discussed the latest adaptive parenting equipment. The newlyweds talked of moving to Berkeley to be closer to the psychologist and her staff.

Tiffany could feed and diaper and carry and play with a baby. She had had regular sessions with a family counselor and had learned how to ease the frustration she once felt whenever David cried.

No mother she knew had ever worked so hard and studied so long to be ready for a child. This one she would have time to hold and tease and comfort and love.

One day that child would leave also, but it would be the child, and no one else, who would choose the moment of departure. And on that day she would insist that her baby, no matter how tall or how full of adult yearnings, bend over for one more nuzzle and a kiss.

INDEX

ABOUT THE AUTHOR

Jay Mathews is the author of *Escalante: The Best Teacher in America*. With his wife, Linda, he coauthored *One Billion,* an account of their experiences as journalists in China. Mathews, a winner of the National Education Reporting Award, specializes in urban issues, including immigration, welfare reform, and disability rights. Until recently the Los Angeles Bureau Chief of the *Washington Post,* he is now a correspondent for *Newsweek* in New York.